Peace without Victory

Peace without Victory

Woodrow Wilson and the British Liberals

LAURENCE W. MARTIN

KENNIKAT PRESS
Port Washington, N. Y./London

PEACE WITHOUT VICTORY

Manufactured by Taylor Publishing Company   Dallas, Texas

TO MY PARENTS

Preface

DURING the first World War a group of British radicals dissented from the view of the war officially adopted by the Liberal and Labour parties. The radicals developed criticisms of national policy which were influential at the time and served as potent sources of dissatisfaction with the peace settlement in later years. Woodrow Wilson, who was steeped in the tradition of British and American liberalism, found himself in close agreement with the radical attitude toward war aims. In his famous call for a "peace without victory" Wilson symbolized the kind of settlement which he and his radical associates in Britain thought essential for the future stability of world order. Even after they had been forced to accept the pursuit of peace through victory, they retained hopes of guiding the victors toward moderation.

The sympathy between Wilson and the radicals had an important effect on British and American policies—the more so as they became fully aware of their community of opinion and worked in conscious harmony. This relationship, the common ideas on which it rested, and its bearing on the Anglo-American peace program have never been thoroughly investigated. Yet, apart from its diplomatic significance, the relationship is of interest as a sidelight on Wilson's thought and character, as an incident in the decline of the Liberal party, and as a decisive stage in the development of Labour's outlook on foreign affairs. Much of the radical argument also deserves notice as an effort to devise a concept of foreign policy capable of reconciling national interests with international harmony. The present book is an attempt to explore this episode in Anglo-American relations.

The Prologue sketches the inheritance of previous thought

and experience with which Wilson and the radicals faced events. I have not attempted a full discussion of the background of liberalism but merely draw attention to common elements in traditional British and American attitudes toward foreign policy. The Epilogue is a similarly restricted endeavor and must not be mistaken for an effort to reinterpret the Versailles conference; it is confined to outlining the aftermath of the war-aims movement and suggesting the most promising directions in which to look for its long-term effects.

It must also be borne in mind that this book singles out a particular theme from the complicated diplomatic history of the war. Although the effort to present a well-rounded narrative has necessarily involved the re-evaluation of broader issues, I have devoted most attention to the exploration of relations between Wilson and the British radicals. I have not undertaken a history of war aims and peace offensives or, especially, a detailed reconsideration of the secret treaties. The treaties are well known and have been debated in numerous works, many of which are cited below. Even more to the point, the precise contents of the treaties did not, in my opinion, greatly influence Wilson's policies, which were calculated to compel acceptance of a peace based upon principles which would render the treaties irrelevant. The question is discussed at some length in the pages that follow.

Although much of the material used here is unpublished, the text has been burdened with quotations only when it seemed necessary to convey the flavor or exact wording of a document, and I have avoided reference to manuscript collections when the material in question is wholly or partly available in published form.

I have received much generous assistance in writing this book, which is based in part upon a doctoral dissertation presented to the Yale Graduate School in 1955. My thanks are due particularly to Mrs. Woodrow Wilson for permission to make use of her husband's papers in the Library of Congress, and to the staff of the Labour Party Research Department for allowing me to explore files of papers which belonged to Arthur Henderson. I am especially grateful to President Emeritus Charles Seymour of Yale for access to the House, Wiseman, and Polk Collections, for painstaking criticism and advice, and for numerous discussions in which he has shared knowledge acquired not only as a scholar but as a participant in American diplomacy during the first World War. For several years now I have profited from an association with Arnold Wolfers, and I owe much to his perceptive counsel, as well as to that of Lewis P. Curtis, Edmund Morgan, and Harry R. Rudin. Above all, Samuel F. Bemis has placed me under an obligation which I can acknowledge but not discharge. His good-humored scholarship has been a constant source of encouragement.

L.W.M.

Cambridge, Mass.
March 1958

Contents

. . . it must be a peace without victory. . . .
Only a peace between equals can last. Only
a peace the very principle of which is equality
and a common participation in a common benefit.
           Woodrow Wilson, January 22, 1917

. . . whilst you can have peace without
victory, history shows that as a rule nations
have had victory without peace.
           Ramsay MacDonald, August 17, 1917

Foreign Relations: Papers Relating to the Foreign Relations of the United States, various series.

H. C. Deb. or *H. L. Deb.: Parliamentary Debates, Official Report,* 5th ser.

"House Diary": Typewritten diary of Colonel House, in House Collection, Yale Library.

Intimate Papers: Charles Seymour, *The Intimate Papers of Colonel House,* 4 vols. Boston, 1926–28. Selections reprinted by permission of Houghton Mifflin Co.

Lansing Papers: Papers Relating to the Foreign Relations of the United States: the Lansing Papers, 1914–1920, 2 vols. Washington, D.C., 1938–40.

Life and Letters: Ray Stannard Baker, *Woodrow Wilson, Life and Letters,* 8 vols. Garden City, N.Y., 1927–39. Selections reprinted by permission of Doubleday and Co.

New Democracy: Woodrow Wilson, *The New Democracy, Presidential Messages, Addresses, and Other Papers (1913–1917),* ed. Ray Stannard Baker and William E. Dodd, 2 vols. in one, New York, 1926.

War and Peace: Woodrow Wilson, *War and Peace, Presidential Messages, Addresses, and Public Papers (1917–1924),* ed. Ray Stannard Baker and William E. Dodd, 2 vols. in one, New York, 1927.

War Memoirs: David Lloyd George, *The War Memoirs of David Lloyd George,* 6 vols. London, 1933–36.

1. Prologue: The Prewar Years

ENGLISHMEN who professed to be liberals in 1914 were heirs to a century-old tradition of distinctive views on foreign affairs. Early in the 19th century a compound of utilitarianism, religious humanitarianism, and the new economics of Adam Smith combined in a reforming movement which earned the name of liberalism. This program of thought and action laid the foundation for a new British foreign policy reflecting a distrust of government shared by the laissez-faire economists.

Certain attitudes established by earlier students of foreign affairs influenced the new liberalism from the outset. The condemnation with which Edmund Burke and Charles James Fox greeted British policy toward the American colonies and the later criticism which Fox and Thomas Paine leveled against the war with revolutionary France offered precedents for a habitual suspicion of the aims and motives of national policy, especially in wartime. Criticism had sometimes broadened into misgivings about the whole apparatus of diplomacy. Paine and Jeremy Bentham assailed the secrecy shrouding foreign policy and made it appear that the causes of international strife were illusions fostered by the narrow cliques conducting foreign affairs. The belief that diplomatic issues were largely artificial lent plausibility to isolation as a third response to international politics. For if controversies with foreign powers were baseless, enlightened nations could withdraw from the game. This idea, which developed from early Tory views, was eloquently expressed by Paine, who helped to make it one of the impulses toward the American

1

revolution and who continued to advocate it as a general principle. A temptation to withdraw from difficulties and deny
their existence became one of the continuing characteristics
of liberal thought on foreign affairs—thought which seemed
always more at ease in criticism, in the advocacy of self-
restraint, than in suggesting practical courses for times when
foreign influences pressed in and could not be evaded.

The liberal movement which developed early in the 19th
century enlisted support from manufacturers and merchants
eager to cast off encumbrances left over from a privileged,
aristocratic, and agrarian age and from those who felt that a
quickened pace of life called for more efficient ways of conducting affairs. Symbolic of entrenched privilege were the
tariffs protecting agriculture and in working for their repeal
Richard Cobden, John Bright, and other representatives of the
Manchester School outlined a restrained and peaceful foreign
policy. The chief ingredient of this policy was free trade, depicted not merely as a method to increase national prosperity
but also as a major contribution to world peace. For the free-
traders argued that the great majority of wars sprang from
quarrels over commercial discrimination between nations or
from the schemes of special interests who hoped to profit from
international tension. Similar arguments were brought against
imperialism. On these premises the liberals constructed a policy of free trade, anti-imperialism, arbitration, and a firm determination to stand aloof from foreign squabbles.[1]

The liberal program won rapid and far-reaching success. It
consorted well with Britain's industrial, commercial, and diplomatic supremacy. By the middle of the century the Corn

1. For a detailed presentation of the foreign policy views of
Smith, Bentham, Cobden, and other founders of liberalism see A.
Wolfers and L. W. Martin, eds., *The Anglo-American Tradition in
Foreign Affairs*, New Haven, 1956; also F. W. Hirst, ed., *Free Trade
and Other Fundamental Doctrines of the Manchester School*, London, 1903; F. R. Flournoy, "British Liberal Theories of International Relations, 1848–1898," *Journal of the History of Ideas*, 7
(1946), 195 ff.

Laws were repealed and protectionism was, as Disraeli put it, "not only dead but damned." Britain enjoyed a comfortable sense of economic and strategic security. But even as liberalism gained its victories, forces were at work to undermine its achievement. Unrestrained industrial enterprise produced an ugly society which cried out for reform. Demands arose for positive action to remedy the defects of laissez-faire. Similar criticisms were leveled against liberalism's lack of concern for world affairs and for the struggling nationalities of Europe in particular.

Cobden's own concept of a liberal foreign policy was not solely negative. He hoped that curtailment of the role of governments in international affairs would open the way for a proliferation of mutually beneficial commercial and social relations between peoples. His proposals were therefore intended to contribute to the ultimate benefit of foreign nations as well as his own. But a deep skepticism as to human capacity for devising positive policies to improve conditions abroad led him to oppose involvement in foreign problems and brought him very close in practice to the simpler isolationism of many of his associates. The strong humanitarian strain in liberalism, however, endowed some liberals with a sense of mission in foreign affairs: a desire to do good works abroad which tended toward interventionism rather than isolation.

When criticism of a purely negative foreign policy became pronounced in midcentury, John Stuart Mill took a lead in developing the case for positive liberal participation in international politics. He concluded that every nation had a duty to promote international welfare actively, not merely to abstain from deliberate injury to other countries. Intervention on behalf of movements for self-government, for example, was therefore justifiable and even required, whenever it seemed likely to succeed.[2]

2. Wolfers and Martin, pp. 206–20; see also L. T. Hobhouse, *Liberalism* (London, 1911), pp. 112 ff.; W. L. Davidson, *Political Thought in England, the Utilitarians* (London, 1915), pp. 116 ff.

Translating this ethical concern in the welfare of all nations into a conscious British foreign policy was largely the work of Gladstone. He believed that Britain could best pursue peace within the cooperative framework of the Concert of Europe. His efforts to apply these principles by encouraging arbitration, assisting struggling nationalities, and resisting certain opportunities to expand the Empire made him a symbol of international morality; and his frequent appeals to public opinion did much to accustom his audience to the idea of measuring national policy by moral standards.[3] But he also encountered many of the hazards which await those who try to devise particular measures to meet such standards in an imperfect world. His good intentions sometimes led him into courses which puzzled and confused his supporters, as when, for example, his policy in Egypt culminated in the extension of British dominion over other races.

Frustration again followed achievement, and liberalism faltered anew in the 1880's. At home, social problems were aggravated by hard times. Radical members of the Liberal party devised remedies to meet these, but Gladstone, now aging, concentrated his energy on Home Rule for Ireland, and many of his followers had little stomach for the schemes of radical reformers. Those who regarded laissez-faire as liberalism's greatest achievement, indeed as the essence of liberalism itself, could not reconcile themselves to reintroducing the state to intimate concern with social and economic affairs. On the other hand, the voice of organized labor became louder and louder. Given encouragement by Gladstone, the radicals might have led the Liberal party in a new wave of reform. Gladstone, however, failed to satisfy his more advanced followers. A large number of these, led by Joseph Chamberlain, spurred

3. Flournoy, pp. 202 ff.; Ramsay Muir, "Mr. W. E. Gladstone," in F. J. C. Hearnshaw, *The Political Principles of Some Notable Prime Ministers of the Nineteenth Century* (London, 1926), pp. 242–51.

on by personal differences and frustrated by their party's neglect of social reform, quit the party in 1886 on the immediate issue of their opposition to Home Rule, and as Liberal Unionists joined forces with the Conservatives. In this curious manner the Liberal party was deprived of the numbers, the leadership, and the initiative to exercise a decisive influence on affairs.

Changing patterns of international power in the closing years of the century presented fresh problems for liberalism. The political and economic security which had permitted Britain considerable freedom of choice in foreign policy was now challenged by German and American industrialism and by a rising tide of militaristic nationalism and imperialism. Under Conservative governments Great Britain rapidly built up the Navy and resumed its own expansion, adding four million square miles to the Empire. Growing fears that British interests were threatened brought a new alertness to the element of conflict in international relations. A new popular press cultivated an atmosphere of crisis and jealousy toward other nations. Free trade principles remained inviolate but no longer unquestioned. By 1896 Chamberlain was sounding out the response to a proposal for imperial preference.

The new, assertive foreign policy gained converts in the Liberal party, including many of the leaders. A group of Liberal-Imperialists became recognizable, lending support to an adventurous colonialism and a strong naval policy. The remaining radicals in the party and those who clung tenaciously to the classic principles of liberalism viewed such developments with alarm. Dissension over foreign policy came to a boil during the Boer War. Officially the Liberal party did not oppose the war and supported annexation of the Boer states. But radical members of the party cooperated with labor leaders in a bitter "stop the war" movement, one result of which was to revive and reformulate the idea of a typically liberal foreign policy, based on morality, free trade, self-determination, and faith in the compatibility of national interests.[4]

After the war the relative decline in British commercial and naval superiority continued to present the leading problem of British foreign policy. By rapprochement with America, alliance with Japan, and entente with France, the Conservative government concentrated British power in Europe to meet the threat. There was considerable talk of consolidating the Empire as an added source of strength. Chamberlain now persuaded the Conservative party to adopt officially a program of protection and imperial preference.

When, in 1906, the Liberals found themselves once more in possession of a firm majority, the Foreign Secretary, Sir Edward Grey, was a Liberal-Imperialist. The government responded to the international situation by continuing the policies of its predecessor. Indeed Grey went further in the direction indicated by these policies. It was he who gave the Entente with France a military content by permitting secret staff consultations with the French. Similar talks took place with the Belgians. In 1907 Grey extended the Entente into a triangular grouping by agreement with Russia. Under Liberal control the Royal Navy continued its accelerating expansion.

There was a small number of articulate Liberals who were alarmed by the growth of armaments and the alignment of Britain with one of the rival continental alliances. These Liberals, most of them radicals, continued to protest in the tradition of Boer War days. This latter-day radicalism offered the possibility of new measures and new leaders for a revived liberalism which would once more offer a genuine alternative to conservatism. The fledgling Labour party, which had not

4. An important example of the protest is J. L. Hammond, F. W. Hirst, and Gilbert Murray, *Liberalism and the Empire*, London, 1900. This work suggests that, should the Liberals fail to meet the challenge of foreign policy, a new party might emerge to do the work. For an effort to reconcile views in the Liberal party see Herbert Samuel, *Liberalism*, London, 1902.

developed any distinctive views of its own on foreign policy, was content to adopt the main lines of the radical approach and provided energetic support.[5] Foreign affairs were the center of attraction for this new grouping.

Much energy was expended upon attacking particular policies of the day but several writers, each pursuing a special interest, made a common demand for reconsideration of the premises of British policy. Three publicists, J. A. Hobson, Norman Angell, and E. D. Morel, were most influential in providing this theoretical framework.

Hobson's chief interest was in imperialism, and his book, *Imperialism*, which appeared in 1902, was one of the earliest and most important contributions to the new thinking. He condemned on several counts the practice of carving up underdeveloped areas into the private possessions of a few states. The policy caused wars for the simple reason that there was not sufficient land to satisfy all the powers. It weakened democracy by breeding a class of autocratic administrators, by consuming the time of legislatures, and by accustoming the nation to the domination of other races.[6] Hobson's self-appointed task was to discover what made such dangerous policy so prevalent.

He rejected the defense that imperialism provided outlets for surplus population or that it was a mission to elevate backward races. Most recent expansion, he pointed out, was in areas quite unsuitable for emigration. As to the lot of natives, Hobson declared that, on balance, they were exploited rather than aided.[7] The real reason why states desired colonies

5. In fact many of the ideas in question became common property to the international socialist movement.

6. J. A. Hobson, *Imperialism* (London, 1902), pp. 25, 132, 155; L. T. Hobhouse, *Morals in Evolution* (London, 1906), p. 68.

7. In an interesting anticipation of the mandate system Hobson admitted a genuine civilizing mission might be conceivable under "true sanction from a society of nations": *The Crisis of Liberalism* (London, 1909), p. 259.

was hope of profit. By amassing a wealth of statistics Hobson proved that colonial trade was a small and diminishing proportion of Britain's total foreign trade, and that only a small and diminishing part of the colonial trade was with the newly acquired tropical areas.[8] The profits of the colonial trade were far less than the cost of the Empire to the nation. Nations became imperialist, he concluded, only because certain special interests profited from the colonies and were able to mold national policy to serve their private ends.

So far this argument was little different from that of the old Manchester School, though it was much better documented. It was in identifying the special interests that Hobson made his most original suggestion: that the class which benefited most under modern conditions was not the merchant but the investor and the manipulator of investments. Here Hobson's opinions on domestic economics became relevant to his thoughts on imperialism. His thesis was that unrestrained modern capitalism gave a few persons far more money than they could spend on current consumption. Accordingly they ploughed this surplus back into production. Efficient industrial methods and the fact that the mass of people had far less purchasing power than would satisfy their needs made it increasingly difficult to dispose of what was produced. The result was underconsumption and overaccumulation of capital. It was the pressure of this capital seeking investment that led to the search for overseas enterprises and hence to imperialism. The answer to the problem of imperialism was therefore the same as the answer to domestic poverty: a redistribution of purchasing power on a pattern more in harmony with the distribution of need.[9] Meanwhile a proper understanding of

8. Hobson, *Imperialism*, p. 44.
9. Ibid., chaps. 6, 7. Cf. P. T. Homan, *Contemporary Economic Thought* (New York, 1928), pp. 283 ff. Dealers in investments were thought to have a particular interest in unsettled foreign relations which caused profitable fluctuations of market.

the origins of imperialism would make it possible to prevent foreign policy being manipulated by financiers.

Hobson had set out to prove that imperialism was, from a national standpoint, not profitable but costly. Norman Angell undertook to do the same for war. He expressed this idea in a book entitled *The Great Illusion*.[10] The illusion was that "military and political power gave a nation commercial and social advantages, that the wealth and prosperity of the defenceless nation are at the mercy of stronger nations." [11] This was an idea inherited from an age of primitive economies and portable loot. Modern wealth consisted of natural resources and productive capacity which could not be captured "because when a province or state is annexed the population, who are the real and only owners of the wealth therein, are also annexed and the conqueror gets nothing." [12] The repressive system necessary to exploit the conquered population would cost far more than it would produce. There was also a more compelling reason why such policies of exploitation must fail. The modern system of international finance was so sensitive that large-scale confiscations would cause disastrous repercussions in the conqueror's own economy. Thus no victor could profitably tap the economy of a defeated nation.

Angell did not claim that every war was preceded by a conscious balancing of profit and loss. He recognized the importance of less material considerations. In particular, wars were often fought for national honor. But Angell held that national prestige was less and less associated with military prowess, more and more with industrial efficiency. Questions of honor would become less significant as causes of war. In any case, since power depended on economic strength, the fact that

10. London, 1910; an expanded version of a pamphlet, *Europe's Optical Illusion*, which had appeared a year earlier.

11. Ibid., p. vii.

12. Ibid., p. 36. Few observations could more sharply emphasize the extent to which the technology of despotism was perfected later in the century.

conquest did not bring economic advantage was a powerful argument against war even where power and prestige were the motive. Economic considerations were thus the dominant ones in any discussion of the causes of war.

A sensible foreign policy, Angell thought, would aim at promoting the friendly cooperation of interdependent nations. Nationalities should express themselves in constructive, not destructive, rivalry. War survived only because of the ignorance of the majority and the self-seeking of a few. The few were those who, like military men, armaments makers and allied industries, made a profit out of war, and reactionaries who profited by the fact that disturbed international relations caused a "check in normal and social progress," wasting national wealth and giving ascendancy to the military, autocratic mind. But Angell did not think all the activities of warmongers were inspired by selfishness. Even special interests might be in the grip of the great illusion and often sincerely believe their policies were to the advantage of the nation as a whole.[13]

The separate lines of inquiry pursued by Hobson and Angell came together in agreement that it was the mistaken idea that war and imperialism were profitable that accounted for the traditional acceptance of international jealousy as the normal state of affairs. Special interests used this illusion to further their own schemes at the expense of the community. The chief instrument for exciting public pugnacity was the press. Yellow journalism was sometimes the tool of other interests, sometimes it was merely concerned with its own circulation. In either case it promoted unrest by presenting an alarmist account of the diplomatic situation. War was therefore a hoax perpetrated on the public by its own ignorance

13. Ibid., p. 86. In 1912 the Garton Foundation was established to promote study of international politics in general and Angell's ideas in particular. The following year Angell made a highly successful lecture tour of the United States. Norman Angell, *After All* (London, 1951), pp. 167–71.

and the machinations of unscrupulous or deluded pressure groups. The solution was to educate the people in the facts of international life.[14]

Some believed that education alone was insufficient because the people did not have adequate control over foreign policy. There had long been a belief that the remoteness of diplomatic issues from the ordinary man's experience, the need for quick decisions, and the advantages of concealing one's hand in negotiation, rendered foreign affairs liable to escape democratic control. Bagehot had pointed this out in his *English Constitution;* more recently Bryce's *American Commonwealth* had drawn attention to the role of the American legislature in determining foreign policy.[15] The organized British peace movement proposed Parliamentary approval of treaties and declarations of war as early as 1886, and in 1888 a motion in the Commons called for a Parliamentary Foreign Affairs Committee.[16]

In 1912 E. D. Morel, a man who had made a reputation championing the lot of the African native, gave new force to the demand for democratic control of foreign policy by writing his *Morocco in Diplomacy,*[17] a powerful denunciation of secret diplomacy. His special fear was that Britain might become committed to aid France in a future war against Germany. He believed that secrecy had forced Germany to

14. These views were shared by many other liberal writers. See, *inter alia,* E. C. Cooke, *The Case Against Protection* (London, 1909), an account of the International Free Trade Congress held in August 1908. See also G. Perris, *For an Arrest of Armaments,* London, 1906; Graham Wallas, *The Great Society,* London, 1913; and particularly Hobhouse, *Democracy and Reaction,* London, 1904, and his *Liberalism.*

15. James Bryce, *The American Commonwealth* (new ed., 2 vols. New York, 1911), *1,* 54, 70, 107–10, 163, 222.

16. A. C. F. Beales, *History of Peace* (New York, 1931), pp. 169, 223, 259.

17. London, 1912. Morel's reputation was made by the publication of *Red Rubber,* London, 1906.

operate on the assumption that such an agreement had existed during the Moroccan crises. Suspicions of this sort, he warned, greatly increased international tensions and encouraged the build-up of armaments and alliances. Echoing the Manchester tradition, Morel declared that friendships which "fetter a nation's freedom" were "unnatural compacts." [18] When the *casus belli* of such secret commitments arose, the people were told that the nation's honor was at stake and the government was tempted to whip up war fever to ensure public support.

In place of this system Morel wanted Britain to reject special alignments and return to the idea of the Concert. British influence should be freely applied according to the merits of each international dispute, not blindly committed in advance. The way to obtain such a flexible, enlightened policy was to arouse a sustained, sober interest in foreign affairs, to break down the "caste" monopoly of the diplomatic service, to set up a Foreign Affairs Committee, and to insist on Parliamentary ratification of all treaties and declarations of war. Actual negotiations would have to remain secret but the broad issues of policy could be put to the public. Morel was convinced that, with education, the people could judge these issues well; "the citizen of education and intelligence . . . is quite . . . well able to arrive at sound conclusions if the facts are placed before him." [19] In this way the circle of liberal thought is closed. War is the enemy of democracy; democracy is the answer to war. Under existing conditions war was threatening democracy. A firm effort by democrats could reverse the process.[20]

18. Morel, *Morocco*, p. 177.
19. Ibid., p. 62.
20. Strong opposition to secret commitments developed in political circles. In 1913 and 1914 M.P.'s several times questioned the Foreign Minister as to the existence of engagements binding Great Britain. *H.C. Deb, 50,* 42–3, 1316–18; *61,* 1499; *63,* 457–8. In 1912 some seventy Liberal M.P.'s set up a foreign affairs group to study foreign policy and thereby increase Parliamentary control.

These were the lines on which British radicals approached foreign policy on the eve of the first World War. They had inherited much from the earlier years of liberalism. Conditions had changed and the radicals looked back nostalgically to the security which nations had enjoyed in a more stable system of international relations. This stability they associated perhaps too much with liberal policies, too little with the fortuitous circumstances in which those policies had been developed. Recognizing that circumstances had changed, the radicals sought to devise new liberal policies which would relax tensions once more and then pass on to establish a greater degree of harmony than had ever previously existed among the nations of the world.

That which truly distinguished liberal from conservative thought about international relations was a refusal to accept the existing system as given and unalterable. Something not only should but could be done to improve matters. This liberal faith in the power of reason and good will in foreign affairs had deep roots in Britain's past, but in 1914 the British had no monopoly of the idea. For the future it was highly significant that similar ideas were well established in America.

Counterparts could be found in the United States for almost all the principles of foreign policy developed by British liberals during the 19th century. Opposition to militarism, war, and imperialism, and faith in arbitration, and even in free trade, were all represented in American thought when the first World War began. Many of these ideas had been deliberately drawn from English sources and developed in striking parallel to them. For all this, it was remarkable, perhaps, that at the outbreak of the war the United States had a President who not merely developed a foreign policy explicitly based on liberal principles but who consciously relied for inspiration on the example of English writers and statesmen.

Tracing the career of American liberalism is made excep-
tionally difficult by the absence of any vigorous and genuine
conservatism to act as a foil. To justify their revolt against
Britain, Americans borrowed all the ideas of Locke which had
vindicated an earlier English revolution and supported the
subsequent development of liberalism. These doctrines endowed the whole American nation with faith in the possibility of a harmonious, equitable and peaceful political order. At
the same time the Revolution went far toward forming some
American attitudes toward foreign affairs.

In itself the Revolution was a practical demonstration of
anti-imperialism. During the quarrel with Britain, American
publicists expounded the thesis that a nation governed by
another, distant, irresponsible power was a nation governed
ill. Following earlier British isolationist thought [21] revolutionary writers also emphasized the entanglement in European
diplomacy entailed by the imperial connection. Independence,
they urged, would permit America to take advantage of geography and obtain immunity from the perpetual wars brought
on by the vain, monarchical pursuit of predominance and
honor. The Plan of 1776, Washington's Farewell Address, and
Jefferson's desperate efforts to maintain neutrality during the
Napoleonic wars all bore witness to the longing to remain
aloof from Europe's troubles. These early leaders believed
that the United States had a role to play in world affairs but
the part should be one of example; an exhibition of democracy
and peaceful prosperity. It was partly on this account that
free trade, the key to liberal policy in Britain, never gained
wide adherence in America. The dominant reason was undoubtedly the absence of suitable economic conditions; the
infant industries of the North were in no position to compete
with British trade. But protection also seemed a peaceful

21. Cf. Felix Gilbert, "The English Background of American Isolationism in the Eighteenth Century," *William and Mary Quarterly*,
3d ser. *1* (1944), 138–60.

policy as part of the general insulation of America from Europe and its dangerous ways.

Early in the 19th century Southern ambitions to acquire additional slave-holding territories in the Southwest gave new relevance to the anti-imperialist tradition. In opposition to any such extension of slavery, the anti-slavery movement of the North mobilized growing strength and became anti-imperialist. The anti-slavery movement owed its origin to the wave of revivals which swept over the North in the early decades of the century, releasing emotional energies and channeling them into a multitude of reforming causes, almost all of them patterned on British models.[22] Another of these movements was the American Peace Society, which joined the other groups in resisting the South's aggressive foreign policy. In this way the anti-imperialism handed down from the Revolution was kept alive by having a real issue on which to work.

After the Civil War, problems of domestic policy and reconstruction overshadowed foreign affairs. The South's special interest in expansion had disappeared and with it the North's chief objection. Despite this, the efforts of Grant and Seward to acquire new territory met determined opposition and achieved no success beyond the purchase of Alaska. Anti-imperialist sentiment, supported by various motives, sufficed to thwart other expansionist schemes in the postwar era, and more or less earnest plans to take over San Domingo, Cuba, and Hawaii came to naught. Anti-imperialism and its accompaniments thus remained a force to be reckoned with at the end of the century, when foreign affairs once more claimed a major share of American attention.[23]

22. For an illuminating account of revivalism and accompanying social movements see W. R. Cross, *The Burned Over District* (Ithaca, N.Y., 1950), esp. pp. 22–5, 56, 156; also G. H. Barnes, *The Anti-Slavery Impulse*, New York, 1933.

23. The most complete narrative of anti-imperialist activity in this period is D. M. Dozer, "Anti-Imperialism in the United States, 1865–1895," dissertation, Harvard, 1936.

The rising swell of assertive nationalism which revealed itself in the war with Spain and the subsequent annexations appeared to be a decisive reversal of traditional American abstention and anti-imperialism. Yet at the very same time the American peace movement was flourishing as never before and winning support for its favorite device of arbitration, even among the most strenuous expansionists.

In effect, the wave of nationalism and the new zeal for international cooperation to secure peace were both reactions to a new pattern of world politics. The United States could no longer be unconcerned with the activities of other powers. Absorption of most of the world's unclaimed colonial areas released European energies to probe tentatively in the Western Hemisphere. Collisions with Britain and Germany in Venezuela sharpened American fears for the safety of the Caribbean. In the Pacific, Japan demonstrated its new power.

The chief prophet of the disappearance of American immunity was Alfred Thayer Mahan, who indicated the fact in the title of one of his earliest and most influential articles, "America Looking Outward." Assertive nationalists and arbitration advocates alike were in tacit agreement that new conditions called for more active participation in world affairs. The solution adopted by Mahan and his noted disciple, Theodore Roosevelt, was to prepare for the forcible defense and assertion of American interests, which, they believed, were thoroughly compatible with the welfare of mankind at large. Supporters of the peace movement prescribed cooperation with other nations to set up methods for the peaceful settlement of disputes and avoidance of war. Proponents of these differing answers to America's new international position debated spiritedly in the decade before the World War.[24] Typi-

24. A provocative discussion of this debate is contained in R. E. Osgood, *Ideals and Self-Interest in America's Foreign Relations* (Chicago, 1953), Pt. I

cal of this debate was a series of Anglo-American exchanges
in which Mahan disputed the theories of Norman Angell.

In domestic politics as well, the early years of the 20th
century formed a watershed. A revolt against big business,
started by Western agrarians in the 1880's, spread to the East
and attracted small businessmen and workers. Like their
British contemporaries, these reformers were rediscovering
the connections between economic and political power. Muck-
raking journalists uncovered channels of influence and cor-
ruption. The dissident groups demanded legislation to loosen
the grip of the banks and trusts. In part, their program impinged directly on foreign policy by including a demand for
lowering tariffs which had mounted higher and higher under
cumulative pressure from special interests.

During the presidency of Roosevelt the movement continued
to grow and win attention. Roosevelt himself espoused the
progressive cause and lent his support to reforms. He was,
however, far from representative of most Republican leaders,
and throughout Taft's ensuing occupancy of the White House
reaction gained ground. The Payne-Aldrich tariff, which Republican leaders produced in 1909, was a sufficiently blatant
piece of log-rolling to wreck any remaining hope that Taft
might continue the work of reform and to materially assist
the Democrats in winning Congress in 1910. As a further result of the activity of the Republican leaders, Roosevelt re-
belled in 1912 and ran for president as leader of a new
Progressive party.

The Democratic candidate was also identified as a reformer.
Progressivism had made a deep impression on the Democrats.
William Jennings Bryan, titular head of the party and three
times its presidential candidate, was himself a representative
of Western agrarianism. In 1912, when he announced he would
not be a candidate, his leadership was already challenged
and several would-be champions were in the field. Woodrow
Wilson, the successful contender, was a latecomer to the con-

test. He had first won a national reputation as president of
Princeton University, where he had fought a bitter struggle
with conservative groups. Fame won in this fight secured
Wilson's election as Democratic governor of New Jersey. In
this position he gained prominence as a progressive leader
who broke with the party machine and enacted an extensive
series of reforms.[25] At the Democratic convention in 1912 he
came from behind to win nomination for president. With
Roosevelt splitting the Republican vote, Wilson was safely
elected. Taft ran after Roosevelt, thereby demonstrating the
strength of progressivism in the country.

The campaign was waged almost entirely on domestic issues. A strong-willed president had an unusually good opportunity to dominate foreign policy. Wilson shared his party's
preoccupation with domestic problems. "It would be the irony
of fate," he remarked, "if my administration had to deal
chiefly with foreign affairs." [26] But, as this remark indicated,
Wilson was aware of his responsibilities for foreign affairs. He
already professed several broad principles which concerned,
or could be applied to, foreign policy—principles closely akin
to those of British liberals. His years of academic experience
had endowed him with intense admiration for British liberalism, and when he cited a precedent or quoted a maxim, it
was more often from Mill, Bagehot, or Gladstone than from
an American.[27] Always closely similar, the British and American liberal traditions of foreign policy came closer than ever
in Wilson.

The President's religious convictions were fundamental
to his political thought. He shared Gladstone's belief that
every citizen and every leader was a distinct moral agent

25. A. S. Link, *Wilson, the Road to the White House* (Princeton, 1947), pp. 123–32, 181, 277 ff., 310 ff., 527; and his *Woodrow
Wilson and the Progressive Era* (New York, 1954), pp. 10–12.

26. Harley Notter, *The Origins of the Foreign Policy of Woodrow Wilson* (Baltimore, 1937), p. 217.

27. Ibid., pp. 18–25, 29–31, 38.

responsible to a transcendent moral law, which was the sole guide to enduring achievement.[28] Experience at Princeton and as governor of New Jersey taught Wilson that it was often necessary to accept a policy that only partially embodied the moral law. Indeed, before entering politics he had observed that "moral judgments have never been simple: they have always been complicated by a thousand circumstances which puzzle the will . . ." [29] But despite these occasional acknowledgments of inevitable imperfection, a compelling desire to be virtuous constantly tempted Wilson to present his own policies as without blemish.

Like British liberals, Wilson had great faith in democracy as the political system best adapted to moral ends. He believed that "the moral judgment would be the last judgment, the final judgment, in the minds of men as well as at the tribunal of God . . ." [30] In skilled hands, public responsiveness to moral issues could be an effective diplomatic weapon. During the disturbances in Mexico Wilson foreshadowed later policies toward Europe by telling his friend Colonel Edward M. House of "his purpose to build a fire back of the British Ministers, through the English public." [31]

Faith in the common man did not dilute Wilson's insistence upon strong leadership. The people could only pass upon broad issues. It was therefore the duty of the executive to devise well-defined policies for the public to judge. This required free and open discussion to give the public control over policy and to assure the executive of popular support.[32] Wilson

28. Link, *Wilson,* p. 94; Wilson, *Mere Literature* (Boston, 1896), pp. 140 ff.
29. August Heckscher, ed., *The Politics of Woodrow Wilson* (New York, 1956), p. 84; cf. Notter, pp. 17, 58.
30. Notter, pp. 118, 306; Woodrow Wilson, *The New Freedom* (New York, 1913), p. 64.
31. Quoted in Link, *Progressive Era,* p. 117, n. 25.
32. Wilson, *New Freedom,* pp. 98, 113–14, 132; Notter, pp. 23, 52, 98, 146; Link, *Wilson,* pp. 312, 473, 490.

feared that American government had fallen under the exclusive sway of private interests. As he gained political experience, he inclined to blame faults of system rather than individuals. The cure lay in improving the system. For the failings of democracy the remedy was to be more democracy.[33] Hence Wilson's program included measures—referendum, short ballot, direct election—designed to give the people more control over government. This program comprised many of the objects and methods of the British radicals.

Progressives believed that no national policy was more subject to the pressure of special interests than the tariff. Wilson also came to share the suspicion that interest groups played a large part in urging the nation into imperialism. To this he opposed the ideal of a "foreign policy based upon justice and good-will rather than upon mere commercial exploitation and the selfish interests of a narrow circle of financiers . . ." [34] Wilson resisted imperialism not merely because it did not benefit the United States but because it denied the right of every nation to self-government. It might be justifiable for an advanced nation to teach one less favored the art of modern government, but a nation undertaking such a task must genuinely strive to equip its subjects for independence. The relationship was a trust to be liquidated as soon as possible.[35] Wilson's declaration at Mobile on October 27, 1913, that America would never conquer another foot of territory, was a sweeping expression of his distaste for colonialism.

This mistrust of coercion and his reluctance to intervene in Mexico reflected Wilson's poor opinion of force as a political method. He agreed with Burke that force is "temporary and uncertain." Wilson did not deny that force might sometimes be unavoidable. With Mill he thought it might be a duty to

33. Link, *Wilson*, pp. 322–32; Wilson, *New Freedom*, pp. 10–28.
34. November 2, 1912, in the New York *Times*, November 3.
35. Link, *Wilson*, p. 28; Notter, pp. 46–51, 69, 205.

use force if a good cause could be furthered in no other way.[36] But force should not be used for selfish purposes. A powerful nation in the wrong should willingly concede its error and make amends. Under Wilson, American policy in Mexico, in the Panama Tolls controversy, and on reparation to Colombia was a practical demonstration of the President's high regard for self-restraint and the reasoned compromise of disputes.

Thus, when war broke out in Europe, Wilson was experimenting with a foreign policy the principles of which bore a marked resemblance to those long professed by the British Liberal party and now most earnestly propounded by its radical members. Wilson shared their suspicion of special interests and their faith in democratic control as a guarantee for the interests of the whole people. He shared their dislike of imperialism and their faith in the rational settlement of disputes. If he did not share their enthusiasm for complete free trade, he established freer trade than any president since the Civil War and maintained traditional American opposition to commercial discrimination.[37]

In his first months of office, Wilson's foreign policy had taken shape as one of nonentanglement but not isolation. He was sure that America must take a part, indeed the most important part, on the international scene. The United States had an obligation to present an example of good government at home and fair dealing abroad. Isolation was not enough to fulfill this obligation in modern times; it would sometimes be necessary for America to cooperate actively in the affairs of the world.[38]

This was Wilson's response to America's inevitable involvement in international politics. The next few years were to subject this answer to a test as stern as could be imagined.

36. Notter, p. 177; Wilson, *Mere Literature*, p. 145.
37. Notter, p. 233; F. W. Taussig, *Tariff History of the United States* (8th ed. New York, 1931), pp. 413–22.
38. Notter, pp. 44, 110, 270.

2. Official British War Aims

August 1914—April 1917

THE INTERNATIONAL CRISIS of July 1914 broke upon an unsuspecting British nation. The country was distracted by internal dissension. In Ireland the perpetual "Question" was nearing a violent answer. In England organized labor planned a general strike for September. Everyone's attention was drawn inward. Lord Northcliffe, soon to be an unrelenting foe of Germany, spent part of that July on his knees with model soldiers planning war games—for Ulster.[1] Even those at the head of government were taken unaware. In January, Lloyd George had demanded economy in armaments in view of improved Anglo-German relations. On July 9 he thought the "sky has never been more perfectly blue." By July 23 he was happy to announce that Anglo-German relations were "very much better than they were a few years ago." [2] The next day the Cabinet read the Austrian ultimatum to Serbia.

Against such a background it was not surprising to find men eager to test every chance of remaining aloof from Europe's trouble. The Liberal party was in office, a party where the tradition was still peace and quiet. Even the Liberal-Imperialists were more and more concerned with appreciation and preservation of the existing Empire, than with risking its existence

1. Angell, *After All*, p. 179.
2. Thomas Jones, *Lloyd George* (Cambridge, Mass., 1951), pp. 47–8; Malcolm Thomson, *David Lloyd George* (London, 1948), p. 228.

in further expansionist adventures. Both the old-style Gladstonian Liberals who—still the mainstay of the party—were devoted to economy and the new radicals who were intent on squeezing out the last penny for social welfare detested the inhumane extravagance of war. There was also a fear that war might sweep the Conservatives back into office as the party most associated with the military.

Exactly what considerations persuaded the Cabinet to enter the war in 1914 is as obscure as any instance of human decision. Undoubtedly it was the blatant invasion of Belgium which won over all the doubters in the Government but John Morley, Lord Loreburn, and Charles Trevelyan.[3] But many Ministers were for war without that excuse. They pointed out that British policy had traditionally insisted on the independence of the Low Countries and that the growth of German power made a strong France essential to British security. In addition they urged that French naval dispositions made under color of the Entente morally committed Britain to assist France despite diplomatic notes to the contrary.[4] It was this sentiment, coupled with reluctance to see the German fleet at large near British shores, that prompted Grey to announce on August 3, 1914, that Britain would oppose any German attempt to attack French Channel ports.

There were thus at least three sets of considerations which resulted in the British ultimatum of August 4, 1914. These considerations were the treaty obligation to Belgium, the moral commitment to France, and the belief that British security and self-interest compelled resistance to this latest manifesta-

3. *War Memoirs, 1,* 72–3; Lord Loreburn, *How the War Came* (London, 1919), pp. 139–218.

4. The most important of such notes is that of Grey to Paul Cambon, November 22, 1912; but see also Grey to Carnegie, July 22, 1912; Bertie to Grey, July 30, 1912; and Cambon to Grey, November 23, 1912. G. P. Gooch and Harold Temperley, *British Documents on the Origins of the War, 1898–1914* (11 vols. London, 1926), *10,* Pt. II, 601, 605–7, 614–17.

tion of German ambition and Austrian decadence. Different
minds combined these motives in varying degrees and no one
of them can be called decisive. While Grey was convinced of
the need to support France, however she was attacked, Lloyd
George had been willing to stand aloof so long as Germany
crossed "only a little bit" of Belgium.[5] Moreover the distinction between these motives is somewhat arbitrary. There were
many who shared Grey's belief that the fulfillment of Britain's
moral and legal obligations and the vindication of the rights
of Belgium and France were themselves essential to British
security.[6]

This was the line taken by the Foreign Secretary on August
3 when he laid the case for war before the Commons and
the people. He claimed to approach the question in the
light of "British interests, British honour, and British obligations . . ." Though he was emphatic in identifying those interests and obligations with international morality, it was on
the interests that he grounded his case. He contrasted French
willingness to guarantee Belgian immunity with the German refusal to promise more than restored "integrity." He predicted
that the fall of Belgium might be followed by that of Holland
and of France, leaving the United Kingdom in grave danger;
a danger increased by the reputation for cowardice which in-
activity would bring upon the British. Grey did not think it

5. Ian Colvin, *Carson, the Statesman* (New York, 1937), p. 20;
Vol. 3 of Edward Marjoribanks, *The Life of Lord Carson,* New York,
1932–37.

6. For this account of Government discussions see, in general,
War Memoirs, 1, chaps. 2, 3; E. Grey, *Twenty-Five Years* (2 vols.
New York, 1925), *2,* 14–39; W. S. Churchill, *The World Crisis* (5
vols. London, 1923–27), *1,* chaps. 8, 9; H. H. Asquith, *Memories
and Reflections* (2 vols. Boston, 1928), *2,* chaps. 1, 2; Colvin, *3,*
chap. 1; G. Riddell, *Lord Riddell's War Diary 1914–1918* (London, 1933), pp. 1–8. Frank Owen, *Tempestuous Journey; Lloyd
George, His Life and Times* (London, 1955), pp. 259–72; Robert
Blake, *The Unknown Prime Minister; The Life and Times of An-
drew Bonar Law* (London, 1955), pp. 219–26.

possible to stand aside and impose mediation at a later date, for as a neutral Britain would be weakened by loss of trade. Any British war effort would be almost exclusively naval, and such hostilities would be cheaper than neutrality.[7]

Undoubtedly the moderate tone of Grey's speech, emphasizing the reluctance with which the Government went to war, did much to unify the nation for the coming conflict. It was extremely fortunate for national unity that a Liberal government with the confidence of labor held office. Lloyd George's well-known distaste for war, evidenced in Boer War days, appeared in itself as a guarantee that everything possible had been done to avoid hostilities. At least one man perceived the value of this arrangement at the time. A. J. Balfour argued against a coalition on the ground that it would facilitate the formation of an antiwar party.[8] As it was, the Government could count on whole-hearted Conservative support in undertaking the struggle against Germany. Conservative leaders cooperated with Lloyd George, the Chancellor, in taking steps to meet the financial crisis—for, somewhat out of harmony with some pacifist theories, the prospect of war threw the City into panic. In this cooperation Lloyd George began an amiable new association with the Right.

Grey's speech set forth the reasons which led the Government to war and with these reasons the history of British war aims begins. War aims in general may perhaps be divided into three classes. First come the immediate causes of the war: the restoration or achievement of those conditions for which the nation decides to accept the sacrifices of war. Second are those old ambitions for which the nation was not willing to start a war but which might as well be obtained once hostilities have broken out. For instance, no British govern-

7. *H. C. Deb.*, 65, 1813 ff.
8. As indeed it did. See below, pp. 64–5. B. E. C. Dugdale, *Arthur James Balfour, First Earl of Balfour* (2 vols. New York, 1937), 2, 78.

ment could fail to perceive the chance of settling German naval rivalry for some time to come. Third are those new war aims which come to mind in the course of the war. These may be new ambitions or the result of new insights into the pre-war world. In spelling out the immediate occasion for war on August 4, 1914, Grey had invoked strictly negative, defensive purposes which could be satisfied by the rebuff and abandonment of the German onslaught. It is, however, one of the commonplaces of history that "war never leaves where it found a nation," and England soon became involved in far-reaching programs of change.

The shock of the outbreak had dismayed and confused the country. In the following weeks the Government attempted to reassure the public by expounding the purposes of the war. Appealing to liberal principles and matching their tone to the attitude of most of their party—an attitude that will later be examined in detail—the Liberal leaders now endowed the war with a broader, more idealistic justification. The defense of Belgium was extended to embrace the vindication of the "sanctity of international covenants" and the right of small nations to enjoy independent existence.[9] Speaking in various parts of Britain, Herbert Asquith, the Prime Minister, widened his interpretation of the war to depict it as a spiritual conflict on behalf of the liberty of mankind. This growing assumption of deep moral significance for the Allied cause brought with it a corresponding indictment of Germany. British leaders condemned "those who control and execute German policy" and declared that the peaceful settlement of Europe would not be possible until "Prussian militarism" was repudiated and Germany reconstructed on democratic lines.[10]

9. *War Speeches by British Ministers, 1914–1916* (London, 1917), pp. 5–7. At this time, of course, Asquith was referring to the independence of such small nations as Belgium and Serbia, not the submerged nationalities of Austria.

10. Ibid., pp. 12, 18, 29, 40–1, 50–1, 149; Grey, 2, 146.

Thus, in seeking to justify the war to the consciences of liberals, the Government soon sketched purposes which the mere repulse of German forces could not satisfy. This, however, was less than half the story of mushrooming war aims, for grim strategic necessities were drawing the nation into more precise commitments on issues which might arise at the peace conference. It was essential to secure the bonds of the Entente, and Britain's allies had extensive territorial ambitions. On November 12, 1914, Asquith promised never to make peace until "France is adequately secured against the menace of aggression." [11] The listener could hardly help thinking of Alsace-Lorraine. Britain had already promised by the Pact of London, September 5, 1914, not to make a separate peace. To this extent she had undertaken to work out a program of war aims acceptable to her allies. By the end of the year Viviani, the French Premier, had declared Alsace-Lorraine a *sine qua non* of peace. Another territorial rearrangement was foreshadowed when Asquith announced the "death knell of Ottoman dominion, not only in Europe, but in Asia." [12] It was indeed in the Levant that Britain, upon declaring war on Turkey in October 1914, became the first belligerent to make territorial gains, by annexing Cyprus and establishing a protectorate over Egypt.

The Russian Foreign Minister Sasonov provided the most striking insight into the latent ambitions of Britain's allies when, on September 14, 1914, he put forward in conversation with the British and French ambassadors a thirteen-point program for completely redrafting the European map. He

11. *War Speeches*, p. 58; H. W. V. Temperley, *History of the Peace Conference at Paris* (6 vols. London, 1920–24), *1*, 169.
12. *War Speeches*, p. 156. The treaties binding the Entente not to make separate peace are printed in *Declaration between the United Kingdom, France, and Russia, Engaging Not to Conclude Peace Separately during the Present European War*, Cd. 7737, January 1915. Later agreements including Japan and Italy are printed in Cd. 8014 and 8107.

favored French annexation of the Palatinate and Rhineland, as well as Alsace-Lorraine. For Russia herself Sasonov claimed a frontier on the Niemen, with East Galicia, while West Galicia and Silesia should be attached to Poland. Austria-Hungary he proposed to divide in three. The Allies should also break German military and political power. To this end Sasonov mentioned the drastic expedient of recreating an independent Kingdom of Hanover. Britain, France, and Japan should share the German colonies and all the Allies should receive substantial indemnities.[13]

The majestic sweep of this plan indicates the complications into which continental politics were drawing England. Her pressing need of allies made it virtually impossible for her to restrain their ambitions. These ambitions, coupled with the antipathy she was herself developing for Germany, with her demands for changes in German internal affairs and in the European system, soon added up to a program that was unattainable short of the crushing defeat of Germany, even if Germany's own terms became unexpectedly moderate.

During 1915 there was little public development of British war aims. Early in the year when President Wilson's personal emissary, Colonel House, tentatively investigated the prospects for peace, he met little encouragement. Asquith and his colleagues believed that all energies should be bent toward victory. Those who talked of peace, the Prime Minister declared in March, were victims of "grievous self-delusion . . . The time to talk of peace is when the great tasks . . . are within sight of accomplishment." Later in the year, a little ruffled perhaps by his slow progress in the great tasks, he dealt less tolerantly with those whom he now called "professional whimperers." [14]

But if the public development of Britain's aims was virtually

13. September 14, 1914, *Die Internationalen Beziehungen im Zeitalter des Imperialismus,* 2d ser. 6, Pt. I (Berlin, 1934), 193–4.
14. *War Speeches,* pp. 72, 168.

suspended, her actual and prospective allies continued to elaborate their expansive projects and to demand British acquiescence as part of the price of Allied solidarity. With the Allies hard pressed by German armies and the Central Powers bidding high for Italian assistance, Britain had no choice but to consent and do what seemed necessary to safeguard British interests. An exchange of notes with France and Russia in March, 1915 endorsed the latter's claim to Constantinople and other extensive acquisitions at Turkish expense. In return Britain and France were assured of vague rights in Asiatic Turkey, subject to later definition. Britain was to bring the larger part of the "neutral" zone of Persia within her sphere of influence. A few weeks later Britain signed the Treaty of London by which Italy agreed to join the Allies in exchange for large slices of Hapsburg territory, including the Trentino, South Tyrol to the Brenner, Trieste and about half Dalmatia, an indemnity, a promise of a share of Asia Minor if it were partitioned, and compensation for any colonial gains the other Allies might make in Africa. These two agreements were the beginning of a process of such bargaining over the next two years which eventually added up to something not very far short of Sasonov's sketch.[15]

The network of secret treaties grew out of varied causes: out of ambitions for national aggrandizement and fears for national security; out of the need to plan ahead and reluctance to alienate allies. Some of the arrangements were in keeping with the idealistic principles expounded by British leaders, many others could not easily be reconciled with those ideals. Certainly the treaties forecast a return to the prewar pattern

15. Italy acceded to the earlier Anglo-French-Russian agreement when she entered the war. There is a convenient summary of secret treaties in Temperley, *Peace Conference, 1,* 169 ff. F. Seymour Cocks, *The Secret Treaties* (London, 1918), prints the texts of the chief secret treaties as published by the Russians. He does not include the agreement of St. Jean de Maurienne or the treaties with Japan dealing with Pacific islands and Shantung.

of international conflict and evidenced little faith in the development of a new order in which armed force would play a reduced role.

The aims expressed in the treaties were not, of course, inflexible. They were plans for action if all went well. But once formulated, revision of the commitments would entail a difficult series of negotiations, and in this way the treaties stiffened the Allied position. Thus these territorial enterprises and Britain's growing moral condemnation of Germany combined to increase the acerbity of the war, rendered compromise difficult, and went far to make a settlement improbable short of the total defeat of one side.

The beginning of 1916 therefore discovered the coalition government in a difficult position. Allied ambitions, German resistance and no less extreme ambitions, and the government's own estimation of the necessary conditions of security made it despondent of an early peace. Yet the prolonged horror of the war sharpened the peace hunger of the British people and increased the impatience of neutrals, especially the prime neutral, America. In the spring of 1916 rumors of German peace moves aroused hopes at home, while President Wilson's interest and impatience evidenced themselves in another visit from Colonel House, this time frankly seeking a chance to make peace.[16]

The Government rebuffed German advances and smothered House's plans with delay, but felt it advisable to appear ready for a moderate peace. Speaking on April 10, 1916, Asquith derided German advances as an impudent demand for surrender but he was careful to add that Britain had no desire to destroy Germany. Britain only desired to set up an international system guaranteeing equal rights to all nations. On the same day Grey proclaimed his eagerness to set the German people free so that a German democracy could pursue a peaceful foreign policy. Lloyd George privately took advantage of

16. See below, pp. 98–106.

House's visit to avow a modest set of war aims, confining Italian gains to Italian-speaking areas and suggesting that France should regain Alsace-Lorraine only in return for colonial territory. Grey used the occasion to display his approval of an organization to enforce the peaceful settlement of disputes. In May, Balfour publicly expressed a similar conviction, inviting neutrals to interest themselves in the project, an invitation which Grey repeated in October, when he praised the work of the American League to Enforce Peace and suggested that the main burden of planning must fall on the undistracted neutrals.[17]

These benevolent generalities did not reflect any strong probability that the peace would be early or moderate, though apparently Grey would have welcomed a genuine American readiness to redress the balance of Europe. Rosy pictures of the postwar world might be used to justify fighting on until the Central Powers accepted Allied terms, but those terms were becoming increasingly severe. The same stresses of war that required these public exhortations also prompted a new round of diplomatic bargain-hunting. Secretly the Sykes-Picot agreement of May 16, 1916, filled in the plans for further expansion of French and British dominions in the Near East. A secret treaty made with the Rumanians in August projected exchanges of territory hard to reconcile with the vaunted principle of nationality. In the same month Bonar Law, the Conservative leader, publicly implied that Britain's occupation of German colonies was to be permanent.[18]

17. *War Speeches*, pp. 104–5, 196–7, 205–6, 292–5; *War Memoirs*, 2, 686–8.
18. August 4, 1916, *War Speeches*, p. 340. The Sykes-Picot agreement has been widely regarded as incompatible with British promises to the Sherif Hussein of Mecca, made in a letter from Sir Henry McMahon in October 1915. See *Correspondence between Sir Henry McMahon and the Sherif Hussein of Mecca*, Cmd. 5957, 1939. For a recent detailed discussion of the Sykes-Picot agreement, which concludes that there was no essential conflict with promises

Equally suggestive that the British government envisaged a punitive peace and a postwar world divided by the same tensions as the old, was the part ministers played in discussing commercial policy. This discussion has received scant historical treatment, and it may be significant that most British memoirs pass over in silence episodes which occupied a great deal of attention at the time.

Toward the close of 1915 influential sections of the British economy began to demand a protectionist policy discriminating against Germany. The demand took several forms. Some pointed to wartime deficiencies in British resources and urged the need to protect strategic industries. Others came out in favor of temporary trade restrictions after the war to ensure Allied priority in facilities for reconstruction. Thoroughgoing protectionists cited alleged German plans for an economic bloc in Central Europe and demanded tariffs to combat unfair trading practices and economic warfare.[19] These various proposals naturally won support from Conservatives, who had long advocated protection, and aroused the suspicion of many Liberals who were equally accustomed to resisting the Conservative demand. Gradually the Government made substantial concessions. In January 1916 the president of the Board of Trade accepted the case for protecting strategic industries and admitted the danger of a German economic offensive after the peace. He went so far as to assert the necessity of denying Germany a "chance of reconstructing her commercial position."[20] In February, Bonar Law told the

to Hussein, see Elie Kedourie, *England and the Middle East—1914–1924* (Cambridge, 1956), pp. 29 ff. The Treaty with Rumania was abrogated by her separate surrender.

19. *Report of a Sub-Committee . . . to the Board of Trade . . .* Cd. 8181 (January 1916), pp. 6–16. Evidence in Cd. 8275. An account of earlier Anglo-German trade rivalry can be found in Ross J. S. Hoffman, *Great Britain and the German Trade Rivalry*, Philadelphia, 1933.

20. The *Times* (London), January 11, 1916. Henceforth the *Times* refers to the London *Times* unless preceded by "New York."

New York *Times* that the war had settled Britain's fiscal controversy in favor of protection and predicted an Allied economic entente and imperial preference. Visiting England in March, the Australian Prime Minister, William E. Hughes, added his voice to the protectionist campaign. Lloyd George, too, endorsed the nursing of strategic industry. The *Times* threw itself headlong into the fight and sought to strengthen the protectionist element in the British delegation to an Economic Conference of the Allies destined to take place in June. These efforts succeeded and the Liberal Walter Runciman was joined by Bonar Law and by Hughes himself.[21]

The resolutions passed at this Conference and approved by the British government were a resounding victory for the advocates of protection. Recommendations called for discrimination against Germany in the immediate postwar period and also in the long-term future. There were to be permanent measures to secure Allied self-sufficiency. Allied nations were to give each other preferential transportation rates and to secure their own economies by subsidies and tariffs. These recommendations were endorsed in November and again in December 1916, by the interim reports of a government committee on industrial policy.[22] Here was a publicly announced policy which ill accorded with idealistic prophecies of a world of harmony and peaceful cooperation.

As the late summer of 1916 advanced, the continued elusive-

21. Ibid., February 21, March 21, 22, 24, 25, 1916. Starting on April 3, 1916, the *Times* published a special weekly supplement to promote its views on trade.

22. *Recommendations of the Economic Conference of the Allies, June 14–17*, Cd. 8271, June 21, 1916, promulgated by the Board of Trade. *Interim Report on the Importation of Goods from the Present Enemy Countries after the War*, Cd. 9033, November 9, 1916; *Interim Report on the Treatment of Exports . . . and the Conservation of the Resources of the Empire . . .* Cd. 9034, December 14, 1916. In a speech on November 9, 1916, Asquith pointedly denied any intent to injure *neutral* trade after the war. *War Speeches*, p. 138.

ness of victory, growing public desire for a statement of war aims and warnings of impending German and American peace moves impelled the Cabinet to undertake its first comprehensive consideration of peace terms. In August, Asquith invited his colleagues to submit their views. There was still no desire at all to encourage public discussion of terms or of the possibility of an early end to the war. In an interview with the United Press on September 28, Lloyd George expressed this attitude somewhat vehemently, declaring British determination to fight on for complete victory. Shortly after this endorsement of a "Knock-Out Blow" Grey himself, while privately regretting Lloyd George's intemperate language, publicly announced his own opposition to any immediate negotiations.[23]

The Cabinet discussions proceeded by means of a series of memoranda. On August 31 General Sir William Robertson, Chief of the Imperial General Staff, submitted a paper urging careful preparation to promote British interests at a future conference. He stressed Britain's interest in maintaining the balance of power. In this connection Robertson laid remarkable emphasis on the continued need for a powerful German military—though not naval—force to balance the continental members of the Entente.

In September, Lord Robert Cecil, the Minister of Blockade, submitted a memorandum of a very different sort, suggesting a determined effort to establish a new kind of international relations on a basis of cooperation. He proposed a territorial settlement of only five years' duration, to be amended by a later, calmer conference. The treaty should also bind signatories to submit all future disputes to conference under pain of economic sanctions. On the other hand, Balfour's memorandum expressed the opinion that it was vain to speculate about such schemes. He predicted that international affairs after the war would continue to be the old struggle of—in his words—

23. *War Speeches,* p. 200; *War Memoirs,* 2, 853–9.

"haves" against "have nots." Britain's chief concern should be the balance of power and the maintenance of maritime supremacy. Territorial arrangements on the continent would, Balfour thought, be largely dictated by the other members of the Entente, but he agreed with Robertson on the desirability of continued German military strength. In view of the current criticism of secret diplomacy, it is interesting to note that some of these secret discussions thus revealed opinions which would have been more congenial to Germany than the public pronouncements of British leaders. It would clearly have been impossible to talk openly of preserving German military might.

So far the Cabinet's discussions had proceeded on the assumption of a decisive Allied victory. On November 13, 1916, Lord Lansdowne boldly forced attention to the most fundamental question of all by querying whether such a victory could be won. For his own part he feared that continued fighting would fail to bring any success proportionate to the costs involved. He therefore suggested that Britain might "accept less than twenty shillings in the pound in consideration of prompt payment."

General sentiment in the Cabinet went againt Lansdowne. Even Cecil's proposals envisaged a German defeat, and it was in fact he who made the most direct rejoinder to Lansdowne in a later memorandum. Lloyd George's views had been expressed in his "Knock-Out Blow" interview, and he had repeated this opinion more recently in a draft speech intended for Asquith's use at an Anglo-French conference on November 15. In this document Lloyd George warned of probable efforts by "powerful neutrals to patch up peace on what would appear to be specious terms" and of the danger that war-weary people "might listen to well intentioned but mistaken pacificators."

Having heard all the arguments, Asquith decided against any moves toward peace at that time. No one questioned this decision which was, in effect, one for peace with victory rather than peace by compromise.[24]

Shortly after this, Asquith's Ministry fell and Lloyd George became Premier. There had long been much discontent with Asquith's slowness and lack of decision as a war leader. As early as May 1915 he had been forced to admit the Conservatives to a coalition and to give Lloyd George extraordinary powers at the new Ministry of Munitions. This Coalition never formed a harmonious team, and Lloyd George, who had revealed an enthusiasm and aptitude for war which shocked many of his old colleagues, was increasingly drawn into association with Conservatives who were more warlike than the Liberals.[25] Gradually Lloyd George, Bonar Law, and Sir Edward Carson came to be in league to secure a more energetic war effort. The unsuccessful and in many cases disastrous conduct of the 1916 campaign exasperated these men. Lansdowne's memorandum emphasized the close connection between war aims and war effort. By deciding to go after maximum war aims and to refuse peace negotiations, Asquith went far toward compromising his position. If the country was committed to aims which demanded the complete defeat of Germany, then it needed leaders who would throw themselves headlong into the fight.

An early sign of trouble came on November 8 in a Commons debate on the disposition of enemy property. This subject which bore upon postwar trade policy came to be a test of Conservative dissatisfaction with the Government. In

24. *War Memoirs*, 2, 832–99; Lord Newton, *Lord Lansdowne* (London, 1929), pp. 450–1; Asquith, p. 176; Robert Cecil, *Great Experiment* (London, 1941), pp. 44, 353–7; Owen, pp. 328–9. Lloyd George's draft for Asquith is in typescript with the Papers of Arthur Henderson at the Library of the Labour Party Research Department, Transport House.

25. Jones, pp. 60, 70–1, 82; Thomson, pp. 241, 256–9; Colvin, p. 48; Dugdale, 2, 118–19; Lord Beaverbrook, *Politicians and the War* (2 vols. London, 1928–32), 1, 175, 216; 2, chap. 7; Blake, chaps. 16–18.

the division almost as many Conservatives followed Carson in opposition as their official leader, Bonar Law, in the Cabinet.[26] A little later Lloyd George, working hand in hand with Bonar Law and Carson, proposed a reorganization which would have secured them control of the war effort. Asquith resisted, and a series of complicated intrigues produced his resignation.[27]

Lloyd George took over and succeeded in forming a new coalition. He set up a War Cabinet of five members which met for the first time on December 9, 1916. The new Prime Minister's reputation for effective leadership enabled him to carry about half the Parliamentary Liberal party with him. The other half continued to support the war but went into an opposition of veiled bitterness under Asquith.[28] To gain the support of the Labour party, Lloyd George promised them a seat in the War Cabinet and certain social reforms. He also accepted demands that labor should have a representative at the peace conference, that militarism should be crushed in the United Kingdom as well as Germany, and that he would not refuse any reasonable peace offer. The latter pledge is less impressive in view of his conviction that a reasonable offer—which he did not define—would not be made.[29]

Although Labour party support was essential for sustaining the enthusiasm of the workers, Lloyd George depended on Conservatives for his Parliamentary strength. Many Conserva-

26. *H. C. Deb.*, 87, 247 ff. Of 286 Conservatives, only 73 voted for the Government, while 65 voted against.

27. For these maneuvers see esp. Beaverbrook, 2, chaps. 10–26; Blake, chaps. 19–21; Owen, pp. 329–44; Austen Chamberlain, *Down the Years* (London, 1934), chap. 7; Asquith, 2, 152 ff.

28. Thomson, pp. 263–4. Some of the Liberals who refused to follow Lloyd George argued that unless some supporters of the war applied a check to his belligerence, many moderates would be driven into league with those who would accept a premature peace; cf. a memorandum of Lord Crewe, December 20, 1916, Asquith, 2, 162.

29. *War Memoirs*, 3, 1048–60.

tive back-benchers were far from forgiving Lloyd George for
his past, but Bonar Law, Balfour, and Carson brought the
party into line behind the war effort. Henceforth it was on
these men that Lloyd George placed most reliance. They were
representatives of the fight-to-a-finish school of thought and
particularly of the mercantilist outlook on trade. The change
of government therefore marked the final ascendancy of men
of this stamp. The resignations of 1914, Balfour's admission to
Cabinet discussions in December, 1914, the coalition of 1915
and Lloyd George's growing control of the war effort had all
been stages in a process which now reached fruition.

Within a few days of the new Government's assuming
office the anticipated peace moves materialized. Replying to
the German and American peace notes of December, 1916,
was, in fact, the first major task of foreign policy under Lloyd
George.[30] The replies had to be written in harmony with the
Allies. Britain's leaders also had to draft their answer so as
to conform to the decision against peace talks at that time
while presenting British aims in a moderate light in order
to retain the sympathy of neutrals and liberal-minded men
in Britain.

Germany's note was the easier to handle, for it was both
vague and peremptory. On December 18 the War Cabinet
decided to reject the advance, leaving the details of a formal
reply for consultation with the French. The next day Curzon
in the Lords and Lloyd George in the Commons discussed the
German offer. Curzon declared that mere territorial restoration and the *status quo* were no longer enough. There must
be reparation and guarantees of security. Lloyd George professed himself always open to any reasonable proposals but
he branded the present German move as insincere, intended
only to weaken and divide the Allies. There must be ample
guarantees, he added, for any arrangement made with the

30. For the American move see below, pp. 80–1, 120–1.

faithless German regime. His whole speech once more took up the attack on Prussian militarism and implied that peace was not possible with the existing German leaders. It was necessary to carry on the war until aggression met an unmistakeable defeat and punishment. Only thus, Lloyd George declared, could the world achieve international good faith, the sole path to lasting peace.[31]

The official text of Wilson's note arrived the next day. The War Cabinet considered it on December 21 and 23 and arranged for Cecil and Balfour to draft replies pending an Anglo-French conference which happened to be meeting on December 26, 27, and 28. The conference approved a final text for an answer to Germany. This reply refused to parley, rejected the German case, and branded her move as a mere "war maneuver." [32]

On the matter of the American note Lloyd George raised two questions for general discussion. "Should we go into any sort of detail? Should we state our terms to America, to the world, and to our own people? The War Cabinet were themselves at present undecided." Secondly, should there be identical or separate replies? Separate replies would allow France, Belgium, and Serbia to "say things to the Americans that this country could not." The French expressed the fear that, if there were not a joint reply, the Belgians might offer terms which would only satisfy their own case. Germany would jump at such a chance and thereby gravely embarrass the other Allies.[33] It was therefore agreed that the Allies should

31. *H. L. Deb.*, 23, 935–9. J. B. Scott, ed., *Official Statements of War Aims and Peace Proposals, December, 1916–November, 1918* (Washington, D.C., 1921), pp. 16 ff.; *H. C. Deb.*, 88, 1333–8.

32. *War Memoirs*, 3, 1108–11; Scott, pp. 26–8.

33. Some civilian German leaders were apparently ready to adopt a tactic of this sort. Cf. H. W. Gatzke, *Germany's Drive to the West (Drang nach Westen). A Study of Germany's Western War Aims during the First World War* (Baltimore, 1950), pp. 139–40.

submit a united answer to Wilson, though in the event
Belgium added a supplementary note detailing her special
grievances.

As to the content of the reply, Cecil urged caution. He
shared the general resentment of Wilson's interference and
announced that he had told the American ambassador that
Wilson's note appeared "almost hostile." But Cecil advised
an answer which would not give America a chance to accuse
the Allies of evasiveness intended to conceal their intention
of destroying Germany. He also feared that a negative reply
would arouse questions in Britain as to why the Allies had
not seized the opportunity to state their case. While the conference agreed the reply would have to constitute an "appeal
to democracy," several of Cecil's compatriots as well as the
French stressed the danger of going too far in the attempt.
Balfour pointed to the "very dangerous fallacy" that the belligerents could make any kind of settlement and then the
nations of the world, led by the United States, create a
universal peace. This was a serious matter "because the United
States had it in their power to compel peace." America must
learn that no peace would last unless the first settlement was
"one such as the Allies desired." The *status quo* would not
do, and Balfour suggested the Allied reply should sketch a
large measure of self-determination in Europe and Turkey as
a *sine qua non* from which Britain itself would gain nothing.
Lord Curzon added his view that any detailed statement at
all would be too dangerous, if only because it would require
considerable negotiation between the Allies.

In the end the conference adopted a French suggestion
to compose a reply calculated to appeal to American opinion,
giving examples of Allied terms but avoiding any complete
or definitive statement. This answer was transmitted in a joint
note on January 10, 1917. The Allies approved the idea of a
league of nations but asserted that such an organization must
follow a satisfactory end to the war. Such a settlement must

include the restoration of invaded areas and of provinces "formerly torn from the Allies" and freedom for economic development subject to the need for strategic frontiers. The submerged nationalities of Austria, Hungary, and Turkey would have to be "enfranchised," though not necessarily independent. Finally, the Allies professed faith in the Tsar's good intentions toward Poland and denied any desire to enslave or exterminate the German peoples.[34]

Balfour made it his first task as Britain's new Foreign Secretary to send a supplementary note expounding British willingness to work for a peaceful world. He repeated his insistence that redrawing the map on national lines was a prerequisite for any international organization. Another necessary preliminary was the discrediting of the German leaders and the establishment of democracy in Germany. Without this condition it was very possible that Germany would once more launch aggression and be sufficiently strong to defeat any resistance. Subject to these reservations, Balfour appealed to Anglo-American liberalism by pledging Britain's devotion to the international reforms favored by the "best thinkers of the New and Old Worlds."[35]

Wilson's note had irritated a great many Englishmen by what they assumed to be an expression of his inability to see much difference between German and Allied aims.[36] He had succeeded, however, in evoking the most comprehensive statement of war aims yet made by the Allies. The detailed terms were obviously not such as Germany could accept until quite badly beaten, but it would be difficult to show that they were

34. Scott, pp. 35 ff. This account of the conference is based on the secret minutes to be found in the Henderson Papers. See also *War Memoirs*, 3, 1108–16.

35. Scott, pp. 45 ff.; Dugdale, 2, 136–7. This note was sent January 13, 1917. See also *British and Foreign State Papers, 1917–1918, 111* (London, 1921), 600–10.

36. Charles Seymour, *American Diplomacy during the World War* (Baltimore, 1934), pp. 190–1. See below, pp. 80–1.

in any exact particular out of harmony with the generalized proposals of self-determination and a rule of international law and democracy. On the other hand, these proposals were indeed extremely general and in the recent Cabinet discussions Balfour had not appeared an ardent internationalist. Viewed from another standpoint, there was little in his note and still less in his secret memorandum which could not be reconciled with a Europe remodeled along the lines of Sasonov's earlier design. There was no clear treatment of economic policy or of colonial questions. The secret treaties were still secret—indeed new agreements were in the making—and their contents gave increased significance to the exception to self-determination made in favor of defensible frontiers.[37] Thus, although the exchanges with Wilson had gone some way to clarify Britain's war aims, there was still plenty of confusion and vagueness.[38]

During the next few months uncertainty persisted in public and in private. Having staved off the danger of immediate negotiations, Lloyd George showed interest in developing the "ideal" side of the British peace program. There was both greater need and increased opportunity to do so. In Britain the public remained uneasy. The Russian Revolution relieved Britain of the embarrassment of Tsarist autocracy and of many Russian ambitions which ran counter to the principle of nationality. But at the same time the Revolution sent a tremor of unrest through the ranks of British labor. This tremor was

37. In February 1917 France and Russia gave each other a free hand in remaking their frontiers with Germany. Also in February, Britain agreed to support Japan's claim to German concessions in Shantung and to divide Germany's island possessions, Japan getting all north of the Equator. France subsequently adhered to this arrangement. In April agreements initiated at St. Jean de Maurienne elaborated the partition of the Near East and specified Italy's share.

38. See below, p. 82. The staff of the Foreign Office also circulated a war-aims memorandum at this time, but it was not discussed in Cabinet. Lloyd George, *Memoirs of the Peace Conference* (2 vols., New Haven, 1939), *1*, 11–22.

all the more serious because the Government felt the need of ostentatious labor support in dealing with the new Russian regime.[39] British leaders hastened to welcome the Revolution and to seize the added opportunity to identify the Allied cause with that of democracy. Speaking at a secret session of the Imperial War Conference on March 20, 1917, Lloyd George declared that the democratization of Europe was the only reliable guarantee of peace. "Liberty," he said, "is the sure guarantee of peace and good will amongst the peoples of the world. Free nations are not eager to make war." [40]

Many others, however, left no doubt that they put little faith in prospects for permanent peace and were intent on reinforcing Britain's position in a world of continued international conflict. On January 23, 1917, a day after President Wilson made a major address summing up his peace moves, the Conservative Solicitor-General, Sir Gordon Hewart, declared that the Allied statement was a minimum not a maximum.[41] Next day Bonar Law himself said that the idea of a league might not be "altogether Utopian" but he cast serious doubt on its practicability. "What President Wilson is longing for," he remarked caustically, "we are fighting for." [42] At the end of the month the Colonial Secretary, Walter Long, filled in another gap by asserting that Germany's colonies could never be returned.[43]

Similar opinions emerged during the meetings of the Imperial War Cabinet and Imperial War Conference which took place in the early months of 1917. One of the purposes of

39. *War Memoirs,* 4, 1881–84. See below, pp. 132–4.
40. Ibid., *3,* 1634–7; *4,* 1767–85. It was at this time that Lloyd George, in consultation with Cecil, set up the Phillimore Committee to study the question of international organization. Henry R. Winkler, *The League of Nations Movement in Great Britain, 1914–1919* (New Brunswick, N.J., 1952), pp. 232–4.
41. Speaking at Manchester; *Times,* January 24, 1917.
42. Scott, pp. 57–8.
43. Speaking at City Hall, Westminster, January 31, 1917; *Times,* February 1, 1917.

these gatherings was to discuss conditions for peace. Two subcommittees of the Imperial Cabinet considered territorial and nonterritorial terms. The reports of these committees recommended that the Empire retain permanent hold on its colonial conquests, that no concession should be made on the freedom of the seas and that, although the proposals of the Paris Economic Conference needed revision, Germany should be denied renewal of trade concessions and there should be imperial preference and protection of strategic industries. As to international organization, the committee decided that "any too comprehensive or ambitious project to ensure world peace might prove not only impracticable but dangerous." The committee's findings on such matters as a league of nations and disarmament were, in fact, so negative as to draw criticism from Lloyd George himself as unduly depressing.[44]

Thus there were, in British government circles, differences between those who favored a fight to a finish and those who would accept a negotiated peace of compromise. There was also a divergence between those who were willing to contemplate a new pattern of international affairs and those who were intent on improving Britain's position in the traditional balance of world politics. A memorandum which General Smuts presented to Lloyd George on April 29, 1917, well portrayed the tension between a concept of war aims calculated to institute a new world order and a concept designed for success in the old. Writing in the light of the Imperial

44. *War Memoirs, 4,* 1747–60 and Appendix D, 1798 ff.; *Resolutions Passed by the Committee on Commercial and Industrial Policy on the Subject of Imperial Preference,* Cd. 8482, February 2, 1917; *Imperial War Conference, Extracts from Minutes of Proceedings and Papers Laid before the Conference,* Cd. 8566, May 1917. Arthur Henderson, leader of the Labour party, dissented from resolutions to retain colonies and to set up imperial preference. At this time Balfour presented an account of British War Aims to the Imperial War Cabinet, an account very similar to his memorandum to the Cabinet in the previous autumn. This account is printed in *Lansing Papers, 2,* 19–32.

Cabinet meetings, Smuts, in one section of his report, defined as a minimum such objectives as the destruction of Germany's colonial empire and the detachment of all Turkish territory which might threaten British power in Asia. By way of contrast, another part of his report underlined the importance of democracy as a guarantee of peace, world opinion as a political force and the importance of pursuing a policy which could be presented in moral terms.[45]

For the moment the proponents of a decisive victory and a return to the old order were in the ascendant. The nature of the ultimate settlement would be greatly influenced by the future course of this debate. Many months were to pass, however, before the collapse of Germany opened the way for peace. Meanwhile America had entered the war under a leader with ideas of his own, and many unofficial but articulate people in Britain itself had been developing their own concept of a desirable peace.

45. *War Memoirs*, 3, 1531–7.

3. *Toward a Lasting Settlement*

THE REVERSAL of feeling in the Liberal party in August 1914 must rank as one of the most remarkable incidents in the history of public opinion; yet historians and political scientists have paid it scant attention. Those who have at least taken note of British liberalism's enthusiastic espousal of a war which it had earnestly opposed have usually been content to accept the invasion of Belgium as sufficient explanation. This answer is inadequate and makes it impossible to appreciate the significance of much that followed.

Liberalism as a whole in England—press, public, and politicians—did not apprehend the possibility of general war until July 27, 1914. When, at that time, they could no longer ignore the imminence of a major war, at least in Eastern Europe, Liberal newspapers saw no reason for British involvement. They declared that no British interest was at stake and congratulated themselves that there were no alliances to drag Britain into the conflict. The Conservative press might talk of the balance of power but that was still the "foul idol," the "chimera," that Bright had christened it. In any case Russia, not Germany, was the greatest menace to the equilibrium and civilization of Europe. A Minister who led the country into this war, avowed the moderately radical *Nation*, "would be responsible for a war as causeless and unpopular as any war in history, and he would cease to lead the Liberal Party." [1]

But from the Cabinet, locked in its own dissension, there came no word of reassurance. The Royal Navy did not dis-

1. *Manchester Guardian*, July 27, 28, 30, 31, 1914; *Daily News*, July 27, 28, 1914; *Nation*, August 1, 1914.

perse from its maneuvers; the Territorial Army mobilized and prepared for embarkation. All the worst liberal prophecies seemed about to be fulfilled; all the specters of a Cobdenite nightmare appeared to be at work. On Friday, July 31, 1914— the day Germany mobilized—the *Manchester Guardian's* leader revealed how deeply the liberal theory of international relations permeated its approach to the current crisis. By "some hidden contract" the *Guardian* complained, "England had been technically committed, behind her back, to the ruinous madness of a share in the wicked gamble of a war between two militarist leagues on the Continent." [2]

Here, in the words "hidden" and "behind her back," was the fear of secret diplomacy. The menace of foreign entanglement rose up in "committed," "leagues" and "Continent"—moreover, the country had been committed "technically" by the maneuverings of bureaucrats. What did this policy lead to but war, "ruinous madness," and a "wicked gamble"? Meanwhile the House of Commons, the public guardian, was seized with the Milk and Dairies bill.

By the weekend some Liberals were belatedly rousing to fend off war. Many public meetings expressed antiwar feeling; letters and telegrams opposing the Government's policy poured into London. The Free Churches passed resolutions for neutrality. On Sunday, August 2, 1914, a mass rally gathered in Trafalgar Square.[3] J. L. Hammond, the social historian, and H. W. Massingham, editor of the *Nation*, were there, vehemently denying that even an invasion of Belgium would be sufficient cause for war.[4]

On Monday, August 3, 1914, the peak of the crisis and the day of Grey's speech, the *Manchester Guardian* carried the

2. *Manchester Guardian*, July 31, 1914.

3. Irene C. Willis, *England's Holy War* (New York, 1928), pp. 64–9. This volume consists of three short books originally published in 1919, 1920, 1921.

4. Margaret I. Cole, ed., *Beatrice Webb's Diaries, 1912–1924* (London, 1952), p. 25.

manifestos of two hastily formed groups working for neutrality. One of these groups, the Neutrality League, included Norman Angell and C. P. Scott, editor of the *Guardian;* the other, such Liberal eminences as A. G. Gardiner, editor of the *Daily News,* F. W. Hirst, editor of the *Economist,* Gilbert Murray, G. M. Trevelyan, L. T. Hobhouse, Hammond, and Hobson. In the Commons, Grey revealed the military conversations which had taken place with France and the joint naval dispositions. A Liberal member shouted, "Something more behind our backs!" Amid considerable commotion dissentient Liberals and Labour members secured the right to debate the matter on the adjournment. When that came round, violation of Belgian neutrality had begun. A large body of members continued to oppose war, repeating all the liberal arguments. The war would be the result of the "old and disastrous system" of diplomacy. It would aggrandize Russia. German conduct had not been perfect but neither had that of any other nation: the war would be against the German people, friends of the British people. It was particularly ridiculous for Grey to pretend that war would do no more harm to Britain's economy than neutrality. On the contrary, said Josiah Wedgwood in terms reminiscent of Angell's *Great Illusion,* war would shatter credit and bring civilization down in financial ruin. The only sane course was neutrality, preserving the national strength for the rescue of civilization.[5]

All the cards were on the table. Germany had violated Belgium. Grey had laid open the ramifications of the Entente and had outlined Britain's vital interest in the balance of power and the immunity of the Channel coast. Conservatives had long made up their minds. On August 3, 1914, the *Morning Post* frankly brushed aside the cause of Belgium and Serbia: "England is driven into war by Germany's attack upon France." Still, most of the Liberal papers were for neutrality. On the night of August 4, 1914, as the British ultimatum ex-

5. *H. C. Deb.,* 65, 1809–80.

pired and the nation went to war, Liberal presses continued to rumble out their protests. Even on the morning of August 6 the *Daily News* was still decidedly of the same mind.

> [It] would have been just and prudent and statesmanlike for England to have remained neutral . . . a mistaken course of foreign policy, pursued over ten years, has led us to the terrible conflict in which we are now engaged. We believe that the conviction that that policy was mistaken will steadily conquer the minds of the English people.

Once the war was under way, the Liberal press reluctantly conceded that the nation must support the war effort. "Being in . . . we must win," admitted the *Daily News*.[6]

The record of the previous few days hardly suggested that Liberals would be very enthusiastic supporters of the war, but with startling rapidity a new note crept into Liberal papers. Those who opened the *Daily Chronicle* on August 7, 1914, were informed by H. G. Wells that "never was war so righteous as war against Germany now." The same day the *Daily News* concluded from Asquith's justification of the war that the Government, with "clean hands and a clear conscience," was fighting to save civilization. At the week end the editor of the *Daily News* proclaimed that "Barbarism, we hope, is fighting its last battle."[7]

And so the Liberal press now approved the war, emphasizing the rights of Belgium and the defense of civilization but saying very little about the national interest or balance of power. Very soon Liberal editors discovered the war was for the "spiritual governance of the world." Britain stood for "the spirit of light against the spirit of darkness."[8] This interpreta-

6. *Daily News,* August 6, 1914.
7. Ibid., August 8, 1914; cf. "Why Britain Is Right," *Nation,* August 15, 1914.
8. "A.G.G.," *Daily News,* September 26, 1914.

tion carried with it a corresponding promise that Allied victory would necessarily create a new and better world. The
supreme architect of this best of all possible worlds was H. G.
Wells, who saw the future with such inspiring clarity that he
rushed repeatedly into print as one of the war's most fervent
advocates. Beginning on August 7, 1914, he wrote a series of
articles in which he coined the phrase "war to end war." [9] He
expected the war to "alter the world for ever," introducing an
age of disarmament, social welfare, and universal peace. Here
and there a note of caution sounded, to be drowned by the
outburst of confidence. Lord Eversley wrote to the *Daily News*
suggesting that a "war to end war" must be a long one and
might not end where its proponents expected. Wells scoffed
at this "pseudo-sage intellectual laziness, this easy dread of
prematurity." [10] Occasionally the editors drew back, but only
for a moment. In September, Gardiner recalled blemishes in
British policy and then dismissed them "because we are fighting the common enemy of humanity." [11] The *Nation* admitted
that in wartime the people were bound to oversimplify the issues. But when on the same day Bertrand Russell wrote placing a share of the war guilt on Britain, the editor was vehe-
ment in dissent.[12]

This change of mind as to the merits of the war implied a
profound shift in attitude toward Germany. Before the outbreak Germany had been a fellow victim of the international
system, sinned against as well as sinning and distinctly less
dangerous than Russia. Now this was changed. German ambition had caused the war against the "entirely defensive" policy
of the Entente.[13] Liberal papers far outstripped Conservative

9. The articles were later collected as: H. G. Wells, *The War
That Will End War*, London, 1914.
10. *Daily News*, August 20, 21, 1914.
11. Ibid., September 26, 1914.
12. *Nation*, August 15, 1914.
13. *Round Table* (September, 1914), pp. 600–13; *Nation*, August 22, October 31, 1914.

in depicting and condemning German iniquities. Atrocity stories in particular fascinated Liberals and by September 26, 1914, the *Nation* was generously conceding, "We do not suppose that the Germans as a whole are less than human." [14]

A new portrait of Germany's role in the war demanded a new perspective on the other Allies, especially Russia. With regard to Russia, Liberals adopted a strategy they were frequently to employ toward painful subjects: that of almost complete silence. A few were bolder and undertook to exculpate Russia of any ill intention.[15] The attitude of the Liberal press toward Russia foreshadowed its later treatment of Italy's entrance into the war on the Allied side in the spring of 1915. The *Daily News* then dared to hail Italy's declaration of war, after months of hard haggling with both sides, as "no mere calculation of expediency." [16]

Quite clearly these Liberals had performed an astounding *volte face*, with startling speed. How could they believe so firmly in the complete justice and beneficent outcome of a war which, all their tradition suggested, sprang from a pernicious international system, would exacerbate hatred, and would do more for woe than weal? Doubtless Belgium and the diplomatic correspondence published in the government White Paper of August 1914 [17] provided many arguments and dominated the impressions of the short-memoried newspaper reader. But certainly this cannot explain the change of front among Liberal leaders. The Liberal press had said that Britain

14. *Nation,* September 26, 1914; cf. "The German Gospel," "Huns, Goths and Vandals," "The Method of Terror," ibid., September 5, 12, 19, 1914; Caroline R. Playne, *Society at War, 1914–1916* (Boston, 1928), p. 259; Lucy Masterman, *C. F. G. Masterman* (London, 1939), p. 274; Wells, *War and the Future* (London, 1917), p. 193. In his excitement A. G. Gardiner demanded that the Kaiser, "if guilty," should be tried. Quoted in Willis, p. 187.

15. Wells, *Nation,* August 22, 1914; Philip Snowden, *An Autobiography, 1864–1934* (2 vols. London, 1934), *1,* 361.

16. *Daily News,* May 22, 1915; cf. ibid., March 30, 31, 1915.

17. *Collected Diplomatic Documents,* Cd. 7860.

should not fight for Belgium and had refused to divorce the
events of July 1914 from the history of the previous ten years.

It seems improbable that wholly rational grounds can be
assigned to the change of front, which must be attributed
rather to the emotional impact of an unforeseen catastrophe
on minds conditioned to a liberal outlook on foreign affairs. In
August 1914 British Liberals found themselves in one of the
most trying political situations, that of opposition to a war in
which their nation was engaged. There is ample evidence that
they felt the strain acutely. Even members of the Liberal party
who favored the war from the first were conscience stricken.
Grey himself was "terribly concerned . . . and suffering." [18]
The unprecedented scale of the war and a lack of accurate
news which now seems incredible, heightened the tension.[19]
Only an overwhelming case for going to war could justify
such a tragedy.

Conservatives had no difficulty. They accepted war as a
necessary risk of international affairs and in 1914 they consistently founded their advocacy of war on the balance of
power and the threat to the national interest. Liberals, however, had specifically rejected these arguments. Once the war
had begun they might have recanted or glossed over their
previous statements and accepted a war of national self-
interest. But such an argument would have rested uncom-
fortably on their whole prewar training in foreign policy.
They had learned that it was never in the interest of a nation
to go to war. Strictly speaking, this traditional liberal doctrine
meant only that in cases of dispute it was always possible to
work out a settlement which entailed less loss to the parties
than a war. The doctrine did not rule out the possibility that
the irrational conduct of some nations might require a per-

18. Cole, p. 28.
19. For the lack of news, and the belief that the war was the
greatest tragedy ever, see Playne, pp. 11, 117; Arnold Bennett, *The
Journal of Arnold Bennett* (2 vols. New York, 1932), 2, 113–43;
Masterman, p. 280; Cole, p. 38.

fectly "enlightened" and reasonable nation to fight in defense of its interests. But this was an unwelcome qualification, especially to the strong humanitarian strain in the liberal theory of international relations, and was seldom expressed. It seemed as if liberals had so often depicted the conduct of nations as it should be, that they demanded such conduct of their own government, as if other nations were already similarly disposed.

In 1914, then, to fight for British self-interest would stress the conflict of national interests when liberals had been accustomed to emphasize international solidarity. Instead, forgetting that they had seen the current European question as just another international quarrel, with much to be said for both sides, they chose to treat this as a special case. The defense of Belgium, however, was not a sufficient cause in itself, for many Liberals had specifically denied this. It was therefore extremely convenient to use the Belgian cause as a symbol, depicting the war as a struggle against exceptional iniquity, the removal of which would produce the kind of world in which war would really be unnecessary. Initially this process was at least partially conscious.[20] Shortly, the events and atrocities of the war rendered it easier to evade the whole question of origins. By February the *Nation* thought it "unnecessary for us to recall [Germany's] pre-war diplomacy in order to make good our main case against the perils of her upstart dominion. She is her own accuser." [21]

Thus Liberals rallied in support of the war and did their part in intensifying its bitterness. It was in this atmosphere

20. For example, Lord Loreburn wrote to C. P. Scott: "Now that we are in for this war we must do our best to win. . . . The question how it came about . . . and who is to blame . . . ought, I feel, to stand over till we are at peace." J. L. Hammond, *C. P. Scott of the Manchester Guardian* (London, 1934), p. 182. Cf. Bennett, 2, 114; Victoria de Bunsen, *Charles Roden Buxton: A Memoir* (London, 1948), p. 62

21. *Nation,* February 27, 1914.

that Asquith and the rest of the Government made their plea for national unity. Such strongly held convictions as to the responsibility for the war would certainly exercise a powerful influence when the time came to consider the terms on which the struggle might be ended.

With varying degrees of enthusiasm the great majority of the Liberal party adopted this attitude. To some it may have seemed that the war would prove a means of reintegrating the party. But the official view did not win universal acceptance. Most of those who dissented were radicals.[22] The interesting fact that the leaders of this dissent had all been associated with prewar Liberal groups devoted to the study of international affairs reinforces the theory that the *volte face* of most other Liberals was closely related to their being taken unaware by the war.

By far the majority of the Government's critics were members of the Liberal party. A remarkable number of eminent Liberals became associated with this dissent from the attitude of their leaders.[23] Very important additional support came from the Independent Labour party—notably from Philip Snowden and from Ramsay MacDonald, who resigned as leader of the Parliamentary Labour party when the party supported the war. This association with labor, and, because the Labour

22. From now on the term "radicals" will be used to distinguish those who dissented from the majority position on the war and its origin. In this broad sense, it embraces some members of the Labour party and a few Liberals whose views on domestic affairs could not properly be described as radical in the conventional sense. This usage follows a general contemporary practice.

23. The names of some of those associated with the radical dissent will give an idea of the range of talent involved: C. R. Buxton; his brother, Noel Buxton, M.P.; Charles Trevelyan, M.P.; Arthur Ponsonby, M.P.; Philip Morrell, M.P.; E. J. King, M.P.; Bertrand Russell; J. A. Hobson; G. Lowes Dickinson (the eminent humanist); E. D. Morel; J. L. Hammond; F. W. Hirst (editor of the *Economist*); Norman Angell; and H. N. Brailsford, a well-known journalist. At least eight of these were associated with the Garton Foundation, as were Snowden and MacDonald.

party supported the war, with the left wing of labor, came to play a major role in attracting numbers of articulate members of the Liberal party leftward. It proved a decisive step in the process whereby Liberals who held radical views on foreign policy moved over to the Labour party where their ideas had been long in vogue.[24]

Those who dissented did so because they could not accept the official view of the war's origins and therefore feared for its outcome. The radicals naturally viewed the origins of the war in the light of their prewar analysis of international affairs. That analysis taught them that war was normally the result of a faulty but universally practiced diplomacy which pursued mistaken ends by dangerous methods. This made it unlikely that any nation could bear sole responsibility for a war. The radicals insisted that the "genesis of the war is to be sought, not in original sin grafted on the German government or nation, but in a universal reign of fear . . ."[25] There was here no effort to exculpate a people by placing all blame on its government: the diplomatic system in general was to blame. Britain had become involved because of a mistaken and undemocratic foreign policy which entangled her in the interstices of continental politics. The particular conflicts which set off the chain reactions of this system lay in Eastern Europe and there Russia had behaved with at least as much intransigence as Germany. Moreover, Russia had rivaled Germany in pugnacity in the closing days of the crisis.[26]

24. On this see Angell, *After All*, pp. 217 ff.; Charles P. Trevelyan, *The Union of Democratic Control* (London, 1919), p. 8, and his *From Liberalism to Labour* (London, 1921), passim.

25. E. D. Morel, *Truth and the War* (London, 1916), p. 51.

26. Morel, "Memorandum," in Seymour Cocks, *E. D. Morel: the Man and His Work* (London, 1922), pp. 220–2; Angell, *Prussianism and Its Destruction* (London, 1914), passim; *H. C. Deb.*, 65, 2089–90; MacDonald to *Nation*, August 15, 1914; Ponsonby to *Nation*, August 22, 1914; *The Balance of Power* (Union of Democratic Control, Pamphlet 14a, 1915), passim, esp. p. 2; Ponsonby, *Democracy and Diplomacy* (London, 1915), pp. 4, 100; Brailsford,

With these and similar arguments the radicals denied Germany's sole responsibility for the war. Such criticism of the nation's policy during a war was in a long-established British tradition embracing Burke, Fox, Bright and Lloyd George's own activities in the Boer War. Occasionally, in their anxiety to refute excessive charges against Germany, some radicals came close to putting all the blame on Great Britain; they seemed to argue that Britain's past misdeeds should inhibit her from any action at all. Most of the radicals avoided this extreme and admitted that Germany was a prime exponent of "militarism" and that there was, on balance, an "overwhelming case against Germany" in this particular war. They therefore accepted the necessity of carrying on the war and repulsing Germany.[27]

It was in contemplation of the settlement after the war that the difference between the radical and the orthodox Liberal view of the war's origin became most important. The radical theory of international affairs implied that a stable and more peaceful world could be constructed only by rationally reforming the whole system of international intercourse. A belief that Germany alone had caused the war and the preceding international tension, and that no problems would survive her defeat, would be fatal to any satisfactory peace. Such a belief implied that only the Central Powers need change their ways. It led to the demand for "unconditional surrender" and sapped all incentive to consider the precise ends of the war and the

The Origins of the Great War (U.D.C., 4, 1914), passim; Russell, War, the Offspring of Fear (U.D.C., 3, 1914), passim. The Union of Democratic Control (see below, pp. 57 ff.) issued two series of minor publications, pamphlets and leaflets. About the beginning of 1915 the code numbers of pamphlets were distinguished by the letter "a," the leaflets by "b." In these references simple numbers indicate pamphlets unless specifically stated. The place of publication is rarely given, the date also is sometimes omitted.

27. The Morrow of the War (U.D.C., 1, 1914); Brailsford, Origins, p. 11.

most economical way to achieve them. A war conducted in such a spirit ceased to be an instrument of policy.[28]

Consequently the radicals thought it essential to dispel the illusion that the mere defeat of Germany would usher in a golden age. Being deep-rooted, the causes of war would still exist when the fighting ended. A lasting peace would have to be "scientific," based not on conquest but on a rational attempt to remove the sources of international friction. The most desirable settlement would be what H. N. Brailsford called a "Peace by Contentment," leaving the enemy nothing to fight about rather than nothing to fight with.[29] Those who desired such a peace had a double task: to devise adequate solutions for international problems and to recommend those solutions to public opinion.

Radical publicists hastened to take up these tasks. The movement was given an early focus by the foundation of the Union of Democratic Control. Four men—Ramsay Mac-Donald, Arthur Ponsonby, Norman Angell and Charles Trevelyan—set up this organization a few days after the war began. E. D. Morel became the secretary and in November the Union published its program of four "Cardinal Points":

1. No province shall be transferred from one Government to another without the consent, by plebiscite or otherwise, of the population of such province.

2. No Treaty, Arrangement, or Undertaking shall be entered upon in the name of Great Britain without the sanction of Parliament. Adequate machinery for ensuring democratic control of foreign policy shall be created.

3. The Foreign Policy of Great Britain shall not be aimed at creating Alliances for the purpose of maintaining the Balance of Power, but shall be directed to concerted action

28. Morel, *Truth,* p. 53; Brailsford to *Nation,* December 12, 1914.
29. Brailsford to *Nation,* December 12, 1914, January 2, 1915; *Morrow,* p. 1; *The National Policy* (U.D.C., 6, 1915), p. 10.

between the Powers, and the setting up of an International Council, whose deliberations and decisions shall be public, with such machinery for securing international agreement as shall be the guarantee of an abiding peace.

4. Great Britain shall propose as part of the Peace settlement a plan for the drastic reduction, by consent, of the armaments of all the belligerent Powers, and to facilitate that policy shall attempt to secure the general nationalisation of the manufacture of armaments, and the control of the export of armaments by one country to another.[30]

These points, deliberately more precise than a simple appeal for peace, were well calculated to appeal to liberal-minded men, for they were all grounded in traditional liberal doctrine. So armed, the U.D.C. began a campaign of public education. It organized local branches and invited the affiliation of other —chiefly labor—groups. Special efforts were made to attract labor support. Within a year there were eighty-one branches; by 1918 there was an affiliated membership of 650,000. The Union sponsored meetings, published pamphlets and leaflets and in 1915 began publication of a monthly magazine.[31] Another outlet was the I.L.P.'s weekly Labour Leader.

Perhaps the U.D.C. was most important, however, as a symbol of the generally critical attitude taken by a number of able and prominent adherents to the Liberal and Labour parties who were otherwise bound by no common program. The U.D.C. itself was a loose and flexible body: its members were committed only to the Cardinal Points, other opinions put forward in U.D.C. publications being solely for information and discussion. Many eminent members of the U.D.C.

30. H. M. Swanwick, *Builders of Peace* (London, 1924), pp. 30–4; Angell, *After All*, pp. 189–92; Cocks, pp. 222–3; Charles Trevelyan, *The Union of Democratic Control* (London, 1919), passim. The Points are taken from *Morrow*, front cover.

31. Swanwick, pp. 50–71; U.D.C., *Annual Report: 1917* (London, 1917), pp. 4–5; Trevelyan, p. 8.

conducted all their research and publicity independently. With similar informality many who did not join the U.D.C. contributed to its funds and discussions and moved in roughly the same direction. Noel Buxton, a prominent back-bencher, fell into this category. Conversely, U.D.C. members and sympathizers were active in other influential groups. Lowes Dickinson inaugurated the "Bryce Group," a group for the study of international organization, which gained its name from the occasional attendances of Viscount Bryce. U.D.C. members gained a dominant position in the influential "Writers Group" of the Reform Club, a stronghold of orthodox Liberalism.[32] The *Nation,* the *Daily News,* and other Liberal papers continued to commission articles from the many well-known radical journalists. Above all, organized and unorganized critics of national policy possessed a splendid outlet in their handful of Parliamentary representatives. Here they had a forum destined to increase in usefulness as the war proceeded. Radical members used this position to publicize their views and to put pressure on the Government. As time passed, they concerted debating strategy.[33]

Thus the radicals enjoyed from the outset an influence of greater proportions than their numbers would suggest. It speaks much for the essential tolerance of their countrymen that, though harassed and impeded by both official and unofficial opposition, radicals were able to persist in their activity and agitation.

Their first chosen task was to undermine the majority Liberals' determination to view the war as a simple issue of right against wrong. Initially this campaign was waged chiefly in the correspondence columns of the *Nation,* which remained open to all shades of opinion. The U.D.C.'s fourth pamphlet,

32. E. M. Forster, *Goldsworthy Lowes Dickinson* (London, 1934), pp. 155 ff.; Winkler, *League of Nations Movement,* pp. 16–17; Bennett, 2, 252–3.
33. Trevelyan, p. 8; U.D.C., *Report, 1917,* p. 5.

The Origins of the Great War, was an expansion of Brailsford's contribution to this correspondence. From then on, discussion of the war's origins remained a constant feature of
the U.D.C.'s work. Soon, however, the radicals extended themselves to more constructive efforts and began to shape their
desire for a "scientific" peace of reconciliation into specific
demands. The first of these was that the settlement should be
negotiated, not dictated. Only if all parties had an opportunity
to express their views could a treaty represent the best possible compromise of interests. The radicals confidently expected that Germany would speedily be swept out of France
and Belgium and would then be ready to negotiate.[34] Allied
failure to achieve this result and Germany's refusal to become
sufficiently accommodating proved a constant stumbling block
to radical aspirations.

Along with the principle of a negotiated peace went a more
pressing demand: that the Allies, especially Britain, should
forthwith define and declare the terms upon which they were
willing to parley. Some of these terms were not in dispute. All
the radicals accepted the need for evacuation and restoration
of Belgium. But other more dubious issues were now in question; Alsace-Lorraine and Poland, for instance. Most radicals
were suspicious of sweeping territorial changes, fearing that
"playing at map-making" might only create new frustrations.
Such ambitious projects also seemed calculated to make it
more difficult to arrive at an agreement, a consideration which
weighed heavily with those who valued peace as highly as the
radicals. The terms declared by the Allies should therefore be
as moderate as possible.[35]

On one point the radicals were determined: it should be
made quite clear that there was no intention to crush Germany
to the point of impotence, partition, or discrimination. A peace

34. Brailsford, *Origins,* pp. 14–15.
35. Ibid., p. 15; *Morrow,* p. 2; *Why We Should State Terms of
Settlement* (U.D.C., 9, 1915).

of this kind would clearly be incompatible with the rational solution of mutual differences. It would also prove tenuous, for history taught that no nation could be artificially enfeebled for long and that the instability of international alignment would offer the vanquished many potential allies in recovery. A punitive peace being unwise, it was obviously advantageous to say so. Failure to do this would stiffen German resistance and arouse attitudes and expectations in the Allied nations which would greatly impede efforts to reach a clear-headed settlement. Assurance of moderate intentions, on the other hand, would, the radicals hoped, encourage equivalent liberal elements in Germany to urge moderation on their own government. The persistent impotence of German liberalism remained another constant source of frustration to its British counterpart.[36]

From the conviction that the Government should declare terms, that the settlement should be moderate, and that it largely depended upon the public temper, it was but a short step for the radicals to begin sketching their own patterns for the peace. At first most of the ideas developed and publicized consisted of fairly general elaborations of themes prominent in prewar liberal speculations. Pamphlets dealt with democratic control, international organization and disarmament. Ponsonby published the first book-length study of democratic control, advocating Parliamentary authority over declarations of war and ratification of treaties, together with devices for increasing the flow of information to Parliament and people.[37]

Schemes for international organization were also pressed

36. Brailsford to *Nation*, August 29, September 19, 1914; *Morrow*, p. 7; Angell, *Shall This War End German Militarism?* (U.D.C., 2, 1914), pp. 2, 10, 15, 18.

37. Ponsonby, *Democracy*; and *Parliament and Foreign Policy* (U.D.C., 5, 1915); Morel, *Morocco in Diplomacy*, was now reissued as *Ten Years of Secret Diplomacy*, London, 1915; *The International Industry of War* (U.D.C., 7, 1915); *Towards an International Understanding* (U.D.C., 10, 1915).

forward. Lowes Dickinson, who set to work on the idea in the first fortnight of the war and probably coined the term "league of nations," quickly established the Bryce Group and later helped to found the League of Nations Society in April 1915.[38] J. A. Hobson, another radical interested in the league idea, published his ambitious scheme in *Towards International Government*.[39] One point very much debated among proponents of a league was whether Germany should be admitted to a league or excluded as untrustworthy, the radicals unanimously declaring that Germany must be a full and equal member. This issue, with its implication as to the origin of the war, went to the heart of the difference between the radicals and the majority of the Liberal party.

Later on, by the end of 1915, the radicals had time to formulate more detailed proposals for the peace. In the autumn Morel and C. R. Buxton published comprehensive drafts for a settlement.[40] The U.D.C. decided that henceforth it would devote a major part of its attention to studying and devising solutions for particular contemporary problems.[41] Probably the crowning achievement of radical research in 1915 was the publication of *Towards a Lasting Settlement*, a symposium which formed almost a manual of liberal theory. On the whole, the authors of the work, who included Dickinson, Hobson, Brailsford, Snowden and C. R. Buxton, struck a note of caution, warning of difficulties in the way of any adequate international organization, the dangers of encouraging self-determination to extremes and the contradiction between economic conditions and many nationalist aspirations. In the

38. Winkler, pp. 50–1. Hobson and Ponsonby were also in the Bryce Group.

39. Hobson, *Towards International Government*, London, 1915.

40. Morel, *Labour Leader* (September 25, 1915), reprinted in idem, *Truth*, pp. 197–8; C. R. Buxton's proposals in *Manchester Guardian*, November 20, 1915, and, in part, U.D.C., *Terms of Peace* (U.D.C., 18b, 1915).

41. Swanwick, pp. 75–6.

liberal tradition these writers reasserted that the causes of war were "definite, ascertainable and removable," but they warned their optimistic colleagues in the Liberal party that victory alone was not enough; peace could be firmly established only by the painstaking solution of the various problems underlying international tensions.[42]

All the time the radicals were conducting these studies they continued their efforts to win support for their program, especially for a statement of moderate terms as a basis for negotiation. This campaign naturally labored under great handicaps. Criticism of national policy aroused angry opposition. But the radicals possessed one potential advantage. Their aims and their methods were squarely in the tradition of British liberalism; they had preserved the traditional viewpoint with greater consistency than the bulk of the Liberal party. For this reason, if the majority of the party should be shaken in its confidence that British policy would produce an ideal peace, it would offer a fertile field for radical propaganda. Meantime the radicals served as a restless conscience.

Very early, certain features of the war sharpened the majority's sensitivity to doubt and criticism. The radicals kept repeating the old liberal lesson that war played into the hands of reaction.[43] Before 1914 was out, the Liberal press was up in arms against censorship and other encroachments on civil liberty, including the threat of conscription.[44] Rapid indications of growing annexationist ambitions on the part of Britain's allies aroused further anxieties. By December 1914 fears

42. C. R. Buxton and others, *Towards a Lasting Settlement* (London, 1915), passim. For radical proposals for the peace, see below, pp. 73–8.

43. See esp. Angell, *Prussianism*, passim.

44. E.g. *Nation*, August 29, October 10, November 21, 1914; January 9, April 24, 1915; *Daily News*, December 5, 1914; Bennett, *2*, 156; MacDonald, *War and the Workers* (U.D.C., 8, 1915), passim.

of such runaway schemes, especially on the part of Russia, had persuaded the *Daily News* and the *Nation* to admit the value of openly discussing desirable peace terms.[45] The spring of 1915 brought rumors of Russia's designs on Constantinople and of the bargains offered Italy. In May came Japan's Twenty-one Demands on China; the same month the *Manchester Guardian* printed a highly accurate account of the Treaty of London. Such terms, the *Nation* exclaimed in horror, "would be to buy victory at any price," and would ruin the peace.[46]

Also in May the Liberal government gave way to the first Coalition. The crisis took the Liberal party by surprise: Asquith did not even forewarn his colleagues in the Government. Accompanying this process, painful enough for Liberals, were several aggravating circumstances; the admission of Sir Edward Carson to the Government, the Conservatives' humiliating insistence that Haldane be thrown out on suspicion of pro-Germanism.

The change of Government undoubtedly dealt a severe blow to radical hopes of securing a statement of moderate terms leading to a negotiated peace. Even the previous Government had given no encouragement. The influx of Conservatives made concession even more improbable. But on a long-term view the cabinet crisis offered the radicals some consolation. It testified to the growing stresses of war which made peace constantly more alluring and strengthened the argument that war was a poor instrument of policy. More important perhaps, the crisis dramatized the ability of the right-wing to oust the Liberal party from the conduct of the war. The most warlike Liberal was now forced to wonder whether the war for democracy might cost his party its power. It became more and more difficult for one trained in the lib-

45. *Daily News,* November 17, 1914; *Nation,* October 10, 1914.
46. *Manchester Guardian,* May 13, 1915; *Nation,* May 15, 1915.

eral tradition to overlook the radical arguments. Although the Liberal press grumblingly accepted the change as a necessary price for unity, the *Nation*, at least, never quite regained its old buoyancy.[47]

For the rest of 1915, Liberals faced similar trials as the strain of war tightened. Before the summer ended, Allied campaigns were going badly. Demands for a more energetic conduct of the war became insistent. Carson resigned from the Government to lead his "ginger" group in opposition. The clamor for conscription increased, and various half-way measures successively failed. A number of Liberals, including C. P. Scott, favored conscription, but most did not. The *Daily News* and *Nation* justified their opposition by denying that the nation's plight was really so grave or that compulsory service would be effective. Very different was the reaction of the radicals, who saw in the lack of military success an added reason to declare terms and negotiate a peace. They did not answer the objection that because the most far-reaching commitments made by Britain stemmed from the demands of her allies, a statement of moderate terms would greatly endanger the alliance at a time when every ounce of strength was sorely needed. This omission reflected a consistent radical refusal to admit that Britain's dire need of assistance provided pressing reasons to make these commitments and that it was not easy to suggest an alternative policy. Nor did they resolve the dilemma that Germany showed no readiness to meet their terms and was especially unlikely to do so when her military prospects appeared so bright.

Early in 1916 the advent of conscription, violent attacks upon civil liberties [48] and indications that the Government

47. For some Liberal press comment see *Nation*, May 1, 22, 29, 1915; *Daily News*, May 1, 22, 1915; *Manchester Guardian*, May 19, 20, 26, 1915; H. Wilson Harris, *Life So Far* (London, 1954), pp. 108–9.

48. Playne, pp. 280; T. P. Conwell Evans, *Foreign Policy from*

intended concessions to protectionism [49] presented orthodox Liberals with so many inroads upon their most treasured principles that the suggestion of a negotiated peace gained a readier hearing. Negotiation appeared all the more attractive in view of the Allies' continued lack of progress toward commanding a settlement on the battlefield. Already the radicals had urged that military deadlock need not mean diplomatic paralysis as well. They claimed the stalemate supported their contention that the war must be ended by the declaration and mutual adjustment of terms, which was, in any case, the only basis for a lasting peace. Those Liberals who demanded the prior total defeat of Germany seemed to assume that the Allies could impose terms so obviously just as to win the willing endorsement of the vanquished. History showed, however, wrote Hobson, that a peace in which one side had no effective voice was always extreme.[50]

In 1916 these views made considerable headway among orthodox Liberals. The *Nation,* never quite at ease in its support of the war, took conscription as its cue to adopt a generally critical attitude which brought it progressively into the radical camp.[51] By spring the *Nation* was joining in the call for a declaration of British terms.[52] A notable indication

---

a *Back Bench, 1904–1918* (London, 1932), p. 152; de Bunsen, p. 67; cf. *H. C. Deb.,* 77, 1420.

49. See above, p. 35.

50. *Nation,* October 16, 30, November 20, 1915. These arguments will be recognized as an anticipation of Lansdowne's memorandum to the Cabinet in 1916 (see above, p. 35) and his letter to the *Daily Telegraph* on November 29, 1917 (see below, pp. 148–9).

51. *Nation,* January 1, 8, 1916; Beaverbrook, 2, 44–5; cf. *Daily News,* December 11, 1915, May 3, 1916. The introduction of conscription also brought the first defection from the Liberal party leadership since August 1914, when John Simon resigned from the Government. *H. C. Deb.,* 77, 1645 ff.

52. "The Sort of Peace We Want," *Nation,* April 15; cf. May 6, July 15, 1916. By May the *Nation* had revised its opinion of the

of the radicals' improved standing was given on February 23, 1916, when members of the U.D.C. managed to stage the first prolonged discussion of war aims in Parliament. Radicals urged the Government to test German intentions and encourage German liberals by clear and continued statements of terms. The time had come, declared Ponsonby, to decide between those who "desire a lasting settlement and those who desire to punish Germany." Overwhelming victory, he warned, "will corrupt the best intentions: elated by a conspicuous victory, a nation practically is forced to go beyond what is just."[53]

It was shortly after this exchange that the Government, in the face of general uneasiness in the Liberal party, made a few conciliatory gestures, denying that its intentions were any obstacle to an early settlement but carefully avoiding any indication of the precise nature of its aims.[54] Successful in initiating a second debate on May 24, 1916, the radicals showed they were far from satisfied. On the surface, they declared, there was little difference between the Government's declarations and those of the German Chancellor. Could it be secret commitments, the radicals asked, that accounted for reluctance to speak out?[55] The Government remained unreceptive but the idea of a negotiated peace continued to gain support as the military situation remained indecisive. In April, Lord Cromer, no radical, drew much attention by writing to the *Times* to argue against fighting on to humiliate Germany.[56] The moderate *Economist* was another victim of anxiety lest

war's origin sufficiently to assert: "We cannot advance . . . to the comfortable legend that the Europe of July, 1914, was a fold of lambs encompassed by the Teutonic wolf" (May 27, 1916).

53. *H. C. Deb.*, 80, 701–40. Cf. Angell, *The Dangers of Half-Preparedness* (Washington, D.C., 1916), passim.

54. See above, pp. 30–1.

55. *H. C. Deb.*, 82, 2185–2213.

56. *Times*, April 11, 1916; cf. Lord Bryce to the same effect, July 5, 1916.

the war drag on until a general economic collapse ensued. A correspondence in this paper during the early summer gave further evidence of support for a negotiated peace in circles far removed from the U.D.C.[57]

Proponents of a negotiated settlement drew much encouragement from Woodrow Wilson's speech of May 27, 1916, in which the President offered to participate in future arrangements to keep the peace. From the first days of the war some radicals had thought of Wilson as a possible agent in building a new world order. The sinking of the *Lusitania* in May 1915 had opened the prospect of American belligerency and prompted many Englishmen to give more careful consideration to America's role. Most radicals decided that American belligerency would be regrettable, preferring to retain the hope of American mediation. The *Lusitania* incident inspired Morel to address a public "Appeal to President Wilson" to act for peace.[58] From the very beginning, the U.D.C. had made efforts to influence American opinion, but was increasingly hampered by British censorship.[59] Radical authors frequently contributed to American journals. Prominent radicals had energetically pressed their views upon Colonel House during both of his visits to England in 1915 and 1916.[60] Wilson's speech of May 27, which the radicals correctly interpreted as including a hint of readiness to help make the peace, thus

57. *Economist,* April 15, May 20, June 3, 10, 17, 1916. In a letter to the *Economist* on June 10 Loreburn appealed to Lansdowne as a moderate realist to lead the movement for peace. Whether so intended or not, the Lansdowne memorandum corresponded to this request. Cf. *Earl Loreburn and Lord Courtney of Penwith in the House of Lords, November 8th, 1915* (U.D.C., 16b, 1915).

58. Published in the New York *Tribune,* July 4, 1915. It bears some resemblance to Wilson's speech of January 22, 1917. See also *Nation,* April 17, May 15, 1915; Morel, *War and Diplomacy* (U.D.C., 11b, May 1915).

59. Swanwick, pp. 127 ff.

60. For a detailed account of these contacts, see below, pp. 95, 103–4.

appeared as an answer to their hopes and exhortations. The probability of American mediation remained an important factor in radical thinking during the rest of the year.

For the moment, however, Wilson's offer was less interesting in itself than the reactions it produced in Britain. These threw much light on the divisions of British and especially Liberal opinion. The radicals were the most enthusiastic. A special U.D.C. leaflet entitled *America and a Permanent Peace* hailed Wilson's offer as the greatest event of recent months, and radical writers hastened to incorporate a new role for America in their plans for future political arrangements. The *Nation* welcomed the speech wholeheartedly; the *Daily News* and *Manchester Guardian* were similarly gratified. On the other hand, the *Daily Chronicle*, a firm supporter of Lloyd George, made a response scarcely less chilling than that of the *Times*, which was openly hostile, expressing the hope that Wilson would not try mediation, because the Allies could only listen to overtures from a defeated enemy.[61]

The mixed reception accorded Wilson's offer measured the conflicting currents swirling around British war-aims policy. Advocates of a moderate, negotiated peace were unquestionably stronger than ever before; but the opposing forces were yet stronger and no less active. The chief product of this activity was the preparation for economic discrimination against Germany after the war. This project, coming to a climax in the Paris Economic Conference of June 1916, constituted the most direct challenge to the aspirations of the radicals. But it also provided them with another effective issue upon which to appeal to well entrenched liberal principles. Not only radicals but all members of the Liberal party,

61. *Nation,* June 3, 1916; *Manchester Guardian,* May 29, 31, 1916; *Times, Daily News, Daily Chronicle,* May 29, 1916; *America and Permanent Peace* (U.D.C., 31b, 1916); A. G. Gardiner to Colonel House, June 15, 1916, House Collection, Yale University Library; Brailsford, *Turkey and the Roads of the East* (U.D.C., 18), passim.

nurtured in the tradition of free trade, were bound to interpret proposals for discriminatory trade as an attempt by protectionists to reverse their prewar defeat.

After the Government countenanced a strongly worded Parliamentary motion on January 10, 1916, tending toward imperial preference,[62] "war after war" had rapidly become the dominant issue in controversy over war aims. All through 1916 the *Nation* printed frequent articles and editorials condemning commercial discrimination.[63] The U.D.C. was, of course, even more vigorously opposed to the protectionist proposals, and on May 2, 1916, it added to its program a Fifth Cardinal Point:

> The European conflict shall not be continued by economic war after the military operations have ceased. British policy shall be directed towards promoting free commercial intercourse between all nations and the preservation and extension of the principle of the open door.[64]

Clearly the protectionist proposals and the commitments made at the Paris Economic Conference did strike at the heart of the radical cause. Permanent economic discrimination perpetuated the idea that Germany was a peculiarly wicked nation. Such measures also entailed the deliberate establishment of exactly those economic conditions which the radicals believed to be the primary cause of wars. A peace of reconciliation, a rational settlement, all were ruled out by the Paris proposals. Yet the Liberal Prime Minister announced that the Government had formally approved the proposals,

62. *H. C. Deb.*, 77, 1299–1394. See above, p. 32.
63. *Nation*, January 15, February 12, March 11, 25, April 8 ("War after War"), June 24 ("War after Peace"), July 15, 29, September 16, 1916; cf. *Manchester Guardian*, June 1, 14, 15, 17, 21, 26, 1916, and Dickinson to ibid., June 26, 1916.
64. Swanwick, p. 39; cf. Hobson, *Labour and the Costs of War* (U.D.C., 16a, 1916), p. 8. Cocks, *Morel*, p. 225, assigns the Fifth Point to 1915 and curiously enough Trevelyan places it in 1917. These errors obscure the relationship between the Point and the protectionist campaign of 1916.

despite an earlier promise that the Conference would not commit the nation.[65]

On August 2, 1916, the Commons debated the Paris proposals and the radicals brought forward all their arguments. They found themselves in the company of many orthodox Liberals, led by John Simon, who branded the Paris program as defeatist because it assumed the continuance of a German menace.[66] Also in August the U.D.C., in the person of Lowes Dickinson, published its considered reply to the Paris proposals. Dickinson condemned them on the grounds that they treated Germany as a "mad-dog nation," encouraged German resistance, emphasized the antagonism between nationalities, and alienated neutrals, perhaps to the extent of making America withdraw its offer of cooperation. The policy would be costly, provocative, and a prolific source of friction between the Allies. Admitting that Germany had indulged in reprehensible trade policies, Dickinson advanced an alternative remedy: an international code of commercial conduct.[67]

Despite all these arguments, the champions of the Paris policy pressed on and in doing so drove home one of the last wedges needed to split the Liberal party asunder, for it was of course the debate of November 8, 1916, on economic policy which did so much to precipitate the downfall of the Asquith government. Signs of an impending crisis for Liberals appeared much earlier. The prospect of another winter of war strengthened peace sentiment in Britain.[68] But, as already related, Lloyd George's "Knock-Out Blow" interview strongly

65. August 2, 1916, *H. C. Deb.*, 85, 339; cf. Asquith's speech, March 9, 1916, *Times*, March 10, 1916.

66. *H. C. Deb.*, 85, 347 ff.

67. Dickinson, *Economic War after the War* (U.D.C., 19, 1916), passim; cf. *What Our Allies Think about Economic War* (U.D.C., 28b, 1916).

68. One indication of this sentiment was a memorial in favor of negotiation presented to Lloyd George on December 16, 1916, signed by 200,000 and endorsed by resolutions passed by almost 600,000. Copy of Memorial in House Collection.

suggested that the Government would set its face against any negotiations. This pugnacious attitude disappointed and angered those who would have welcomed at least an attempt to negotiate. Lloyd George's pronouncement convinced the *Nation* that "war is . . . more and more conceived as an end in itself." [69] The outlook seemed bleak for the radicals. Grey, it is true, had given further indications of an interest in international organization, but his utterances now carried little weight compared to those of Lloyd George.[70] All but a few of the Conservatives were eager supporters of a fight to a finish; most of the Liberal party either endorsed Lloyd George's energetic program or were tied to the Government by allegiance to the party.

Lloyd George's accession to the premiership in December 1916 was therefore in itself a grievous defeat for the forces of moderate liberalism. Yet once again, a Cabinet change had its compensations for the radicals; for they were no longer in isolation. The passage into opposition of Asquith and his followers gave a new freedom to those Liberals, centering round the *Nation* and *Daily News,* who had shown an increasing sympathy with the radicals but had been restrained by party loyalty. Most Liberal papers deeply resented the change of government. The *Daily News* was no less alarmed than the *Nation* by the "squalid conspiracy." [71] Gardiner became en-

69. *Nation,* October 7, 1916. Cf. Hammond, *Scott,* p. 200; Conwell Evans, p. 123. The U.D.C. passed a resolution condemning Lloyd George and welcoming the prospect of mediation; Swanwick, pp. 78–9. Cf. C. R. Buxton, *Peace This Winter,* London and New York, 1916.

70. For the decline of the Foreign Secretary see Gordon A. Craig and F. Gilbert, eds., *The Diplomats* (Princeton, 1953), pp. 16–21. For evidence that Grey's colleagues by no means accepted his views see the exchange between Cecil and Snowden, November 25, 1916, *H. C. Deb.,* 88, 448.

71. *Daily News,* December 5, 11, 1916; *Nation,* December 16, 1916; the *Westminster Gazette,* often a supporter of Lloyd George, had opposed the change and though now accepting the new Gov-

raged at what he considered Lloyd George's underhanded conduct and henceforth the *Daily News* sustained an implacable hostility to the new Prime Minister. Even the *Manchester Guardian's* editor, C. P. Scott, who had encouraged Lloyd George, had his doubts: "There will be force in the new Cabinet," he wrote, "but will there be wisdom?" [72].

The Cabinet crisis thus widened the ranks from which the radicals might draw recruits. But because the change in government was a triumph for advocates of a fight to a finish, immediate prospects for a statement of terms and for other radical projects were gloomy. There was little reason to expect any but the roughest treatment for the peace overtures that Germany made within a week of Lloyd George's promotion. But before the radicals had had time to acclimatize themselves to the new situation, help arrived from America. Wilson made his long awaited and eagerly expected move toward mediation. The President's venture provided the climax to the war-aims campaign in the period of American neutrality, cast a new light on the subject, and established a pattern for the remaining months of the war.

By the time Wilson acted, the radicals had developed a comprehensive outline of the peace they desired. In the fore-front of their plans was the demand that the peace be mutually arranged on a basis of compromise of interests. Otherwise every nation with a sense of injury would lie in wait for a chance "to exchange the politically unprogressive position of equilibrium for the progressive and expanding position of victory over others." [73] The radicals also believed that a stable Europe required a vigorous Germany.[74] In this connection they emphasized their belief that a complete victory would probably lead to excesses in British policy. Paradoxically, the

---

ernment as a patriotic duty, warned the Liberal party to prepare to defend its principles; December 2, 4, 5, 7, 8, 1916.

72. Harris, p. 109; Hammond, *Scott,* p. 202.

73. Angell, *Prussianism,* p. 58.

74. Cf. Morel, *Labour Leader,* May 13, 1915.

radicals, who claimed to abhor the balance of power, were here arguing for a balance, asserting that only countervailing strength could render national power innocuous. This makes it less surprising that the only other body of British opinion in favor of allowing Germany continued power was the military leadership. The *Economist*, at least, caught a glimpse of this relationship and, protesting against plans to remap Europe at the expense of the Central Powers, invoked traditional British devotion to the balance of power, "a doctrine which, whatever absurdities of policy it may have promoted in the past, will at least always operate against the crowning absurdity of endeavoring to crush great nations out of existence." [75]

A similar mistrust of wholesale rearrangements tempered radical enthusiasm for national self-determination. The dictum of the Liberal-Imperialists that "hopes of lasting peace are largely bound up with uniting races and nationalities now divided . . ." [76] won widespread acceptance in the Liberal party but was at once too simple and too sweeping for the radicals. They heartily endorsed the principle of self-determination and opposed a peace of conquest and compensation which treated peoples as "moveable goods." [77] But radical publicists believed it was impossible to draw perfect frontiers. Many of the proposed new nations would be economically unsound, and there would always remain some minorities. The radicals therefore mooted the idea of modified self-determination, with provision for economic cooperation and international standards for the treatment of minorities. [78]

75. *Economist*, February 26, 1916. See above, p. 34.
76. *Round Table* (December 1916), p. 6.
77. Morel, *Truth*, p. 174; cf. the U.D.C.'s First Point; also Vernon Lee, "Democratic Principle and International Relations," in Buxton, *Towards a Lasting Settlement*, pp. 206–9.
78. Angell, *Prussianism*, 77; Morel, *Truth*, 265; *Nation*, March 13, April 10, 1916; C. R. Buxton, "Nationality," in *Towards a Lasting Settlement*, pp. 39–46.

This cautious scheme had an added appeal because it moderated designs for breaking up Austria-Hungary and thereby increased chances of a compromise peace.

Suspicion of nationalism, of "enshrining mere statehood," also influenced proposals for international organization. The radicals were eager to discover a substitute for the balance of power. They considered the balance defective because it laid undue emphasis on territorial adjustment to the neglect of other power factors and because it purported to preserve an arbitrary *status quo* and was therefore the "equivalent in international politics of the worst kind of Toryism in home politics." The balance did not provide security, "because the defensive efforts of each merely cancel one another." Really, the system was a see-sawing struggle for preponderance which occasionally prevented wars but only by creating the risk of bigger ones.[79]

Power could not be abolished but it might be organized. Henceforth there could be no more neutrals.[80] There must be international machinery for the adjustment of disputes. Though radical proponents of international organization differed among themselves as to the possibility of enforcing decisions, all agreed that there must be compulsion to resort to set procedures. This, it was thought, was the only way to create an atmosphere of security. Such procedures would also make it easier to define and detect aggression. Most radicals agreed with Brailsford, however, that it would be useless to attempt to perpetuate the *status quo* because "the *status quo*

79. *Balance of Power*, pp. 4–8; Angell, *The Prussian in Our Midst* (U.D.C., 13a, 1915), p. 4; idem, *War Aims: the Need for a Parliament of the Allies* (London, 1917), p. 36.

80. For Angell's promotion of this idea see *Nation*, May 5, 1917, and below, pp. 110–11; cf. *New Statesman*, August 7, 1915; Swanwick, *Women and War* (U.D.C., 11, 1915), p. 5. It should be noted that a few radicals, including Morel, were cool to plans for international organization, preferring to rely upon the development of enlightened national policies, thus avoiding the need for coercion.

may be morally indefensible." [81] There must be provision for
peaceful change; for security *plus* the satisfaction of other
wants. Radicals consequently laid greater stress upon the settlement of disputes than upon the prevention of violence.
They hoped that the mere availability of convenient machinery would do much to encourage peaceful adjustments.[82]
Many members of the U.D.C. confessed, however, that there
were great difficulties ahead. Hobson feared that processes
of enforcement might create more conflict than they resolved.
In particular, he warned that economic sanctions possessed
no "moral" superiority over military measures and would prove
no less expensive and dangerous.[83] Brailsford wondered
whether, in overlooking the greater risks which continental
states would run in trusting to novel methods of achieving
security, the schemes for international organization were "too
Anglo-Saxon." [84]

Radical writers hoped that the league of nations might
rapidly become indispensable by performing positive functions
in the solution of such problems as the treatment of minorities
and regulation of the Straits. It is difficult to exaggerate the
importance that such men as Hobson and Brailsford attached
to using the league for international economic cooperation.
They suggested supervisory powers over trade routes, commercial practices, postal communications, and perhaps even labor
standards and migration. League members should offer each
other most-favored-nation privileges. In part these proposals
were an answer to the demand for economic war after the
war on the theory that assurance against economic aggres-

81. Brailsford, "The Organization of Peace," in Buxton, *Towards
a Lasting Settlement,* pp. 150–9.

82. Ibid., pp. 150–76; Swanwick, *Women,* p. 7; and esp. Brailsford, *The War of Steel and Gold* (3d ed. London, 1915), appendix;
idem, *League of Nations* (London, 1917), passim, esp. on the need
for change, pp. 76–8.

83. Hobson, *War and Peace,* Supplement to the *Nation* (January 1917), pp. 58–62.

84. Brailsford, *League of Nations,* pp. 6–7, 76–7.

sion would rob discriminatory schemes of their appeal. In addition, it was hoped that a league with such functions would possess a powerful sanction in the threat of exclusion from its privileges.[85]

Colonial areas were thought to offer special opportunities for international regulation. Hobson had suggested international trusteeship as long ago as 1902.[86] Now, in the war years, he and Morel paid particular attention to this idea. Believing that the ultimate goal of universal free trade could not be quickly attained, Hobson suggested an internationally supervised open door in the colonies as a practical step in the right direction. There should also be a Charter of Native Rights recognizing the interest of the natives as the paramount consideration in colonial territories. Most writers agreed that international administration was impracticable. Instead colonial governments should regard themselves as trustees accountable to the league organization.[87]

International organization was also expected to facilitate democratic control of foreign policy by providing a forum for debate.[88] Several schemes already provided for the registration and publication of treaties. Democratic control was still one of the radicals' most cherished projects. Revelation of Britain's prewar engagements with France and reports of secret treaties among the Allies had done nothing to allay

85. Brailsford, "Organization," in Buxton, *Towards a Lasting Settlement,* p. 175; Buxton, "Nationality," ibid., p. 42; Hobson, "Open Door," ibid., p. 88; Angell, *War Aims,* p. 123.

86. See above, p. 7.

87. For the best presentation of radical schemes for colonial areas see Hobson, "Open Door," in Buxton, *Towards a Lasting Settlement,* pp. 87–107; idem, *The Open Door,* The Hague, 1916; Morel, *Africa and the Peace of Europe* (London, 1917), esp. pp. 52–3, 63, 70; Brailsford, *War of Steel,* pp. 335–6. This group far outdistanced all others in moving toward the trusteeship idea.

88. Radicals were careful not to assert that only democracies should be allowed in a league. Hobson, *League of Nations* (U.D.C., 15a), pp. 17–18. Brailsford laid particular stress upon the fact that democracies could be aggressive; *League,* p. 86, n. 1.

suspicion of secret diplomacy. The radicals did not ask for the open conduct of negotiation; that, Ponsonby admitted, "would be disastrous." [89] What was needed was better public information on the general lines of policy and especially on national commitments, so that the people could face crises with some perspective, could appreciate proposed courses of conduct, and support necessary preparedness.[90] Democratic control was in this respect a means of ensuring that the nation's foreign policy was adapted to the needs and aspirations of the citizens.

There was also a fairly general conviction that democratic control would reduce the risk of war. Some asserted that the people possessed a higher moral sense than their existing rulers and would therefore pursue a less provocative policy. More commonly, advocates of democratic control argued that the "real interests of two peoples are never opposed, whereas the interests of the ruling castes of two countries, or of the business groups controlling them, often are opposed." [91] A refined version of this view admitted that national interests might conflict but asserted that it was always to the advantage of all concerned to settle peacefully. This meant not that any settlement was better than war—the U.D.C. accepted the need to continue fighting the current war—but that it was always possible to discover such a preferable settlement. The most cautious radicals qualified their hopes even further, merely claiming that a peaceful solution was best in all but a very few cases. If wars still occurred, at least the peoples would be paying for their own mistakes.[92]

89. Ponsonby, *Democracy*, p. 25.
90. One of the radicals' most bitter complaints was that there had been no chance to foresee the crisis of 1914 because the British people had been kept unaware of their Government's commitments.
91. *Morrow*, p. 6.
92. For this discussion of democratic control see above, pp. 11–12, and Ponsonby, *Democracy*, passim; idem., *Parliament*, passim; Snowden, "Secret Diplomacy," in Buxton, *Towards a Lasting Settle-*

By the end of 1916, then, the radicals had developed comprehensive proposals for the future peace and had made some headway toward popularizing their ideas in the Liberal party. They had met with little success, however, in their purpose of extracting a declaration of terms from the successive governments, let alone a declaration consonant with radical principles. Only with regard to economic policy had official plans become at once public and precise, and here they ran directly counter to radical wishes. Of course any British government, however innocent its own intentions, must have been conscious of the damage a declaration of terms might do to Allied unity. There seemed good reason to believe that the new Lloyd George regime would prove especially adamant against conciliatory gestures.

The German Peace Note of December 12, 1916, gave the radicals little comfort. Against the trend of public opinion they urged the Government to make a reasoned reply which would appeal to neutrals and to moderate elements in Germany. All the Liberal press except Lloyd George's satellite, the *Daily Chronicle,* joined in this plea.[93] In a debate on December 21, radical M.P.'s urged the Government to recognize that terms reached by conquest were not thereby better than those reached by negotiation.[94] But the radicals were forced to admit that the tone of the German note was more appropriate to a proclamation of victory than to an overture of peace. Not for the first time, and not for the last, the more open-

---

ment, pp. 191 ff. The following passage from Angell, *Half Preparedness,* p. 22, illustrates that the demand for democratic control did not stem merely from an optimistic view of men: "I am a Pacifist because I have in some respects little faith in human nature; because I believe that that nature unless we watch it, will betray us into very stupid courses."

93. *Daily Chronicle,* December 13, 1916; *Westminster Gazette,* December 13, 14, 1916; *Daily News,* December 13, 1916; *Manchester Guardian,* December 13, 1916; *Nation,* December 16, 1916.

94. *H. C. Deb.,* 88, 1714–32. There was also a brief exchange on December 14, 1916, ibid., 942–50.

minded radicals were obliged to confess that Germany showed
no sign of reciprocating their moderation, that the vaunted
German liberals were rarely in evidence, and that the German
government's behavior gave little hope for a "reasonable"
peace, even if the Allies were to join the U.D.C. in a body.
Because its uncompromising tone made it easier for the British
government to reject the German note, it did not assist the
radicals as much as they had expected.

Wilson's *démarche* was another matter. Even before the
President's speech of May 27, 1916, the radicals had decided
that American "intervention may be Europe's only means
. . . of obtaining a tolerable, desirable peace." [95] After May
27, hope of American help grew steadily, and in this connection
the radicals cast themselves in a vital role, for they believed
that intervention could not be successful unless they kept
a liberal spirit alive in Britain. They also made it their business to inform Wilson of their work and to urge him, both
publicly and privately, to act.[96]

The note which Wilson dispatched on December 18, 1916,
was a double answer to radical prayers. At a time when their
fortunes were low, the President did not simply intervene;
he did so by the chosen radical method of inviting statements
of terms as a basis for negotiation. All the more alarmed were
the radicals, then, at the hostile reception Wilson encountered.
The *Times* and other right-wing elements demanded that
Wilson be rebuffed with a declaration that the Allies would
fight on to overwhelm and occupy Germany.[97] Worse, Wilson's

95. *Nation*, March 11, 1916.
96. Cf. "Wayfarer" (H. W. Massingham), "American opinion
. . . has let it be seen very clearly that it draws a sharp distinction
between the England of Gladstone and an England that might
look more like an England of Castlereagh," *Nation*, August 16,
1916; cf. open letter to Wilson by Charles Trevelyan, November
25, 1916, also reported in *Westminster Gazette*, December 5, 1916,
and Russell, *An Open Letter to the President* (leaflet of American
Neutral Conference Committee, December ? 1916). For a full
account of the radicals' relations with Wilson see below, Chap. 4.
97. *Times*, December 22, 1916; Playne, *Society at War*, p. 347.

assertion that the "objects which the statesmen of the belligerents on both sides have in mind in this war are virtually the same, as stated in general terms to their own people and to the world," was widely interpreted as placing the belligerents on an equal moral footing. This aroused much resentment among many Englishmen who were otherwise well disposed to an early peace. The radicals quickly tried to undo this mischief and win support for Wilson. They explained that Wilson had passed judgment not on the belligerents' aims but on their pronouncements. Nor had he asked the Allies to make peace; he had merely inquired as to what kind of peace they would accept. Britain could not afford to alienate America, the radicals argued, because only America had the power to tip the balance of the war and make a substantial contribution to stabilizing the peace.[98] In what can only be interpreted as another invocation of the much maligned balance of power, the *Nation* suggested that Wilson's offer provided an opportunity "not only to arrest war at the point of security but to fix it there . . ."[99]

Radicals with access to the Government did their best to encourage a respectful response to America. Noel Buxton, who had returned from a visit to America completely converted to a negotiated peace, circulated a memorandum to the Cabinet urging it to take the opportunity to test Germany's intentions. He advised a confidential answer on the grounds that inter-Allied diplomacy and the tactics of bargaining would compel a public reply to be a statement of maximum demands.[100]

Those who took this line received some satisfaction. By the

98. *Westminster Gazette,* December 23, 1916; *Nation,* December 30, 1916; Morel, "President Wilson's Message and the *Times,*" *Labour Leader,* December 28, 1916.

99. *Nation,* December 30, 1916; cf. Noel Buxton in the Commons, December 21, 1916, *H. C. Deb.,* 88, 1768–72.

100. Conwell Evans, pp. 124–8. There is a copy of the memorandum in the House Collection. Cf. U.D.C., Memorandum, January 18, 1917, Swanwick, *Builders,* p. 80.

end of the year even the *Times* conceded that Wilson must have a civil answer. When the Allied Note and Balfour's supplementary remarks provided that answer, the radicals gave it a warm welcome. It would have been strange had they not done so, for here at last was a statement of terms and one more moderate than many had expected. The radicals qualified their welcome, however, for they spied several ambiguous corners in which illiberal ambitions might lurk. Were the proposed territorial changes to be only those readjustments which everyone regarded as necessary for a lasting peace, or did they constitute a thinly veiled program of imperialism? Did the references to Austria mean autonomy for the various nationalities or dismemberment of the Empire? Did the passages on Turkey foretell liberation, internationalization, or Russian annexation? The editor of the *Nation* decided that the key lay in the demand for "guarantees." Were these to be a league of nations or annexations and compensations; were they "the shadow of a batch of specific agreements among the Allies?" [101] Pending answers to these queries the radicals concluded that the Allied reply and Balfour's Note were open to either a moderate or an extortionate interpretation.

The generally angry comments of the British press upon Wilson's speech of January 22, 1917, in which he called for "peace without victory," and the subsequent uncompromising statements of Government spokesmen, increased radical fears that the immoderate interpretation was correct. Once again the radicals rallied in support of Wilson. "Peace without victory," the *Nation* argued, merely excluded a vindictive peace; a peace without victory could be a decisive defeat for aggression.[102] This was, of course, exactly what the radicals had always preached. Naturally enough the U.D.C. eagerly took up Wilson's case and devoted a special leaflet to endorsement of his

101. *Nation*, January 20, 1917.
102. Winkler, *League of Nations Movement*, p. 140; *Nation*, January 27, 1917. See above, p. 43.

speech. Other radicals contributed their various appraisals, welcoming Wilson's apparent readiness to commit America to a "community of power," praising his insistence upon a just peace and concurring in what they took to be his warning against excessive devotion to self-determination.[103]

In a more sustained effort to win support for Wilson the radicals pressed the Government to give a moderate interpretation of the Allied terms which would bring them into closer harmony with Wilson's proposals. This endeavor assumed even greater importance after the renewal of unrestricted submarine warfare made American participation in the war almost inevitable and thereby increased the opportunity for Wilson to influence the peace. When Parliament reassembled in February radicals lost no time in airing their doubts. On February 20, 1917, in a debate initiated by members of the U.D.C., critics of the Government acknowledged that the Allied declarations marked a step forward but deplored the ambiguities and the subsequent hints of concealed imperialist aims. Members urged the Government to remove these suspicions, renounce economic discrimination, support international organization, and withdraw support from exaggerated nationalistic claims which must impede the making of peace. All this activity drew no favorable response, either from the Government or from Asquith and his followers. Bonar Law charged the critics with lack of patriotism. Neatly turning the tables, he expressed surprise at hearing such complaints just when "the greatest of neutral nations has recognized that there is a difference between right and wrong"—a back-handed compliment indeed for the prospective new belligerent.[104]

103. *President Wilson's Message to the World* (U.D.C., 33b, 1917); *British Working Men—Observe!* (U.D.C., 34b, 1917); Angell, *War Aims*, pp. 20, 113–15; *Round Table* (March 1917), 204–7, 314–17; Brailsford, *League*, pp. 81–4, 100–15; Noel Buxton to W. H. Buckler, January 25, 1917, House Collection.

104. *H. C. Deb.*, 90, 1179–1299. For the staging of the debate, U.D.C., *Report—1917*, p. 5. See also interventions in debate, Feb-

Unabashed, the radicals resumed their campaign for the adoption of moderate war aims. Recent events had greatly improved the radicals' position in debate. Their opponents could no longer argue that the declaration of terms was bad strategy because the Government had already made one such pronouncement. Wilson had made statements of terms respectable. As Charles Trevelyan drily remarked in the Commons debate on February 20: "We kept on saying that there ought to be a declaration of policy. It was deplorable lack of patriotism on our part. I am glad, however, that when, on the invitation of President Wilson, the same demand was put forward, it was put forward by a person who could not be disregarded." [105]

Active support from many Liberals who had hitherto remained silent demonstrated the increasing prestige of the war-aims campaign. Many members intervened in the debate on February 20 who had never before spoken out for moderate terms. In March 1917 the first mass meeting held in London on behalf of temperate war aims gave further evidence of growing influence.[106] Another obstacle disappeared when the Russian Revolution swept away fears that Tsardom would taint the Allied cause. The collapse of the Russian armies and the consequent strengthening of German imperialism were not yet foreseen.

Despite these hopeful events, the outlook was by no means unclouded. The Government maintained its refusal to follow up its declaration of terms or interpret it in a moderate sense. Renewed manifestations of intolerance culminating in the suppression of the *Nation's* foreign circulation served as an additional reminder that the radical cause was far from tri-

---

ruary 12, 1917, *H. C. Deb.*, *90*, 270 ff., 348–55, and questions on February 14, 1917, ibid., 602–4.

105. *H. C. Deb.*, *90*, 1189.

106. Conwell Evans, pp. 138–40; Morel to W. H. Buckler, February 15, 1917, House Collection.

umphant.[107] Moreover, it did not bode well that, whether they realized it or not, the radicals owed most of their new support to war weariness and factional differences in the Liberal party, rather than to conversions to the radical analysis of foreign affairs.

Distrustful of their own national leaders, the radicals committed their hopes more and more into the hands of President Wilson. Liberal aims survived, declared the *Nation*, but "since the new Government arrived their most conspicuous champions are to be found in American rather than British statesmanship." What was needed was an "Anglo-American alliance of temper and policy." Earlier in the war radicals had viewed the possibility of American belligerency with disfavor because it would remove the world's last important neutral as a source of mediation and possibly debase American intentions. These fears remained, but now that mediation had failed and American intervention seemed inevitable most radicals persuaded themselves that it could be welcomed as an opportunity for Wilson to purify the Allied cause from the inside. Wilson's policy in Mexico and as a neutral was taken as proof of his ability to keep a cool head. The radicals urged the President to insist on "limited liability" and endorse only liberal war aims. The *Nation* predicted that Wilson would not accede to the treaties binding the Allies not to make separate peace and would certainly not accept the Paris resolutions or the secret treaties.[108]

107. At the same time F. W. Hirst's monthly *Common Sense* suffered a similar penalty. See *Nation*, April 14, 28, May 5, 1917. Much indignation among radicals was occasioned by Bertrand Russell's expulsion from his fellowship at Trinity, Cambridge, at this time.

108. *Nation*, February 3, 10, 17, 24, March 17, 1917; *Labour Leader*, April 12, 1917; Swanwick, *Builders*, p. 112; Brailsford, *League*, pp. vi, 40–8; Memorandum by Noel Buxton, February 8, 1917, House Collection; W. H. Buckler to House, February 23, 1917, ibid. See below, p. 129.

The British radicals regarded Wilson as the heir and director of progressivism. With his full participation in the war they believed that "American liberalism comes into action." [109] They expected the President to lead them to a liberal and lasting peace—now confidently called "an American peace." [110] Nothing, therefore, could be more important to the radicals than Wilson's concept of what that peace should be.

109. "Wayfarer" in *Nation*, February 10, 1917, quoting Walter Lippmann.

110. "February 5, 1917 [someone expounded] an American peace, that is an unbiassed peace, which was received with silence not altogether hostile" (Bennett, *Journal*, 2, 214).

4. Woodrow Wilson and

Europe's War, 1914-1917

NEWS of general war in Europe took America even more
unaware than the British Liberals. As he sat by the bedside of
his dying wife, President Wilson's reaction to this "incredible
European catastrophe"[1] seems to have been typical of his
fellow citizens. Americans were highly confused as to how the
war had come about but were generally agreed that it concerned the United States only as a grievous nuisance and a sad
demonstration of Europe's political and moral failings. It
seemed, as Wilson was to observe when it was all over, "like
a natural raking out of the pent-up jealousies and rivalries of
the complicated politics of Europe."[2] Very few had any doubt
that America should stand aloof. Wilson fully shared the common view, fearing not only the horrors of war but the inter-
ruption of domestic reform. Underlining his determination
to stay out, the President went beyond his obligations as a
neutral, ordering United States officers to refrain from comment
on the war, pleading with the people to be neutral in thought
as well as action, and placing an informal ban on loans to
belligerents. With such restraints, he declared, America could
and should keep out of war.[3]

1. *Life and Letters*, 5, 1 (Doubleday, Doran and Co., Inc.).
2. *War and Peace*, 1, 527 (Harper and Bros.). Cf. *Life and
Letters*, 5, 94; *Intimate Papers*, 1, 285–6.
3. Link, *Progressive Era*, pp. 150–1; *Life and Letters*, 5, 18 n. 2,
and 174–5; and *New Democracy*, 1, 151 ff. (Harper and Bros.).

The decision for neutrality had no reference to the causes of the war. But American judgment, and particularly Woodrow Wilson's, as to the responsibility of the belligerents would clearly exercise a strong influence on American ideas of a desirable outcome, of a good peace, and of how to obtain such a peace. Most attentive Americans of non-German origin seem to have quickly decided that the Central Powers, especially Germany, bore a major share of the guilt. Ignorance of Balkan politics, the invasion of Belgium, reports of German atrocities, the German reputation for autocracy and militarism, and long-established fears of German colonial ambitions in the Western Hemisphere all contributed to this conclusion.[4] By contrast there had developed a general recognition that Britain was too fully occupied with her existing Empire and European interests to offer any menace to America. Wilson himself observed that the British were "safe" because they had all they could handle and knew it.[5] The knowledge that Britain and France were democracies and that democracies were supposedly peaceful fortified this confidence in the harmlessness of a British victory.

Officially Wilson was neutral—in thought as well as deed —and in private, too, he was more open-minded than most. He made several remarks early in the war which indicated that he shared the general predilection for the Allies and there is nothing to indicate that he ever completely abandoned this.[6] But on other occasions the President's comments suggested considerable impartiality. He declared that postwar Germany would be too exhausted to threaten the United States. A proposal by President Eliot of Harvard that America cast its

4. Frederick Sondermann, "The Wilson Administration's Image of Germany" (dissertation, Yale, 1953), pp. 212–18.
5. Wilson to May Hoyt, October 4, 1914, *Life and Letters*, 5, 290.
6. Ibid., p. 169; G. M. Trevelyan, *Viscount Grey of Falloden* (Boston, 1937), pp. 355–6; House to Wilson, September 20, 1914, House Collection; "House Diary," August 30, 1914.

lot with the righteous cause of the Allies "amazed and distressed" Wilson, and he firmly rejected it.[7]

Probably Wilson gained his first firm impression of the war's origins from an article in the New York *Times* which explained the Balkan aspects of the crisis and, while laying the chief blame on Austria-Hungary, also sketched Russia's expansive policy in relation to the interlocking and often secret system of European alliances. The article moved Wilson to comment, "the more I read about this conflict across the seas, the more open it seems to utter condemnation." [8] This was closer to "a plague on both your houses" than a simple indictment of Germany. Three months later in a confidential interview with a New York *Times* correspondent, Wilson predicted that "it will be found before long that Germany is not alone responsible for the War," though he added his conviction that a reform of her government would contribute to the peace of the world.[9] Showing similar reluctance to judge the strident counterclaims of the belligerents on the disputed evidence available, Wilson took a strong stand against official cognizance of atrocity stories. So much more evidence would shortly come to light, he argued, that it would be unwise not merely to express but even to "form" opinions so soon. To at least two inquirers he went so far as to suggest that the invasion of Belgium itself should not be finally condemned until the whole moral situation could be known.[10] This unwillingness to condemn Germany out of hand is striking when set against the anti-German tone of most of the Eastern press and of Walter Hines Page, Wilson's ambassador to Britain.[11]

7. Wilson to Nancy Toy, December 12, 1914, *Life and Letters*, 5, 71; for the lack of a German danger, "House Diary," November 4, 1914, *Intimate Papers, 1*, 298 (Houghton Mifflin).

8. *Life and Letters, 5*, 62.

9. December 14, 1914, ibid., pp. 214, 219.

10. Ibid., pp. 161–8.

11. Link, *Progressive Era*, p. 147; Notter, pp. 326, 333; Page to Bryan, December 28, 1914, *Lansing Papers, 1*, 259–61.

Recognition that the Allied case was far from perfect strengthened these reservations to what, it must be repeated, was a predominantly pro-Allied view. It was no paradox for some Americans to feel that, undesirable though a German victory was, an Allied triumph would not be entirely satisfactory either. The blackest smudge on the Allied escutcheon was, of course, autocratic Imperial Russia. Wilson and House thought it very likely that Russia would be the greatest future menace to world peace and also suspected her of carrying an undefined but appreciable share of responsibility for the war. When attention turned to England, the record, though lighter, was by no means lily white. The President and his advisers were well aware of Britain's bitter naval feud with Germany. Could Britain be fighting for naval supremacy, not international justice? Suspicion of British sea power was destined to grow as the exercise of that power increasingly encroached upon American interests.[12]

Looking more precisely to the future settlement, there were signs that an Allied peace might not be one that Wilson or Secretary of State Bryan could readily reconcile to their highly developed consciences. With characteristic bluntness Page told Wilson that the Allied agreement not to make separate peace signaled their intention to fight Germany until one side was completely exhausted. Offsetting reports of militarism in Germany, Page added that the British Admiralty would take over government if necessary to ensure a vigorous naval policy.[13] House, who was more trustful of Britain than Wilson and who believed German militarism needed a salutary beating, nevertheless warned the British ambassador that moderate elements in Britain could easily lose

12. "House Diary," August 30, September 18, 1914; *Intimate Papers, 1*, 271–8, 284–5.
13. Page to Secretary, September 7, 10, 1914, *Foreign Relations* (1914), Supp., pp. 99, 100–1.

control of the Entente, which might go careening on to a
dictated and annexationist peace.[14]

Thus although the indictment of Germany was more elaborate, more damning, and more widely heard than that against
Britain and her allies, both sides were under some suspicion.
This belief that neither side was wholly in the right was closely
similar to the arguments of the British radicals, and it led
Wilson to a similar conclusion: that "it might be well if there
were no exemplary triumph and punishment." He agreed with
House that if the war were unduly prolonged either the Allies
would crush Germany and rend her apart or a ruinous deadlock would ensue. Peace could not endure under such circumstances, and above all Wilson wanted the coming pacifica-
tion to be "permanent." The only satisfactory ending to the
war, the President concluded, was a decision "reached wholly
by the forces of reason and justice after the trial at arms is
found futile . . ." Only such a negotiated peace, worked
out reasonably, would be "for the advantage of the European
nations regarded as people." [15]

Wilson's vision of a desirable outcome was thus already
remarkably akin to that of the British radicals, and, of course,
it largely stemmed from a similar liberal inheritance of dissatisfaction with the existing methods of foreign policy and of
distrust for European governments. But this unwillingness to
contemplate the complete triumph of either side did not
present Wilson with a dilemma as acute as that of the British

14. "House Diary," September 19, 1914. In January 1915 Grey
sent Wilson an indication of British aims, through the agency of
C. P. Anderson of the State Department. The aims included resti-
tution of Belgium, return of Alsace-Lorraine and indemnity for
France, and transfer of the Straits and Constantinople to Russia.
Link, *Progressive Era*, p. 155.

15. Wilson to Hoyt, October 4, 1914, *Life and Letters*, 5, 290;
Wilson to H. B. Brougham, December 14, 1914, ibid., p. 214;
"House Diary," September 19, 1914, January 13, 1915; *Intimate
Papers*, 1, 328, 351.

radicals, for while they, as members of a belligerent nation, were forced into active criticism, the President could fulfill his conceived duty by neutrality. He could even weight his neutrality according to his relative estimation of the belligerents, who, though both were suspect, were not equally so.

Wilson soon identified two ways in which America might encourage the conclusion of a rational, negotiated peace. The first was to provide as a neutral a conspicuous example of that calm, benevolent reasonableness which should inspire the peace.[16] A second and more active policy was mediation. As early as August 5, 1914, Wilson formally proffered his good offices. This offer met a polite and unanimous refusal. In September an attempt to discover whether the belligerents were ready to negotiate received a similar repulse.[17]

Despite discouragement from House, Page, and the Allied ambassadors, Wilson and Bryan continued to discuss the project of mediation throughout the autumn. These discussions produced no immediate diplomatic results but they served to fix in Wilson's mind certain ideas of a desirable peace and how to obtain it, that influenced him for the rest of the war. Rebuffed by the belligerents, Bryan developed the idea that mediation might be public; that an open offer might bring the suffering peoples to force their governments to be reasonable. Mediation might proceed by demanding from each belligerent a declaration of the kind of peace it desired and the terms it would accept. Bryan hoped that in this way extremists would either be shamed into silence or exposed to public condemnation. The President and he also hoped that the terms so declared would prove not hopelessly disparate and that once the narrowness of the differences lay revealed, public opinion would compel a compromise. Failing this the world would at

16. *New Democracy, 1,* 157–9.
17. "House Diary," September 28, 1914; Notter, pp. 342–3; *Foreign Relations* (1914), Supp., pp. 99 ff.

least know which powers were responsible for the unreason-
ableness which alone, it was assumed, could account for the
continuation of the war.[18] Building on the same faith in public
opinion and the amenability of international disputes to reason,
Wilson had thus begun to entertain methods of obtaining a
good settlement which were identical with those favored by
British radicals.

Meanwhile Colonel House was pursuing a different approach. The Colonel disapproved of Bryan's ideas not because
he was less anxious to secure peace but because he thought it
more promising to refrain from public action until a basis for
agreement had been discovered by confidentially ascertaining
and exchanging the terms of the belligerents. More partial
to Britain than Wilson, House also hoped that by clearing each
step with the British, whom he believed to be reasonable, he
could avoid any action which would aid Germany by embarrassing Britain.

With some encouragement from Grey and from Spring-
Rice, the British ambassador, Wilson permitted House to go to
Europe on behalf of his plan in the winter and spring of 1915.
House hoped to ease the impact of the war on neutral commerce by bringing about a naval *modus vivendi* between
Britain and Germany. He expected to use this as an opening
to begin the exchanges called for in his plan.[19] The *modus
vivendi* never materialized but the attempt had the important
result of bringing to the fore the phrase "freedom of the seas,"
symbolizing rules of maritime warfare which henceforth be-

18. *Life and Letters*, 5, 279–85, 292; Bryan to Wilson, December
1, 1914, *Lansing Papers, 1*, 10–11; W. J. Bryan, *The Memoirs of
William Jennings Bryan* (Philadelphia, 1925), pp. 389–92.

19. The planning of the House mission can best be followed in
Link, *Progressive Era*, p. 161; *Intimate Papers, 1*, 331–2, 340 f.;
cf. Page to Secretary, January 15, 19, 1915, *Foreign Relations*
(1915), Supp., pp. 5–6; Bryan to Wilson, December 17, 1914,
Lansing Papers, 1, 182–3.

came a constant ingredient in American plans for the peace. Another important result originated from Grey's demand that if he were to agree to freedom of the seas, America must join an international organization to help Britain in case some future enemy broke the rules. House resisted any suggestion that the United States could become involved in a general organization, but he did agree that she might accept an undertaking to enforce the laws of war.[20] Thus the idea that America might join in a guarantee of at least part of the settlement entered the diplomacy of her efforts to obtain a good peace.

House and Grey also discussed terms of peace. The Colonel suggested disarmament by moratorium and guarantees of territorial integrity and commercial freedom. But his immediate efforts to promote negotiation made no headway at all. Grey mentioned very moderate terms but confessed that this was not an official British, much less an Allied, view. House left England for Germany with no peace message.[21] In Germany he gathered that the military were in complete control and firmly opposed to peace. The Colonel concluded that there was no hope of a negotiated peace for the moment. He placed the chief blame on Germany, which had aroused his strong distaste by its militaristic display.[22]

Wilson had also decided that negotiations were not yet possible and turned his mind to other pressing matters, notably the disturbances in Mexico. He seems to have accepted House's judgment that German ambitions formed the chief obstacle, but he probably did not go so far as House in accepting the British viewpoint. The President was well aware of his friend's tenderness for Britain; he had sarcastically prodded House into leaving the atmosphere of England to explore

20. *Intimate Papers, 1,* 363, 381–2. Wilson offered to come to Europe for the peace conference, ibid., pp. 356–7.

21. Ibid., pp. 347, 363, 381–2, 387–8, 400, 414–15; "House Diary," March 7, 1915, partly ibid., pp. 392–3; House to Wilson, April 11, 1915, House Collection.

22. *Intimate Papers, 1,* 400, 417; "House Diary," April 14, 1915.

German thought through some less partisan medium.[23] Even House had gained a far from entirely favorable impression of British intentions. He reported highly nationalistic talk from George V, from Northcliffe, and from Curzon—the "worst jingo I ever met." The new Cabinet, House noted, was less likely to prove accommodating and he conceded that there might be some grounds for German fears of economic discrimination.[24]

These doubts must have received considerable nourishment when House established contact with the British radicals. This was another aspect of House's visit destined to exercise a very important influence on Wilson's part in the coming peace. For House this was "an entirely new kind of Englishman." Spring-Rice had warned House against these "copperheads," but the Colonel found them "sane, reasonable, able men." He met Loreburn and found his views "largely coincide with mine." At other times he talked with A. G. Gardiner, John Burns, and F. W. Hirst. The latter told House that British public opinion wanted peace, and he urged that Wilson stand up for neutral rights and a new code of international law. House drew the conclusion that these men were Wilson's most ardent supporters in Britain. He had tapped a stream that was to bear him to unexpected places.[25]

By this time Wilson's search for a way to end the war had

23. Wilson to House, cable, February 20, 1915, *Life and Letters,* 5, 262; *Intimate Papers, 1,* 280–1; *Lansing Papers, 1,* 378–80.

24. "House Diary," March 9, 1915; *Intimate Papers, 1,* 385, 390, 448.

25. "House Diary," February 9, 25, March 4, 7, 8, 1915. Neutral rights did not occupy a major part of radical attention. In general whereas Conservatives condemned Wilson's attitude out of hand, Liberals were more inclined to see some justice in his arguments and to defend British practice as justified by the moral superiority of Britain's cause. Radicals and their journals showed the greatest readiness to accept Wilson's position and urge modification of British conduct. For some examples of press comment see Armin Rappaport, *The British Press and Wilsonian Neutrality* (Stanford, 1951), pp. 19, 23, 62–7, 73–8, 91–2, 126.

brought no sign of peace, but he had at least made it plain that he considered the United States had a real interest in the peace. The President had indicated readiness to help make the peace, perhaps even to engage America as a guarantor of some international arrangements. He had demonstrated that he attached great importance to arriving at a settlement by negotiation. In addition he had publicly or privately approved certain general features of a future world order, including provision for bringing disputes under international discussion, disarmament, freedom of the seas, and guarantees of territorial integrity.[26]

Many of Wilson's ideas might have been written into the program of the U.D.C. in England. The most significant divergence between him and the radicals was his disclaimer of any concern in the particular terms of settlement.[27] This was perhaps natural in the leader of a nation traditionally fearful of entanglement in European affairs. Certainly Europe's leaders would not have welcomed American interference. Grey had suggested that America leave peace terms alone and stand solely for the restoration of Belgium and schemes for stabilizing the postwar order.[28] The question was bound to arise, however, as to whether Wilson could reasonably expect to establish his general principles without close application to the detailed arrangements of the world in which those principles would have to operate. Otherwise there was a danger implicit in Grey's suggestion, that the United States would be allowed to endorse or even guarantee a world order upon the soundness and justice of which she was not to pass.

26. In particular Wilson's remarks to Axson, August or September 1914, quoted in Notter, *Origins*, p. 328. The President gave territorial integrity a prominent place in his projected Pan-American Pact, avowedly an example for Europe. Seymour, *American Diplomacy*, pp. 258–9; *Lansing Papers*, 2, 459 ff.

27. Wilson to House, December 24, 1915, House Collection; Seymour, p. 260; *Life and Letters, 5,* 292.

28. *Intimate Papers, 2,* 54, 67–8.

For the moment, thoughts of peace were expelled by acts of war. The torpedoing of the *Lusitania* on May 7, 1915, brought American diplomacy to a crisis in which the President stood up firmly for American rights. This stand cost him his Secretary of State and brought forward the more belligerent though equivocal Robert Lansing. But for all his firmness Wilson showed a desperate anxiety to keep the peace. His speech containing the phrase "too proud to fight" was only one of many intimations of a deep desire to remain aloof and in a position to mediate.[29] It cannot, of course, be said that the desire to mediate was Wilson's leading motive to remain neutral. Clearly his chief concern was to preserve America from the costs of war. But in the light of continued advice that American belligerency would be amply repaid by an early settlement,[30] Wilson's eager pursuit of neutrality represented a decision against seeking a solution by aiding the Allies to victory.

The sinking of the *Lusitania* ushered in a period of progressive deterioration in American relations with both sets of belligerents. American irritation with Britain was chiefly occasioned by the blockade, which some members of Wilson's Cabinet believed to be partly a device to steal American commerce. Rumors of the Treaty of London and the inclusion of right-wing members in Asquith's new Government served further to impair Britain's reputation. The decline in Anglo-American good will was greatly outweighed, however, by increased friction between Germany and America. German offenses against Americans were more spectacular, irrevocable, and of a sort to arouse resentful emotion. Drawn-out negotiations over the *Lusitiania*, punctuated by the torpedoing of the *Arabic* and other sinkings, brought America to the brink of

29. Link, *Progressive Era*, pp. 164–6; *Intimate Papers, 1*, 458–9; Joseph Tumulty, *Woodrow Wilson as I Know Him* (New York, 1921), p. 234; David F. Houston, *Eight Years with Wilson's Cabinet, 1913–1920* (2 vols. Garden City, N.Y., 1926), *1*, 131 ff.; *2*, 226–9.
30. *Intimate Papers, 1*, 434; *2*, 54, 58.

war. Aggravating these offenses were continuous subversive
activities by official agents of the Central Powers in America
and melodramatic threats as to what Germany would do to
the United States after the war.

Wilson still resisted warlike counsels, but even he began to
harden against Germany and give more credence to the
view that German defeat was a necessary preliminary to a
good peace. Modifying his call for neutrality in mind, he declared on October 11, 1915, "neutrality is a negative word.
It is a word that does not express what Americans ought to
feel." But Wilson continued to shrink from the idea of going
to war. In the same speech he made it clear that he believed
America's duty was to keep out and "preserve the foundations
upon which peace can be rebuilt." [31]

Merely passive neutrality was rapidly becoming an unten-
able position in the face of a growing demand for a positive
policy toward the many problems raised by the war. A *New
Republic* editorial by Walter Lippmann published on December
25, 1915, under the title "Uneasy America," well typified the
general mood of insecurity. Colonel House was himself deeply
impressed with the need for a more active course, and spurred
on by him Wilson adopted a twofold policy. He lent himself to a program of military preparedness and set on foot
a further attempt to promote a negotiated peace.

This time Wilson's increased differentiation between the
merits and reasonableness of the belligerents induced him to
adopt a method favored by House. The Colonel proposed to
secure a promise that Britain would accept a call to negotiation. In return for this promise Wilson would offer to inter-
pose American influence on behalf of a good peace, including
disarmament and a league of nations. Wilson summed up the
general idea in a letter to House: "If either party to the present
war will let us say to the other that they are willing to discuss peace on such terms it will clearly be our duty to use

31. *New Democracy, 1,* 378.

our utmost moral force to oblige the other to parley and I do not see how they could stand in the opinion of the world if they refuse." [32] Grey having expressed his approval of the suggested terms, but not of the projected peace move, House sailed for Europe in December 1915.

In England, House and Grey, after numerous conferences with members of the Cabinet, drew up on February 17, 1916, an agreement subsequently known as the "House-Grey Memorandum." This document, initialed by Grey, declared that: "President Wilson was ready, on hearing from France and England that the moment was opportune, to propose that a conference should be summoned to put an end to the war. Should the Allies accept this proposal, and should Germany refuse it, the United States would [probably] enter the war against Germany." Colonel House expressed the opinion, the memorandum continued, that such a conference, if held at a time when the Allies were in a sound military situation, would secure terms favorable to them, and that should it fail to achieve a peace the United States would leave the conference as a belligerent on the side of the Allies. The memorandum suggested that reasonable terms might include restoration of Belgium, transfer of Alsace-Lorraine to France, Russian acquisition of an outlet to the sea and perhaps compensation for Germany outside Europe.[33]

President Wilson never heard that "the moment was opportune." But although the House-Grey memorandum was never used, its negotiation was highly significant for the development of Wilson's concept of the peace. The very draft-

32. Wilson to House, December 24, 1915, quoted in Link, *Progressive Era*, p. 199; Robert Lansing, *War Memoirs of Robert Lansing, Secretary of State* (Indianapolis, 1935), p. 45. Page had suggested something similar in 1914, Burton J. Hendrick, *Life and Letters of Walter H. Page* (3 vols. Garden City, N.Y., 1922–26), 3, 173–4. See also the discussion in Seymour, pp. 140 ff., 259–60.

33. *Intimate Papers*, 2, 201–2.

ing of the memorandum indicated the President's growing sense of involvement in the coming settlement. More substantial evidence of involvement was Wilson's promise at this time to "cooperate in a policy seeking to bring about and maintain permanent peace amongst civilized nations." [34] This pledge, though vaguely worded, was more definite and much broader in scope than the pledge made during House's earlier visit. Coupled with earlier intimations that Wilson favored a league of nations as a part of the peace, the new pledge made it appear that the President was moving toward an intimate relation with the new European order.

It might seem that the offer not merely to intervene but to enter the war constituted an even more remarkable commitment to involvement in Europe. But such an interpretation almost certainly mistakes Wilson's intentions. Colonel House does indeed seem to have regarded decisive American alignment with the Allies, on the issue of Germany's rejecting reasonable terms, as an acceptable alternative result to his *démarche,* even at the price of war, though he had moments of doubt in which he showed much greater caution.[35] That Wilson could contemplate this contingency, however conditional and remote, confirms his awareness that the international situation carried with it the possibility of America being involved in the fighting. This possibility existed entirely independent of the House-Grey episode. It arose from American disputes with the belligerents and was, in fact, the reason why Wilson approved House's effort to bring the war to a close. Ending, not entering, war was Wilson's overriding purpose. He thought of the venture not as a step to war but

34. Wilson to House, January 9, 1916, House Collection; House interpreted this to Balfour and Grey as "bring to bear all our power in behalf of peace and the maintenance of it." House to Wilson, January 11, 1916, House Collection.

35. Thus on January 16, 1916, he wrote Wilson from Europe, "I am more and more certain that it would be a mistake for us to come in." *Intimate Papers, 2,* 133.

rather as an exploration of "the possibilities in the direction of peace." [36] It was "moral force" to secure a settlement, not military intervention on behalf of the Allies that he had in mind. This he showed by inserting the word "probably" in the promise to leave the conference on the side of the Allies. The proposal that America should join the Allies if Germany refused even to enter a conference was already qualified by the same word. Wilson had now made no absolute commitment to intervene at all, other than by the expression of opinion. This accords with the view that he regarded his move as an effort to make peace, and thought of the other outcome, going to war, as an unavoidable but relatively remote risk entailed by his policy, not as a satisfactory alternative outcome. [37]

36. Wilson to House, December 17, 1915, *Life and Letters*, 6, 138–9. Cf. Wilson to House, December 22, 1915, House Collection; "House Diary," October 19, November 25, 27, 28, December 27, 1915.

37. The extent of Wilson's commitment, and the difference in purpose between him and House, has been subject to argument. *Intimate Papers*, 2, 201, n. 1, suggests that the insertion of the word "probably" did not fundamentally weaken the document, which already contained conditional words, including more than one other "probably," as indeed it must have done in view of the U. S. Constitution. But at least the insertion indicates Wilson's sensitivity to the limited nature of his pledge. The fact that the addition was not absolutely necessary strengthens this interpretation. However, the strongest suggestion that the insertion was a significant modification of House's ideas comes from House himself. On October 17, 1915, House drafted an outline of the proposed action. Wilson inserted the word "probably" in the following sentence: "If the Central Powers were still obdurate, it would [probably] be necessary to join the Allies and force the issue." In a passage which I do not believe has been published, House noted that Wilson had added two words to the letter, "Allies" and "probably," and the Colonel commented, "The first was unimportant, the other quite important." "House Diary," October 19, 1915. At this time Wilson explained to House, "I do not want to make it inevitable quite that we should take part to force terms on Germany, because the exact circumstances of such a crisis are impossible to determine." That this alteration, which seemed important to House, did not seem so to Wilson supports the belief that they

Wilson's caution is related to another illuminating aspect of the House-Grey negotiations: the light cast on his intended attitude toward the various belligerents when the time came to make the settlement. The procedure adopted in the memorandum showed that Wilson believed the Central Powers were the greater obstacle to peace and that his influence should be exerted on the side of the Allies. This did not mean, however, that he would help the Allies crush Germany. He would have gladly accepted German cooperation, but he simply did not believe it would be forthcoming. True, the memorandum was cast in terms of an assurance to Britain against defeat while Germany received no such guarantee, but at that time the German army seemed the best possible security.[38] In effect Wilson was offering Britain his advice and influence on condition that she accept a moderate peace. He hoped that his offer of postwar cooperation would facilitate such a peace by rendering extreme demands based on security requirements unnecessary.[39]

Britain was now in a somewhat delicate situation. Not to accept Wilson's offer would imply a determination to fight

---

had different concepts of the mission. Wilson to House, October 18, 1915, *Life and Letters, 6,* 128. Link, *Progressive Era,* pp. 203–4, suggests that certain assurances of support given to the French at this time constitute the only occasion on which House was less than frank in reporting to Wilson.

A highly critical account of the mission as a warlike move is Edwin Borchard and William P. Lage, *Neutrality for the United States* (New Haven, 1937), pp. 108 ff. There is an effective attack on this view in pp. 46 ff. of A. S. Link, *Wilson the Diplomatist* (Baltimore, 1957), which appeared while the present work was in press.

38. "House Diary," September 28, 1915, January 29, 1916; *Intimate Papers, 2,* 87, 107; for Wilson's belief that the German army could take care of itself see Sondermann, "The Wilson Administration's Image of Germany," pp. 232–4.

39. *Life and Letters, 6,* 208. On December 24, 1915, Wilson wrote "the only possible guarantees that any rational man could accept are (a) military and naval disarmament, and (b) a league of nations" (ibid., p. 138; "House Diary," January 15, 1916).

on for unreasonable gains. Already Wilson and House thought
they perceived signs of such an intention. House noted that of
all the British leaders only Grey and Balfour showed real
interest in his scheme.[40] Grey himself had disappointed House
by refusing to put the plan into operation at once and by insisting that it must be up to him to decide the proper time in
conjunction with the other Allies.[41] In his efforts to encourage
early action House revealed his suspicion as to what the
Allies would do if their power were unchecked. He told Grey
that if the Allies won a complete victory, Russia, France, and
Italy would make outrageous demands. House also warned
Lloyd George and Balfour of the danger that British public
opinion would demand a punitive peace if completely victorious. They were, noted House, "inclined to take the
risk"![42] He gained the distinct impression that the British
were dragging their feet.

House's renewed contacts with the radicals provided him
with further reasons for distrusting the British Government.
F. W. Hirst took House to see Lord Loreburn, who "excoriated"
Grey for deceit at the outbreak of the war. House urged
Loreburn to try to stem the flood of extremist declarations and
to pitch the Allied cause on a note of high idealism. The
Colonel hoped he had persuaded Asquith and Grey to do
this, but he thought they might renege, and if so Loreburn
should try to fill the breach.[43]

The radicals also gave House frequent personal assurances
of the strength of peace sentiment in Britain. Howard Whitehouse, M.P., visited him and urged that Wilson offer mediation.
House received much information from Whitehouse, including an estimate that a public offer of mediation from Wilson
supported by Grey and Balfour could obtain a Parliamentary

40. "House Diary," January 6, 1916; cf. House to Wilson, January 3, February 3, 1916, House Collection.
41. "House Diary," November 25, 1915; *Intimate Papers, 2,* 175.
42. "House Diary," February 11, 1916.
43. Ibid., February 21, 1916, partly in *Intimate Papers, 2,* 192.

majority of a hundred. Whitehouse also passed on his opinion of the Cabinet, warning House that Lloyd George was an extremist at heart.[44]

C. R. Buxton sent House a similar account of British public opinion, affirming that there was considerable potential support for a moderate proposal for peace made by any government, belligerent or neutral. Buxton explained that press opinion was distorted and sent House one of his pamphlets. House replied that he had read it and found himself in substantial agreement.[45] More assurances of good will were brought by A. G. Gardiner of the *Daily News.* House briefed Gardiner for an article which, as "Mr. Wilson's Policy and the Pact of Peace," subsequently met with great approval from Wilson himself.[46]

Thus at the end of House's second mission the British government stood as it were on trial. It could demonstrate willingness to work with Wilson for a moderate peace or it could refuse and leave him to draw his conclusions. The foundations of doubt were already firmly laid in the minds of Wilson and House. At the outset of his mission House told Wilson he had admonished Grey that "if we failed to come to a better understanding with England and failed to solve the problems brought about by the war properly, it would be because his Government and people could not follow you to the heights you would go." On March 10, 1916, House wrote Grey, "it is now squarely up to you to make the next move." [47]

This was scarcely comfortable for Britain. Neither Wilson nor House had shown much appreciation of the difficulty of

44. "House Diary," February 22, 1916, partly in *Intimate Papers, 2,* 184–5.

45. The pamphlet was probably *Terms of Peace* (U.D.C., 18b). C. R. Buxton to House, February 19, March 2, 1916, House Collection.

46. "House Diary," March 29, 1916; R. S. Baker to House, April 8, 1916, House Collection.

47. House to Wilson, January 7, 1916, *Intimate Papers, 2,* 118; House to Grey, March 10, 1916, House Collection.

reconstructing Europe or of the strength of the passions at loose. Although House had discussed territorial questions he had, at Wilson's behest, refused to contemplate American participation in making the actual territorial terms. He had appeared to be most interested in such extreme generalities as the "elimination of militarism and navalism." [48] This vagueness spared British leaders the necessity of spelling out their intentions, but it also suggested that American support might prove unreliable when detailed arrangements became unavoidable. The British government had not abandoned hope of securing a decisive victory and imposing terms much more severe than Wilson could be expected to approve. But even had they been resigned to a compromise peace, it would have been a risky procedure indeed for Britain to begin talks with a view to reaching a compromise which Grey believed neither his allies nor the enemy were ready to accept. It would entail the risk of the other Allies making a separate peace to get what terms they could. Even in the dubious event of America entering the war and aiding in the defeat of Germany, it was surely not proposed that Britain and America fight the other Allies to restrain their ambitions against Germany. Here again was the true tragedy of those who wanted a moderate peace. Germany would not grant moderate terms unless beaten, yet efforts to beat her and the free hand which total victory would give the Allies were themselves inimical to moderation. So long as Germany remained intransigent, peace would not be possible without her defeat, and in that

48. ". . . we have nothing to do with local settlements, territorial questions, indemnities and the like, but are concerned only in the future peace of the world" (*Life and Letters*, 6, 138). House showed a tendency to use broad terms which it would be difficult to put into precise proposals. This tendency is perhaps best illustrated by his recurrence to the remarkable idea that a basic *condition* of peace was that it should be "permanent." He even suggested that negotiations should not begin until "this condition had been agreed to by all the belligerents" ("House Diary," January 13, 1915).

case the settlement could be moderate only so far as the judgment and self-restraint of the Allies permitted.

Wilson demonstrated his reluctance to cast in his lot with the Allies and assist them to an "exemplary triumph" much more clearly in the events following the torpedoing of the Channel packet *Sussex* in March 1916. This crisis brought German-American relations to a new low point; Wilson referred to the Germans as responsible for the war and in his negotiations removed all room for diplomatic maneuver should Germany again give her U-boats free rein.[49] But he again did his utmost to stay out of war, and after the Germans submitted, the atmosphere between Germany and America settled down to a new calm. Wilson took German submission as a sign that the German civil authorities were now dominant and prepared to be reasonable.[50]

Meanwhile the causes of Anglo-American friction continued. During the *Sussex* crisis Wilson had shown no sign of being impressed by House's repetition of the argument advanced after the sinking of the *Lusitania,* namely that an American declaration of war would be amply repaid in influence at the peace conference.[51] British standing had been further diminished in Wilson's eyes when Grey rejected an appeal to invoke the mediation called for in the House-Grey memorandum. Grey, of course, had no reason to do so when it seemed highly probable that America and Germany would soon be at war over the U-boats and Britain would receive American assistance without limiting her own freedom of action. The Foreign Secretary gave a broad hint of this reasoning, which did not endear him to Wilson.[52]

Immediately the *Sussex* issue was settled (at least for the

49. *Intimate Papers, 2,* 239.
50. Ibid., p. 247.
51. Ibid., p. 228; "House Diary," March 29, April 11, 1916; cf. Lansing, *Memoirs,* pp. 133–7.
52. *Intimate Papers, 2,* 229–31; Page to Secretary, March 26, May 6, 1916, *Lansing Papers, 1,* 706–7.

time being), Wilson turned once more to problems of peace. His recent narrow escape from war provided a strong incentive, and for the first time he appears to have given the matter his full attention.[53] He was still eager to work with Britain to secure a good peace, and this demonstrates his appreciation that the British cause was more akin to his own purposes than that of Germany. But the method he adopted confirms the impression that he was increasingly unwilling to allow Britain to dictate how and when he should act. Wilson's procedure also revealed that his idea of a peace and how to secure it was moving yet closer to that of the British radicals.

On May 10, 1916, acting on Wilson's instructions, House informed Grey that the President proposed to announce America's readiness to join an international organization to keep the peace and to couple this with a declaration that if the war lasted much longer he would issue a call to negotiation. House explained that this offer rested on a belief that Germany had been sufficiently chastened and that if America were forced to enter the war and so crush Germany, dividing the spoils would take precedence over the conclusion of a lasting peace. There was now no promise to secure terms to the Allies' liking. In terms of strong disapproval Grey immediately declared the project inopportune. House was sufficiently disappointed to speculate on a postwar collision between America and the Allies, flushed with victory and devoted to militarism. This might happen, he decided, even if America helped the Allies win.[54]

Wilson refused to bow to Grey's wishes. The President told House that the United States must either move for peace or hold Britain to a stricter observance of neutral rights.[55] Under Wilson's supervision House drafted another cable

53. He may also have been influenced by an implied threat in Germany's note of submission that if Wilson did not secure modification of the blockade the U-boats would be unleashed again.
54. *Intimate Papers*, 2, 278–83.
55. Wilson to House, May 16, 1916, House Collection.

warning Grey of the alternatives and clearly showing suspicion of British intentions. "If England is indeed fighting
for the emancipation of Europe," it read, then we will cooperate. But "any nation that rejects peace discussions will
bring upon themselves a heavy responsibility." House expanded American ideas in a letter. Declaring that if Germany
were "completely crushed," then certainly a "new set of
problems will arise to vex us all," House returned to the
theme that only a negotiated peace could endure.[56] Once more
Britain's favored position faced her with choices that Germany
was spared by her ill repute. When the British still failed to
respond, it began to look, House complained, "as if a club
were necessary before they would take any notice." [57]

President Wilson would not be denied. Together, House
and he prepared a pronouncement for delivery before the
League to Enforce Peace on May 27, 1916. On the eve of
his speech the persistent lack of any British cooperation persuaded Wilson to abandon any explicit call to peace. He would
confine himself to suggesting the essentials of a lasting settlement in the hope that this would lead the belligerents in the
right direction. The whole speech remained an implied criticism of European diplomacy and a closer approach to impartiality than ever before. "I cast the speech," Wilson confided a day or two later, "in a way that it would be very hard
for the Allies to reject, as well as for Germany." [58]

The peace outlined by Wilson might well have been designed
to please a gathering of British radicals. Declaring that he
was not concerned with the particular causes and objects of
the war, Wilson nonetheless thought it essential to assert
that the conflict had arisen out of "secret counsels." The
peoples of Europe had been given no chance to discuss the

56. House to Wilson, May 17, to Grey May 10, 19, 23, 1916,
Intimate Papers, 2, 278–88.

57. "House Diary," May 24, 1916; *Intimate Papers*, 2, 310.

58. Wilson to House, May 29, 1916, House Collection; *Life and
Letters*, 6, 223.

issues. Had the alignments of the nations been known, "those who brought the great contest on would have been glad to substitute conference for force." In future the world needed a "new and more wholesome diplomacy," in which nations observed as strict a code of morality as individuals.[59] For this new diplomacy Wilson laid down three principles: that every nation had a right to choose its sovereignty, that all nations should have equal rights, and that the world should be secured against "every disturbance of its peace that has its origin in aggression." To call these principles into existence Wilson proposed a league of nations which would use public opinion, economic pressure, and, if necessary, force to safeguard the freedom of the seas and to prevent any war begun contrary to "treaty covenants" or without having exhausted peaceful procedures. This would be "a virtual guarantee of territorial integrity and political independence." [60] The President concluded his speech by suggesting that the belligerents should settle terms among themselves, presumably in accordance with Wilson's principles. Then Wilson was ready to cooperate in a league. He hoped that this promise would facilitate the application of his principles by creating a feeling of security and making strategic considerations less compelling.[61]

Thus it was that Woodrow Wilson publicly endorsed a

59. Wilson took this idea from House. The idea is of course standard in Anglo-American liberalism.

60. The emphasis on aggression and territorial integrity was something of a divergence from the views of the U.D.C. Apparently Wilson saw "aggression" as the central problem. The U.D.C. argued that what looked like aggression was often a reaction to injustice. International organization should therefore be a medium of adjustment, not a guarantee of the status quo. Nevertheless Wilson's scheme did not forbid war and thus tacitly admitted it might be justifiable to change the status quo by force. In later pronouncements Wilson showed increasing interest in the process of peaceful change.

61. *New Democracy*, 2, 184–8. Mr. Seymour compares the address with a draft by House, *Intimate Papers*, 2, 337–8.

league of nations and American participation in it. As the
circumstances of its delivery revealed, the speech was much
more than a declaration on that one point. It marked increasing distrust of the methods by which the British government
proposed to end the war and make the peace. Wilson was now
defining an approach of his own, an approach which closely
resembled that of the British radicals.

Besides the general influence of their propaganda—this
was, for example, the time that Lowes Dickinson was touring
America on behalf of international organization [62]—the radicals actually had a small part in preparing Wilson's speech.
Norman Angell, who had been in America for some time,
lecturing, writing, and advising House, heard of Wilson's
intention and suggested that the President use the tactic employed by the U.D.C. in its sixth pamphlet and thereafter: that
of quoting the idealistic utterances of Allied statesmen with
the purpose of holding them to fulfillment. Failing to lay
his hands on a copy of the pamphlet, Angell sent Wilson a
selection of utterances by Allied statesmen drawn from the
heyday of idealistic propaganda in 1914. House also gave
Wilson his own five-page draft of a speech embodying these
quotations.[63] The influence of this material appeared most
plainly when Wilson justified his appeal by declaring: "repeated utterances of the leading statesmen of most of the great
nations now engaged in war have made it plain that their
thought has come to this, that the principle of public
right must henceforth take precedence over the individual
interests of particular nations." Nor was the impact of the
U.D.C. at this juncture confined to these direct communications. Editorials and articles in recent issues of the *New Re-*

62. Forster, pp. 166–8.
63. Angell to House, an undated letter "Tuesday" and May 19,
1916, House Collection. The pamphlet would be *The National
Policy: Extracts from Speeches by British Statesmen* (U.D.C., 6).
House to Wilson, May 19, 21, 1916, and folder of material used by
Wilson in Woodrow Wilson Papers, Library of Congress, File 2.

public, especially some written by Angell, had much influence on Wilson's speech. From Angell's editorials, principally that of May 20, 1916, the President drew in particular his emphasis of the idea that America could not evade participation in efforts to keep world peace because it could no longer avoid entanglement in the world's wars.[64]

The mixed reception given to the President's speech by Allied governments and right-wing opinion has already been described.[65] Grey wrote to House objecting that a league must be founded on a peace sufficiently favorable to the Allies for Germany to recognize the futility of militarism.[66] Page reported that British opinion assumed Wilson had aimed his words at "the gallery filled with peace cranks." [67] This treatment accorded his considered views did little to halt Wilson's growing suspicion that his aims were widely divergent from those of the Allies. House now expressed such doubts more outspokenly than ever before. He remarked to Noel Buxton that he was tired of the British claim that they entered the war for Belgium. Echoing the "stop the war" arguments of 1914, House suggested that Britain went in because Germany insisted on a dominant army and navy.[68]

64. See esp. *New Republic,* April 22, May 13, 20, 1916, and H. N. Brailsford in ibid., May 6, 1916, "On Crushing German Militarism." A typed memorandum very similar to the editorials of April 22 and May 20, dealing with possible conditions for American intervention, found in the Wilson Papers, is partly printed in Edward Buehrig, *Woodrow Wilson and the Balance of Power* (Bloomington, Ind., 1955), pp. 173–80. For the influence on Wilson see *New Republic,* September 16, 1916, and Angell, *After All,* p. 205. Cf. Wilson's declaration on October 26, 1916, that "the business of neutrality is over," *New Democracy,* 2, 376–82. Of course the constant impingement of the naval war on American interests was the most compelling argument that America must be involved.

65. See above, p. 43. Cf. Sir Horace Plunkett to House, June 7, 1916, House Collection

66. May 29, 1916. *Life and Letters, 6,* 225.

67. May 30, 1916, *Intimate Papers, 2,* 302.

68. *Intimate Papers, 2,* 265–6; cf. Buxton to House, June 29, 1916, and his Memorandum on British response to Wilson's speech,

Other events combined to increase Anglo-American tension. The Paris Economic Conference of June 1916 aroused considerable apprehension in the United States and the British "blacklist," published on July 19, 1916, appeared to some Americans as a stop-gap attempt to apply discrimination at once.[69] Suppression of the Irish Rebellion and the Allied occupation of Greece further tarnished Britain's reputation. In August, Page came home on a visit, and while his fervent pleading of Britain's cause irritated Wilson, the Ambassador's chill reception displayed the President's coldness toward Britain. Even House complained to Page of British "cant and hypocrisy" and predicted that if the United States joined the Allies, they would grumble during the war that America was ungenerous in assistance and after the war that she had forced them to be lenient to Germany.[70] Impassioned British charges that an American warship had assisted a U-boat moved Wilson to remark, "how difficult it is to be friends with Great Britain without doing whatever she wants us to do." [71]

Above all, British persistence in pouring cold water on the idea of mediation aroused Wilson's impatience. In August, Grey put an end to hope in the House-Grey memorandum by flatly and apparently finally rejecting American mediation. Lloyd George's "Knock-Out Blow" interview was a bold confirmation of this decision. Page reported the interview as "a restrained expression of governmental and public opinion." [72] By November, Wilson was advising the Federal

House Collection. It will be recalled that Buxton returned to England a whole-hearted convert to a negotiated peace. See above, p. 81.

69. Brailsford wrote articles in the *New Republic* expounding radical ideas on economic discrimination, May 8, 1915, July 29, 1916. *Lansing Papers, 1,* 311–12; *Life and Letters, 6,* 312–15.

70. Link, *Progressive Era,* p. 222; Lansing, *Memoirs,* pp. 169–70; Hendrick, 2, 183–8; *Intimate Papers, 2,* 319–20.

71. October 10, 1916, *Life and Letters, 6,* 331.

72. Link, *Progressive Era,* p. 219; *Foreign Relations* (1916), Supp., p. 56.

Reserve Board not to approve loans to Britain on account of strained relations. The President spoke of outbuilding the British navy and of not shrinking from war with the Allies if they wanted it. In fact the President's distaste for the Allies and their methods made House genuinely fearful lest America find itself in the war on the wrong side.[73]

The wrong side was, of course, the German side. Wilson realized that as well as House. Dubious sinkings and persistent rumors of an impending resumption of unrestrained U-boat warfare served as a reminder of German misdeeds. By drawing a pointed distinction between offenses against life and those against property in his speech accepting nomination for the 1916 campaign, Wilson made it quite clear that he still considered Germany the greater menace.[74] Nevertheless the Presidential campaign gave additional evidence of decline in the Allied reputation for moral superiority over Germany. In his comments on the war Wilson displayed growing cynicism as to Allied motives. The election also provided a severe setback for those who favored intervention on behalf of the Allies. Wilson's re-election was a virtual endorsement of peace and neutrality.

He emerged from the election having fused peace and Progressivism. As the leader of a pacific liberalism he was now more than ever set upon mediating in the European war. Growing public exasperation with the British blockade and with continued U-boat sinkings kept Wilson alive to the danger that he might be pushed into the war at any moment by public indignation or his own sense of the national right and honor.[75] German civilian leaders were now anxious to have the President act and were dropping broad hints that if he delayed, the military command would insist on unlimited use of the U-boats.[76] There was strong reason however to

73. "House Diary," October 26, 27, November 15, 17, 1916.
74. *New Democracy, 2,* 275–91.
75. "House Diary," November 2, 1916.
76. *Foreign Relations* (1916), Supp., pp. 55 ff.

doubt whether Wilson could secure a hearing. The British government's readiness to resent any peace move was well advertised, but the Germans too, though apparently eager for some initiative toward peace, were widely suspected of harboring impossible terms.[77]

Despite the obstacles confronting him, Wilson did not regard his intended *démarche* as a forlorn gesture. He really hoped to make peace. This optimism rested on his conviction that there was "sufficient peace sentiment in the Allied countries to make them consent." [78] He believed that such sentiment was particularly strong in Britain. To tap this resource the President now abandoned House's method of confidential overtures and proposed to adopt a plan he had conceived in June 1916. At that time Wilson had written: "it will be up to us to judge for ourselves when the time has come for us to make an imperative suggestion. I mean a suggestion which they will have no choice but to heed, because the opinion of the non-official world and the desire of all peoples will be behind it." [79]

Thus Wilson turned to the British radicals exactly as they looked to him. This alliance is understandable. Both acknowledged the same heritage of English liberal political thought, and their views of the war had moved steadily parallel toward a rational peace by negotiation. Both agreed a German victory would be deplorable; neither believed that an Allied victory would itself be sufficient to create a better system of international relations.

The radicals had worked hard to obtain a hearing in America. Authors such as Lowes Dickinson, Brailsford, and Angell had impressed their mark on periodicals like the *New Republic*, one of the few organs to influence Wilson. House had brought

77. These fears were justified. On November 7, 1916, Hindenburg and Bethmann-Hollweg agreed on a severe set of terms. Gatzke, pp. 142 ff.

78. November 14, 1916, *Intimate Papers*, 2, 391.

79. Wilson to House, June 22, 1916, House Collection.

back favorable impressions of the radicals from his missions
to Europe. Occasionally radicals had made direct public appeals to Wilson. The American Neutral Conference Committee
had reprinted U.D.C. publications. Radicals had supported
Wilson's efforts to end the war ever since the first mediation
offer in 1914.

Wilson's assurance of support in England did not, however,
rest on these evidences' alone. By the autumn of 1916 the
radicals were sending him a swelling stream of information
and encouragement. This stream came into spate as Wilson
began to prepare his peace move and flowed unabated during
the following months of diplomatic activity. Most of these
communications passed through the hands of William H.
Buckler, an American attached as a special agent to the Embassy in London. Buckler had been a friend and contemporary
of Trevelyan at Trinity College, Oxford, and enjoyed extensive contacts with British radical leaders. Beginning in 1916
he sent regular reports on radical opinion to Colonel House
for Wilson's information and also forwarded messages from the
radicals themselves. In this way the information avoided the
British censorship; it also evaded the censorious eye of Ambassador Page.[80] Wilson's interest in the radicals may be
partly measured by his use of these special channels to obtain
their views at a time when he no longer bothered to open his
Ambassador's letters.[81]

80. Cf. a typewritten note by Buckler in the House Collection.
Most of these communications have so far escaped notice because
until very recently the only fairly complete files were still in Buckler's possession. Allan Nevins in his *Henry White, Thirty Years of
American Diplomacy* (New York, 1930), pp. 336–49, gives some
information on some later communications between Buckler and
White, his half-brother. But as will be explained, White only came
into the picture some time after America entered the war. The
Henry White Papers in the Library of Congress do not even contain all the material used by Nevins. Some of Buckler's later work
in connection with the Labour party is mentioned in Henry Pelling,
America and the British Left (London, 1956), pp. 109 ff.

81. "House Diary," December 14, 1916.

As early as July 1916, Wilson received a letter from Lord Loreburn promising cooperation whenever the President should decide to make a move for peace.[82] A few days later House passed on Noel Buxton's account of moderate elements in England and suggested that Page be replaced by someone more able to encourage this support. Following his discussions with Buxton, House told Wilson that reactionaries were gaining the upper hand in Britain but that he believed the major part of public opinion would support a peace move if Wilson spelled out the nature of the peace. "It may be necessary," House continued, "to arouse the latent feeling of the people in both England and France in such a way that they will compel their Governments to act." [83] For the rest of the year reports from the radicals continued to keep up Wilson's hope. On August 19 Noel Buxton sent House a letter which, House replied, "heartened us greatly. I read it to the President and he was pleased to know that 'there was a strong drift of opinion towards reasoned calculation.'" [84] A further memorandum from Buxton on November 3, 1916, evoked the promise that Wilson would soon be "paying more attention to these things." [85]

After the Presidential election the presence in America of Howard Whitehouse, M.P., facilitated the transmission of radical thought. "The most interesting caller," House noted on November 18, 1916, "was Mr. Whitehouse . . . he would like for the President to intervene." House immediately sent an account to Wilson:

82. House to Wilson, July 3, 1916, House Collection; Wilson Papers, File 2.
83. Buxton to House, June 29, July 10, House to Wilson, July 3, 5, 20, House Collection.
84. Buxton to House, August 19, 1916, House to Buxton, n.d., House Collection.
85. House to Buxton, November 24; cf. Buxton to House, November 20, House Collection.

Whitehouse is a pacifist, is perfectly reliable and is anxious for a move to be made for peace. He gave me as clear insight into the situation, I think, as it would be possible to get even if I were in England. When I cornered him and put specific questions I got this result. He believes if you made an open move for peace at this time it would be taken into the House of Commons for discussion, that it would probably result in a close vote with the pacifists losing. Then would come resignations from the most advanced Liberal members of the government and their place would be supplied by reactionaries. Military dictatorship would probably ensue and within the year there would be an overthrow of the Government unless they succeeded in making a victorious peace. . . . Whitehouse . . . believes [our entry into the war] would be in the nature of a calamity. He sees, as all clear sighted men see, that the salvation of the situation is in our neutrality.[86]

The next day House told Wilson of another memorandum on peace moves written by Buxton, adding that this represented an important body of opinion. Wilson replied that the letter about Whitehouse and others "has given me a great deal to think about . . . corroborating in some degree the impression I expressed to you, that this is very nearly the time, if not the time itself for our move for peace." [87] This encouragement and assurance of vigorous support goes far to explain Wilson's persistence in his mediation effort.

86. "House Diary," November 18, 1916; House to Wilson, November 20, 1916, House Collection. This letter is quoted fully because Baker, *Life and Letters*, 6, 369, refers to it in a footnote, asserting that Whitehouse thought a *peace move* would be "disastrous." It is quite clear that Whitehouse was strongly recommending a peace move and Wilson so understood him.

87. House to Wilson, Wilson to House, November 21, 1916, House Collection.

In the next few days Wilson sketched a peace note. He consulted numerous reports on opinion and editorials on policy, taking particular notice of a *New Republic* editorial of November 25, 1916, suggesting the need to discover the "precise nature of the political objects" at stake in the war.[88] Wilson's draft noted that the war had become one of attrition which, if continued to a knock-out, would endanger civilization and at best result in a peace of "exhaustion, reaction, political upheaval and a resentment that can never cool." The belligerents had all professed willingness to renounce conquest and seek peace resting not on an "uncertain balance of alliances" but on an organization to preserve international justice. And yet, Wilson complained, "the reasons for this upheaval of the world remain obscure, the objects which would, if attained, satisfy the one group of belligerents or the other have never been definitely avowed." America was ready to cooperate in a good peace but would have to revise its neutral policy if it became clear that no end was in sight. Wilson therefore proposed a conference or some other means of discovering what guarantees the belligerents wanted besides a league. In this powerful appeal Wilson had chosen exactly the method advocated by the radicals, that of demanding statements of terms from both sides.[89]

Wilson read his draft to House on November 27, 1916. House found it rather too strong for his taste. At his advice Wilson removed the statement that the causes of the war were obscure, but he refused to add any indication of sympathy for the Allied cause. Lansing made further criticisms which Wilson and he discussed on December 1. House and Lansing counseled delay, House arguing that a "background should be laid in both France and England." [90]

88. *Life and Letters, 6*, 380, n. 1; Wilson Papers, File 2.
89. The full draft is in *Life and Letters, 6*, 380–6. Wilson was again using the tactic of quoting belligerent statesmen's milder moments to embarrass them.
90. *Intimate Papers, 2*, 393–5; *Life and Letters, 6*, 380–7. For

The President did delay about three weeks, hoping the Germans would cease deportations from Belgium which were incensing American as well as Allied opinion. On November 29, 1916, Wilson ordered the American chargé in Berlin to press an informal protest, pointing out the bad effect on American opinion "at a time when that opinion was more nearly approaching a balance of judgment as to the issues of the war than ever before." [91] Further cause for delay was the change of government in Britain. This distressed Wilson and House. Writing to the President, House showed he had the radicals' advice well in mind by exclaiming that if Lloyd George came to the top, "England will then be under the military dictatorship that Whitehouse spoke about." Wilson decided that an ingratiating note of congratulation which House had prepared for Lloyd George would do no good.[92]

The change of government strengthened the conviction that any peace move must rely heavily on the radicals.[93] House suggested that Whitehouse and his friends might undertake the necessary preparation of British opinion and also that Buckler be given the task of piloting peace moves in London. Buckler, he told Wilson, was the one man in the London Embassy who "has not lost his bearings . . . he is friendly with Trevelyan, Massingham of the *Nation* and men of that kind." [94]

During these days of waiting the radicals continued to offer encouragement and advice. Whitehouse sent Wilson several memoranda declaring the time unusually favorable and ad-

---

Lansing's negative attitude see Buehrig, pp. 137–9. Wilson did not show House his final text.

91. *Foreign Relations* (1916), Supp., pp. 70 ff.

92. House to Wilson, December 3, 6, 7. Wilson to House, December 9, 1916, House Collection.

93. *Intimate Papers*, 2, 397. Cf. Gavit to Wilson, December 2, 1916, Wilson Papers, File 2.

94. Ibid.; House to Buckler, December 6, House to Wilson, December 4, 1916, House Collection.

vocating what Wilson had already decided upon, a reference
to the similarity of the belligerents' declared intentions. Even
if Lloyd George were in power, Whitehouse thought Wilson's
action must open up debate and consolidate opinion.[95] House
also sent Wilson a letter from Trevelyan which, the Colonel
assured Buckler, "will be of especial interest to him at this
time." Trevelyan told Wilson that many were "yearning for
a great solution." Buckler added his own comment that "Massingham of the 'Nation' has now come round in favour of
'peace by negotiation'" and that the radicals' prospects were
"distinctly improving." "That was a most impressive letter
from Mr. Trevelyan,—and a most interesting memorandum
from Mr. Whitehouse," Wilson replied. "The time is near at
hand for *something*." [96]

When Wilson's Note finally emerged on December 18, 1916,
it showed the effects of his subordinates' criticism and of
embarrassment by Germany's own peace move. Wilson no
longer proposed a conference but simply asked each belligerent to define its terms. Nor was there any threat of a
re-appraisal of American policy if the answers were unsatis-
factory. This may reflect Lansing's warning that Germany
might adroitly maneuver America into an alignment against
the Allies. But the President still declared, to House's dis-
comfort, "that the objects which the statesmen of the belligerents on both sides have in mind in this war are virtually
the same, as stated in general terms to their own people and
to the world." [97]

The Central Powers precipitately cut off discussion by thank-

95. Whitehouse to House, December 5, House to Wilson, December 7, 1916, House Collection. Cf. Wilson Papers, File 2.

96. Buckler to House, November 24, House to Buckler, December 6, 1916; House to Wilson, December 6, 7, 1916. House
Collection; Wilson Papers, File 2; Wilson to House, December 8,
1916, *Life and Letters*, 6, 395. For chronology of Wilson's drafts
see R. S. Baker Collection, Library of Congress, Series C, December,
1916, page 85, attached memorandum.

97. Text in *New Democracy*, 2, 402–6.

ing Wilson for his interest and referring him to their own Note. On January 6, 1917, a declaration by the Kaiser indicated German abandonment of the current peace moves before the Allies had replied to Wilson. As already related, the Allies were more cooperative—especially the British, prodded on in part by the radicals—and gave a statement of terms. They made it quite plain, however, that they were not willing to begin negotiations.[98]

Wilson was not surprised by his comparatively unfavorable reception. He had expected to succeed not with the governments but with the peoples, especially the British. The British radicals were indefatigable in their encouragement. Whitehouse assured House that it would now be impossible to stifle peace talk and that the belligerents would soon be unable to carry on much longer. House asked Josiah Wedgwood, another radical member of Parliament then in America, to write an outline of terms for Wilson. Wedgwood complied on December 26, 1916, suggesting among other things that Turkey might come under American protection and the Straits be administered by an American executive under an international commission. House thought the latter proposals "fantastic" but Wilson was interested. The President was also impressed by Wedgwood's insistence that only Wilson could lay down acceptable terms.[99] This thought was soon to bear fruit.

Exhortation continued to come directly from the radicals in England. Buckler sent a copy of a memorial to Lloyd George, signed by 200,000. On December 29 Noel Buxton sent memoranda and messages urging Wilson to continue his de-

98. On January 26, 1917, after the British government, but not the American, knew of Germany's decision to launch unrestricted submarine war, Wiseman gave House the impression that Britain was ready for a conference. With a German-American clash imminent, this was an easy gesture. *Life and Letters*, 7, 441–2.

99. "House Diary," December 28, 1916, January 3, 1916; cf. Noel Buxton to House, December 25, 1916; Wilson to House, December 26, 1916, January 6, 1917; House to Wilson, August 4, 1917, House Collection.

mand for terms.[100] Buckler himself reported that since the
inception of the Lloyd George government the radicals were
profiting by the split in the Liberal party. He predicted that
the radical group would "be almost certain to gather strength
like a snowball when peace once begins to crystallize and when
the very large number of people who feel that to speak out
their moderate sentiments would help the enemy, become convinced that they can talk or vote frankly." There was no
doubt, he reported, that the Government knew the peace
sentiment was too strong to be taken lightly. On January 11,
1917, House assured Buckler that his reports and enclosures
reached the President who "is very much interested in all you
send, for he appreciates as I do the good work you are doing.
I hope you will continue to keep us informed. Your viewpoint
seems to be unprejudiced and quite similar to our own." [101]

Thus encouraged, Wilson decided that if he could not
extract a sketch of a reasonable peace from the belligerents,
he would provide one of his own, round which liberals might
rally. The radicals, of course, had consistently taken this line
of attack and had recommended it to the President. Wilson
began to prepare an address to the Senate even before he

100. Buckler to House, December 16, 30, 1916; Buxton to
Buckler, December 29, 1916, House Collection. Buckler also sent
a copy of Buxton's memorandum to the Cabinet and of his speech
in the Commons. See above, p. 81. House to Wilson, January 5,
16, 1917, Wilson Papers, File 2.

101. Buckler to House, December 27, 1916; House to Buckler,
January 11, 1917, House Collection. At this time House had received all of Buckler's letters up to that of December 30, 1916.
On January 17, 1917, House assured Buckler he had taken excerpts
from all his later reports for Wilson's information.

House was now quite enthusiastic for peace moves. When Sir
William Wiseman, chief of British intelligence in America, blamed
the rejection of Wilson's peace move on public opinion, House
replied that if it were so it was because the Government misled the
public. House added: "in my opinion the worst that could happen
would be a decisive victory for either side." "House Diary," January 18, 1917.

had received his final answers from the European governments. At the very end of December he began to write out a draft. Discussing this with House on January 2, 1917, Wilson gave the opinion that security against future war should be the "keystone of the settlement arch" and that territorial adjustments be subordinate to that purpose. House agreed that the terms should be scientific, "the fairest and best that the human mind can devise." For once Wilson went on to discuss territorial arrangements. He agreed to a free Poland and the restoration of Belgium and Serbia. The two men could not decide on the fate of Alsace-Lorraine.[102] In the final speech Wilson abandoned all reference to territory except a free Poland, which both belligerents had endorsed.

Wilson made it clear that his speech, ostensibly a statement of conditions on which America would join a league, "actually would be a proposal of peace terms." He was now very determined in his effort to end the war and in the conviction that more fighting could not secure a good peace. To House, Wilson declared, "this country does not intend to become involved in this war . . . it would be a crime against civilization for us to go in." [103] As late as January 24, 1917, he wrote: "If Germany really wants peace she can get it, and get it soon if she will but confide in me and let me have a chance. Do they want me to help? I am entitled to know because I genuinely want to help and have now put myself in a position to help without favour to either side." [104] By January 11 Wilson had completed his draft and again called House into consultation. The Colonel brought letters from Lord Bryce, Noel Buxton and Buckler. After hearing them read, Wilson significantly remarked that he did not intend to let Lansing make any changes this time. [105]

102. *Intimate Papers*, 2, 412–16.
103. Ibid.
104. Quoted in Link, *Progressive Era*, p. 263.
105. "House Diary," January 11, 1917. At House's request Wilson did strike out a statement that the war arose out of mutual distrust.

As finally delivered on January 22, 1917, President Wilson's address was first and foremost an appeal to peoples over the heads of their governments. To ensure publicity he had had the full text cabled to London, Paris, Berlin, and Petrograd several days earlier. The speech openly sought to mobilize the peace sentiment of the world. Wilson claimed to speak "for liberals and friends of humanity in every nation and of every programme of liberty," and his debt and appeal to liberalism were evident throughout.[106]

The President declared that a settlement could not be long postponed. If the United States was to help guarantee that settlement, as it should, the peace "must be worth guaranteeing and preserving, a peace that will win the approval of mankind, not merely a peace that will serve the several interests and immediate aims of the nations engaged." The nations should agree to cooperate to obtain a secure peace, one in which the balance of power gave way to a "community of power." Following his by now established tactic, Wilson observed that fortunately all the belligerent leaders had disavowed a desire to crush their opponents. The implications of this promise, however, had not been clarified. Wilson intended to clarify them now. Peace on such lines must be one without victory: "Victory would mean peace forced upon a loser, a victor's terms imposed upon the vanquished. It would be accepted in humiliation under duress, at an intolerable sacrifice, and would leave a sting, resentment, a bitter memory upon which terms of peace would rest, not permanently, but only as upon quicksand. Only a peace between equals can

---

Wilson's persistence in such impartial references to the origins of the war is further evidence that he shared the radical conviction that the fault lay in the system. In a draft he had written: "Why did the war occur? Because ultimate alignment was unknown, the processes established insecurely, the objects conjectural." *Life and Letters*, 6, 414.

106. *New Democracy*, 2, 413; full text, pp. 407–14; *Life and Letters*, 6, 425.

last. Only a peace the very principle of which is equality and
a common participation in a common benefit." This complete
endorsement of the principles long advocated by the British
radicals was the heart of Wilson's message. It was carefully
considered and deliberately phrased. He had retained the
words "peace without victory" over the explicit objections
of both Lansing and Page.[107]

Wilson went on to enunciate more detailed requirements.
No peace could endure that did not foreswear any right "to
hand peoples about from sovereignty to sovereignty as if
they were property." Minorities should be assured civil liberties; otherwise a constant ferment of unrest would undermine the peace. Freedom of the seas was also essential; it
was indeed the *"sine qua non* of peace, equality and cooperation." To strengthen this peculiarly American proposition
Wilson invoked the traditional liberal faith in the power of
free intercourse to develop international amity: thereby condemning by implication plans afoot for commercial discrimination. Linked to the freedom of the seas was the question of
naval disarmament, and to that, disarmament on land. Wilson
declared that some limitation of armament was a necessary
step in creating an atmosphere of general security.

To crown the peace Wilson proposed an international organization wielding such power that no nation could resist
it. He assured his listeners that an organization of this kind
would be no entangling alliance: "when all unite to act in the
same sense and with the same purpose all act in the common
interest."

With the one omission of a careful treatment of economic
questions Wilson's speech was exactly calculated to appeal
to the British radicals. Their enthusiastic response has already
been chronicled. On the other hand it was not surprising that
the Allied governments and Allied sympathizers in America lost
no time attacking the President, especially for his leniency

107. Lansing, *Memoirs,* p. 195; Hendrick, 3, 316–8.

toward Germany. These attacks depressed Wilson for a few days, because he knew that ultimately he would have to work with governments and with the Senate. But his immediate object had been to appeal to the peoples, and he had by no means despaired of his purpose. He revealed this by an unusual request that the Carnegie Foundation take up the task of disseminating his principles.[108]

All this was in vain. Even as Wilson spoke to the Senate, German U-boats were at sea with orders to sink on sight after January 31, 1917. On that day Germany communicated the news to Wilson together with an extreme set of peace terms. This came as a bitter defeat to the President at a time when his hopes were high and his intention toward Germany at its mildest. As a neutral, his days of seeking to bring peace to the world were almost over. Almost, but not quite; for though Wilson met the challenge firmly, he did so reluctantly and continued to hope to avoid war. He still was dubious that American belligerency could conduce to the good of the world or bring a just settlement. Even on February 1, angered though he was at Germany, Wilson "reiterated his belief that it would be a crime for this Government to involve itself in the war to such an extent as to make it impossible to save Europe afterwards." He was also much impressed with the danger of crushing Germany. In the Cabinet on February 2, he declared he did not "wish to see either side win." With such doubts the President broke off diplomatic relations with Germany on February 3, 1917. Announcing that only overt acts would make him go further, he left the door wide open for peace.[109]

108. *Life and Letters, 6*, 431; Wilson to House, January 26, 1917, House Collection. On January 23 House had written to Wilson: "The *Manchester Guardian*, so far, has the best comment and warns the British Government in no uncertain terms." "Whitehouse," he added, "is tremendously pleased." *Intimate Papers, 2*, 419.

109. *Intimate Papers, 2*, 440; Lansing, *Memoirs*, pp. 219–20; *Life and Letters, 6*, 455.

Immediately Wilson took up two projects to avoid war. The first was an effort to win over Austria-Hungary by persuading Britain to assure her against dismemberment. This scheme made no headway. Wilson's second project was an armed neutrality. His original idea of a league of neutrals collapsed when other neutrals refused to cooperate, but Wilson continued to toy with the idea of an armed neutrality of his own. He still had this in mind when the reluctance of American ships to sail forced him to arm them.[110]

In connection with this plan Wilson drew up, between February 7 and 9, 1917, his last neutral design of a settlement. These "Bases of Peace" were founded on the principles of January 22. But there were two important additions. Much more explicitly than before the President now made his guarantee of territorial integrity conditional on the "reasonableness and natural prospect of permanency" of the settlement. This was coming nearer to the radicals' belief in the intimate relation between the general principles and the particular terms of the peace. Bringing himself even more into line with radicals, he added another requirement for a stable peace: "Mutual agreement not to take part in any joint economic effort to throttle the industrial life of any nation or shut it off from fair and equal opportunities of trade."[111]

Wilson had earnestly tried to avoid war but Germany pressed him too hard. On February 28, 1917, the publication of the "Zimmermann Telegram," in which Germany offered to help Mexico regain the Southwestern United States if a German-American war broke out, served to arouse public opinion and lend weight to fears of German designs against

110. *Life and Letters*, 6, 454, 472; Carlton Savage, *Policy of the United States toward Maritime Commerce in War* (2 vols. Washington, 1934), 2, 565–8.

111. The "Bases of Peace" in various stages of drafting, plus Lansing's comments, may be found in *Life and Letters*, 6, 465–7; Lansing, *Memoirs*, pp. 199–201; *Lansing Papers*, 1, 19–24.

the Monroe Doctrine.[112] It also strengthened Wilson's conviction that Germany's leaders were untrustworthy and her methods inimical to world order. Thus it confirmed his longheld belief that prevention of a German victory was a necessary if not a sufficient condition of a good peace. More decisive was the occurrence of several "overt acts," notably the sinking on February 26, 1917, of the liner *Laconia* with loss of American life and the torpedoing in the same month of several American-flag vessels. Reluctantly Wilson called Congress and asked it to acknowledge that Germany was waging war on America.

President Wilson retained grave doubts as to the wisdom of his action, as to whether it would serve American interests or foster the kind of peace he desired. The whole history of the previous two years provided ample evidence of his deep mistrust of his prospective co-belligerents, including Britain. Russia's revolution of March 1917 did much to make the Allied cause more respectable in liberal eyes, but it did not reverse Wilson's opinion of the Allies, nor was it decisive in his resolve. He himself referred to it as merely "additional justification." The President still thought the Allied struggle could not fitly be called one for democracy against autocracy.[113] He continued highly suspicious of the company he was proposing to keep. Sir William Wiseman confidentially reported to his Government at this time that such misgivings were fairly general. Most Americans, he warned, believed Britain was fighting not for Belgium but for trade; while they accepted the need to curb Prussia, they imputed militarism and imperialism to Britain. There was, Wiseman added in another report,

112. The telegram was intercepted earlier in the year by British intelligence. Some have surmised that Britain delayed communicating the information until a moment favorable for the maximum impact on American opinion.

113. Houston, *1*, 243–4; George B. Kennan, *Russia Leaves the War* (Princeton, 1956), p. 15.

no pro-Allied feeling to speak of and certainly no pro-British feeling.[114]

But at least Wilson knew there were liberal elements in Britain. Though they were aware of the danger involved, the radicals were now largely reconciled to the idea of American belligerency. Continuing to send their encouragement, they pointed out Wilson's opportunity to exert his influence for a moderate peace. Buckler reported great Conservative reluctance to have America in the war lest it should "swing the balance" for moderation. The radicals urged Wilson to design his war policies to favor a just settlement and curb his fellow-belligerents.[115] Knowledge of these sympathetic elements was a great comfort for Wilson as he faced his problem. House wrote to Buckler: "I wish you would tell Mr. Massingham, Noel Buxton, A. G. Gardiner and other friends like them, how their support heartens us here. One cannot lose hope for the future when such men as these maintain their equilibrium under such trying conditions." [116]

These frequent and intimate exchanges between the British radicals and Wilson cast a fresh light upon his whole approach to international relations and to the problems of the war in particular. It may be wondered indeed if Wilson could have made his much pondered decision to go to war had he not been able to sustain his faith in reasonable men by recalling the existence of these increasingly active radicals whose war aims, springing from a similar heritage of liberalism, were so congenial to his own.

114. Wiseman Collection, Yale University Library.
115. Most important are Buckler to House, February 23, March 1, 10, 16, 1917; Memorandum from Noel Buxton to House, February 8, 1917, House Collection. Walter Lippmann asked Angell to send an article to the *New Republic* justifying the war on "liberal and international grounds." Angell wrote "An Appeal to American Pacifists," but the British censor stopped the article. Angell, *After All*, pp. 217–19.
116. House to Buckler, February 25, 1917, House Collection.

Although the President had made his decision, he was still painfully aware of the risks. The very night before he delivered his war message—already written—he poured out his fears to Frank Cobb, progressive editor of the New York *World*. Wilson predicted that the war would mean "illiberalism" at home and a foolish egotism in foreign policy. Germany would be crushed and there would be a dictated, a victorious peace, an effort to rebuild the world with wartime standards. This was what the Allies wanted; it was just what America had tried to avoid. There was, however, no apparent alternative. "It is," mourned the President, "just a choice of evils." [117]

The war message Wilson delivered later that day breathes confidence in action regrettable but salutary and right. But against the background of the President's soul-searching the speech is not only a rallying cry for a nation at war; it forms a defense against his own doubts and an explanation to fellow liberals. Wilson urged the people to remain moderate and temperate. Germany, he pointed out, was attacking the rights of the United States; rights which were essential to the welfare of all nations. Every nation was therefore under attack; each must decide its own course. America would have defended its rights by methods short of war, but technical reasons made that impossible. Consequently the nation must go to war; "we are clearly forced into it because there are no other means of defending our rights." The German government had proved itself hostile to the United States, prepared to attack at any opportunity. But America had no quarrel with the German people and genuinely looked forward to the re-establishment of "intimate relations of mutual advantage." [118]

Wilson had now proclaimed a righteous cause. The nation gave him strong support, feeling, like most of the British Liberal party in 1914, a need to believe the war was for noble

117. John Heaton, *Cobb of "The World"* (New York, 1924), pp. 269–70.
118. *War and Peace, 1,* 6–16.

ends. Was not Wilson's reputation a guarantee of this? Across the country the press echoed his words in a remarkable display of bipartisanship. But privately the President had made it clear that although he believed in the justice of the war, he had far from resolved his doubts as to its outcome, that he did not trust the Allies to establish a just world order or deal fairly with Germany, and that he hardly dared hope that he could restrain war fever in his own country, let alone in the Allies.

For all his pessimism Wilson had chosen to keep his fears from the Congress and the people. Perhaps he believed he had spoken often enough of the hazards of war. He knew of course that he had to muster a resolute nation and years earlier he had decided that the public were "much readier to receive a a halftruth which they can understand than a whole truth which has too many sides to be seen all at once." [119] But he certainly went very far, using sweeping language which might well be interpreted as a promise of an ideal outcome rather than an exhortation to strive for its realization. In keeping his doubts from the nation Wilson clearly ran grave risks. He might conjure up the devil he feared by encouraging a self-righteous and intolerant spirit. He might even fall victim to his own rhetoric.

The President's self-questioning to the last moment apparently indicates that he had not yet made this mistake. His noble predictions must have been intended as aspirations, not promises. It remained to be seen how successful he would be in finding as a belligerent what had eluded him as a neutral.

119. Wilson, *Leaders of Men* (Princeton, 1952, written 1890–95), p. 20.

5. British Liberalism and

the Fourteen Points

AFTER America entered the war, the British radicals continued their campaign for a joint Allied declaration of revised and moderate war aims, arguing that this was the only way to keep Russia in the war and encourage German liberalism, which was showing signs of restiveness. The war-aims campaign had now secured a wider basis of support. The *New Europe, Daily News, New Statesman,* and even the Liberal-Imperialist *Round Table* and a disillusioned H. G. Wells joined the call for a reformulation of terms.[1]

New possibilities opened up in organized labor. The need to exact even greater efforts from the workers increased their restiveness and, at the same time, sharpened the Government's anxiety to avoid industrial unrest. A series of strikes during the spring of 1917 greatly alarmed the Cabinet and prompted a number of official investigations aimed at discovering and removing the sources of disturbance.[2] Labor was also deeply stirred by the Russian revolution, which was a revelation of

1. Buckler to House, June 29, 1917; Trevelyan to Buckler, June 28, 1917 (partly printed in Nevins, pp. 345–6), House Collection. Cf. *Daily News,* August 10; *New Europe,* May 10, July 19, *New Statesman,* July 14, 1917; *Round Table* (June 1917), pp. 491 ff.; (September 1917), pp. 641 ff.; Bennett, *Journal, 2,* 239; *Then Why Go On?* (U.D.C., 38b), 1917; Wells, "A Reasonable Man's Peace," *Daily News,* August 14, 1917 (this and other articles were collected in Wells, *In the Fourth Year,* London, 1918).

2. Lloyd George, *Peace Conference, 1,* 3–4.

the power which the left might wield. Allied governments found themselves forced to call upon their own labor leaders for assistance in dealing with the new Russian authorities. These, in their turn, initiated a strenuous war-aims campaign of their own.

The internal politics of the British labor movement also came to bear in favor of liberal war aims. Labor had always given radical war aims their kindest reception. Now the renewed wave of interest forced moderate leaders to take up the cause to prevent its falling into the hands of the extreme left, which might thereby usurp the leadership. Thus Arthur Henderson, a member of the Cabinet, became so associated with the project of an international socialist conference at Stockholm that his activities forced him to break with the Government.[3] His resignation in August restored powerful independent leadership to labor and proved a landmark in its progress toward full stature as a party. For this emancipated force the radicals' familiar ideas provided a ready-made program. In August a special conference of the party produced a "Memorandum on the Issues of the War" affirming, in the radical tradition, that the war had arisen from "general causes" and calling for an end to secret diplomacy, for democratic control, trusteeship of colonial areas, and renunciation of economic war after the war.[4]

Russian events, which played their part in widening labor support for the war-aims campaign, presented the Allied governments with several other embarrassing problems. The perilous condition of their country's political, economic, and social

3. The conference was initially proposed in April by the Bureau of the International and subsequently endorsed by the Petrograd Soviet and the Second Provisional Government.

4. Labour Party, *Memorandum on the Issues of the War*, London, 1917. William P. Maddox, *Foreign Relations in British Labor Politics* (Cambridge, Mass., 1934), p. 110; Arno Mayer, "The Politics of Allied War Aims," dissertation, Yale, 1953, pp. 232, 286–7, 294–8. The memorandum was also presented to an Inter-Allied Socialist Conference later in August.

structure, and the fear of being ousted by extreme factions on the left which were eager to make the war-aims issue their own, impelled moderate Russian leaders to strive for a revision of Allied objectives. For the Russian provisional governments such revision was a step toward making the early peace which seemed to offer the only hope of stabilizing the domestic situation. Hence a series of declarations emanated from Russia, most of them revealing a heavy debt to the radical and Wilsonian programs. On May 15, 1917, for example, the Petrograd Soviet called upon the belligerents to make forthwith a peace "without annexations or indemnities on the basis of the self-determination of peoples." The Second Provisional Government accepted this formula three days later. In June the Government formally requested its Allies to convene an official conference on war aims.

The pressure on the British government to make some response to these approaches became considerable as the year wore on. In addition to their part in aggravating labor unrest, which could not be ignored, the Russian declarations commanded official attention by creating the widespread illusion, shared by liberals as well as ministers, that a satisfactory revision of war aims might encourage Russia to continue the war. It now seems certain that Russia was incapable of further organized resistance. But whatever the real possibilities, the Russian situation, the belligerency of America under a president virtually personifying a liberal program, and the weariness of another winter of war ensured that henceforth the war-aims campaign in Britain developed in an atmosphere of increased interest and support.

Lloyd George's cabinet would probably have welcomed a genuine opportunity to make peace during the spring and summer of 1917, perhaps even at the price of considerable concessions to German ambitions in Eastern Europe, but it strongly suspected that enemy overtures were intended merely as a trap. The continued activity of those who, like Sir Edward

Carson, still put their faith in a knock-out blow and a dictated peace, placed a further curb on any inclination the Government might have to conciliate the radicals.[5] Under pressure from two sides the Government steered an erratic middle course fully satisfactory to no one. Spokesmen denied that Britain had any acquisitive ambitions, and in a major address at Glasgow on June 29, 1917, Lloyd George pleased radicals by professing himself open to any reasonable peace offer. But the Government still firmly refused to renounce the secret treaties, offering only to revise any from which Russia would release them, thus tacitly excluding the important British commitments which did not involve pledges to Russia.[6] Moreover, the Government steadfastly insisted on acting in step with its Continental allies, and these showed no sign of modifying their intentions. The radicals therefore made no progress toward securing a joint statement of Allied terms.

Most of the radicals had counted on Wilson's using his prestige to obtain Allied endorsement of his program. They were willing to work under the President's leadership to secure the "Americanization" of war aims.[7] To their surprise, Wilson did not immediately continue the outspoken exhortations which had become their accustomed spiritual food. The President had several reasons for reluctance to press the Allies to declare terms. He feared that such a move would open fresh rents in the already tattered network of Allied cooperation, at a time when the Allies were reeling before the U-boats and Germany's Eastern successes.[8] On this account Wilson re-

5. Buckler to House, April 13, 20, June 14, July 5, 1917, House Collection; *War Memoirs*, 3, 1708; 4, 1882–93, 1946; Dugdale, 2, 179; Carson to *Nation*, September 7, 1917.

6. Scott, *War Aims*, pp. 107–12, 117–19; Buckler to House, July 5, 1917, House Collection; *H. C. Deb.*, 93, 1667–75.

7. The word is that of Wells, *Fourth Year*, p. 50. For expressions of faith in Wilson see, *inter alia*, Buckler to House, April 27, May 24, 1917, House Collection.

8. *Intimate Papers*, 3, 37, 138–9, 144–6; *Life and Letters*, 7, 155, 203.

frained not only from speeches but from any official discussion
of aims with the French and British missions which visited
Washington in the spring of 1917. His eagerness to reverse the
Central Powers' military successes, not just for strategic reasons
but to discredit the German military regime, further inhibited
his consideration of war aims, and the tasks of mobilization
left him correspondingly less time for diplomacy. Moreover,
though Wilson agreed with radicals upon the importance of
encouraging moderate elements in Germany, he believed that,
for the moment, it would be most effective to press Germany
for a declaration of *her* aims and to hold up the German government's refusal as proof to the German people that their
rulers were not to be trusted.[9]

The President maintained the same firmness in dealing with
Russia. He sympathized with the new democracy and responded to its appeal for a revision of war aims with an elo-
quent restatement of his own liberal aspirations. But he flatly
condemned the Stockholm project and refused to countenance
those aspects of Russian policy which he regarded as inspired
by short-sighted eagerness for peace. He criticized the "no
annexations" formula, stressing the need for positive and particular arrangements in any stable settlement.[10] So concerned
did Wilson become lest liberals should unwittingly assist German militarism by rashly joining the cry for peace that on Flag
Day, 1917, he made a major address, chiefly devoted to warning liberals and labor and roundly indicting Germany with
responsibility for the war and its continuance.[11]

This was a very different tone from that of the "peace without victory" speech to which the radicals had become attuned.

9. *Intimate Papers, 3,* 132–8; "House Diary," March 20, May
19, 29, 1917, partly ibid., pp. 57–8, 129; *Lansing Papers, 2,* 328;
War and Peace, 1, 47–8.

10. Message to Russia, May 26, 1917, *War and Peace, 1,* 49–51;
"House Diary," October 13, 24, 26, 1917.

11. *War and Peace, 1,* 60–67; *Life and Letters, 7,* 96–7; *Intimate Papers, 3,* 137–8.

and it caused them no little anxiety. The President's blowing hot and cold puzzled and confused them. Many feared that Wilson had caught war fever and abandoned his former emphasis on the political dimension of the war. They thought that his attacks on the German government might undo their long struggle against the oversimplification which placed all the blame for the war on one country.[12] Some suspected that Wilson himself now subscribed to that illusion. The President's change of front irritated the radicals all the more because it enabled their opponents to claim Wilson's attitude as an endorsement of Allied aims.

Some of the radicals were quick to air their grievances; Hobson, for instance, wrote a letter to the *Nation* entitled "An American Victory in 1920?" Most radicals were more restrained in public but privately expressions of uneasiness were frequent. Brailsford and Noel Buxton told Buckler of their own concern. A member of the previous Cabinet plumbed the depths of disquiet when he exclaimed, "President Wilson has broken in our hands." [13]

News of this despondency flowed freely to Colonel House and on to the White House. Buckler sent even more copious reports, forwarded communications from radicals, and plied House with records of Parliamentary debates and with liberal publications, including the *Cambridge Magazine, New Statesman, Labour Leader, Nation,* and *Common Sense,* the latter two now banned from foreign circulation by the British government. In addition, Wilson received such books as Dickinson's *The Choice before Us* and Morel's *Africa and the Peace of Europe.*[14]

12. Cf. Brailsford to *Nation,* September 15, 1917, referring to the "current popular view, Mr. Wilson's view, that one evil will, the will of the rulers of Germany, deliberately made the World War . . ."

13. *Nation,* June 23, 1917; Buckler to House, April 27, June 25, 29, 1917, House Collection.

14. See the Buckler-House correspondence in general at this

Some of the radical messages deserve special mention. On June 21, 1917, Buckler reported that Massingham, Whitehouse, Noel Buxton, all agreed upon the urgent need for a full restatement of Allied aims and that they all hoped House would come over to judge for himself. A week later Massingham sent his views in greater detail, declaring that the Allied failure to renounce annexationist claims strengthened German reaction. He hoped that Wilson would force a change in this policy and thereby encourage the German—and Russian—moderates.[15] The same day Buckler forwarded extracts from a letter in which Trevelyan urged Wilson to press the Allies to accept the President's program. Trevelyan affirmed his continued confidence in Wilson and admitted that Germany was probably not yet ready to accept a moderate peace, but he prophesied "one of the most tragic reverses in history" if Wilson "finds himself isolated with the Western European powers who have not adopted his policy, and sees Russia, which has adopted it, forced into anarchy or a separate peace . . ." Wilson, he warned, could not reassure Russia and the British government at the same time. Whitehouse echoed the warning: he admitted the need to expose German failings but America would never win the trust of the German people unless it also made obvious efforts to convert the Allies to moderation.[16]

The most comprehensive account of radical anxieties came later in the summer when, on August 17, 1917, Ramsay MacDonald gave Buckler a memorandum of several pages. MacDonald confessed that "amongst political sections miscalled 'pacifist' President Wilson's recent pronouncements have been regarded with disappointment . . ." The whole difference be-

time and esp. Buckler to House, July 16, 1917; House to Buckler, July 20, August 11, 1917, House Collection; House to Wilson, May 24, 30, 1917, Wilson Papers, File 2.

15. Buckler to House, June 21, 29, 1917, House Collection.

16. Trevelyan to Buckler, June 28, 1917; Buxton to House, June 28, 1917, ibid.

tween the "war" and "peace" divisions of labor was disagreement on how to achieve commonly held ideal ends. By apparently abandoning political methods, Wilson had gravely injured the moderates. MacDonald hoped the President would declare that "the utility of war was severely limited by the political objects which it could gain, and that whilst you can have peace without victory, history shows that as a rule nations have had victory without peace." He also hoped that Wilson would use his influence to encourage liberty of discussion in Allied countries.[17]

House read this material with interest, passing much of it to the President.[18] In June, when assuring Buckler that his reports reached Wilson, House added that they were "of more real value than any coming to me." This interest reflected the great importance House attached to the good opinion of British liberals. The Colonel was deeply concerned to hear of their fears and hastened to allay them on Wilson's behalf: "Do not let our liberal friends be fearful of the President's attitude," he wrote, "you can assure them that when the time comes for action, they will find him on the right side." [19]

Whether his tactics were wise or not, Wilson was in fact still largely in agreement with the radicals, despite appearances. When a British mission under Balfour visited America in May, the President revealed a continued awareness of the

17. MacDonald to Buckler, August 17, 1917. Printed in Nevins, *White*, pp. 342–5. About the same time Angell submitted a lengthy proposal for a "Parliament of the Allies" to promulgate liberal aims. House received this via Lippmann and sent it on to Wilson. House to Wilson, August 9, 1917, Wilson Papers, File 2.

18. On May 29, 1917, the whole Executive Committee of the U.D.C. addressed a letter directly to Wilson, urging him to demand an Allied declaration of terms. House delayed forwarding an advanced copy of this letter because he did not feel the time was ripe. Buckler to House, May 25, June 8, 1917, House Collection. Also *Life and Letters*, 7, 91; *Intimate Papers*, 3, 139.

19. House to Buckler, June 10, July 1, 1917; House to Wilson, August 4, 1917, House Collection.

significance of war aims and of the differences between him and the Allies on this issue. Both House and Wilson had long discussions of war aims with Balfour, taking great care to keep the talks unofficial.[20] During the conversations Balfour revealed the commitments of most of the secret treaties.[21] House expostulated against plans to partition Asia Minor as calculated to create a "breeding place for future war." He urged Balfour not to regard Germany as a permanent enemy and called on him to join America in working for a just peace against the greed that would appear at the peace conference. Both House and Wilson expected more trouble with the Continental Powers than with Britain, which they regarded as the Ally most inspired with a kindred liberal tradition. At a later meeting House urged upon Sir Eric Drummond, Balfour's influential private secretary, the importance of encouraging German liberalism by proclaiming moderate aims. The two men drew up a draft statement of determination to fight on for Wilson's aims but not to dismember Germany. But this movement toward a joint program came to nothing.[22]

Wilson's refusal to adhere to the Allied commitment to make peace jointly and his insistence upon the title of "Associ-

20. *Intimate Papers*, 3, 37–8, 41.

21. On May 18, 1917, Balfour sent Wilson copies of the treaties. He did not send copies of the agreement with Japan concerning Shantung and Pacific islands, nor an Anglo-French agreement disposing of Togoland and the Cameroons, i.e., an agreement impinging closely on American interests and one very directly advantageous to Britain. The recent Franco-Russian understanding on their respective frontiers with the Central Powers and the incomplete arrangements of St. Jean de Maurienne were also omitted. There is nothing to indicate clearly that these omissions were deliberate. House's discussions with Balfour did not deal with colonial questions or the Far East. *Life and Letters*, 7, 40, 74–5; Seymour, *American Diplomacy*, pp. 267–8. See also the interesting exchange between Grey, Drummond, and Balfour in 1919 in E. L. Woodward and Rohan Butler, eds., *Documents on British Foreign Policy*, First Series (London, 1954), 5 (1919), 1015–17.

22. "House Diary," April 28, 30, May 13, 1917; *Intimate Papers*, 3, 42–6, 54–9; *Life and Letters*, 7, 180–1; Seymour, p. 267.

ated Power" was a public and therefore more striking indication of his differences with the Allies. He was meticulous in maintaining this distinction, forbidding American military commanders to attend an Allied War Conference in July lest it should give the impression of discussing "ultimate purposes to do with peace terms." For the same reason he had been reluctant to receive the Balfour mission itself.[23] Although he preferred Britain to her Continental allies, Wilson still believed the aims of the British government were widely disparate from his own. In July he wrote to House, *"England and France have not the same views with regard to Peace that we have by any means."* This was not the time to argue: later on, America could use its economic power to force the Allies into line.[24] So marked was Wilson's detachment from the Allied outlook that he approved a memorandum in which Wiseman warned the British government that Americans felt themselves "arbitrators rather than collaborators" and urged his superiors to make some liberal declaration to satisfy American opinion.[25]

Thus Wilson had not strayed as far from the radicals as they feared. The secret treaties and discussions with Balfour suggested that the Allied concept of a desirable peace conflicted in many important ways with his own.[26] This strengthened a conclusion he had formed much earlier. But the particular provisions of the treaties seemed less important to Wilson

23. *Life and Letters,* 7, 2, 177; *Intimate Papers,* 3, 34, 364, n. 1.

24. Wilson's italics. July 21, 1917, *Life and Letters,* 7, 180–1; *Intimate Papers,* 3, 18, 113. House, too, retained his doubts, fearing that "if Germany is defeated too completely, there will be difficulties to be met because of the rapacious demands of the Allies." "House Diary," June 30, 1917.

25. *Intimate Papers,* 3, 30–1.

26. Wilson's statement in 1919 that he had been largely in ignorance of the secret treaties until the peace conference has caused much confusion. Whatever the reasons for this remark there can be no doubt that in 1917 he knew of the treaties—their general tenor and some important particulars. For a good brief discussion of this see Seymour, pp. 266 ff.

than the basic principles of settlement. Perhaps closer study of the detailed arrangements of the treaties would have improved his understanding of the diplomatic situation and of the fears and ambitions which a new order would have to satisfy. Be that as it may, when he judged the time ripe for bringing the Allied peace program into line with his own, he devoted his energies not to securing specific modifications of the secret treaties but to rendering their objectionable provisions obsolete by developing a temper and program in which their realization would be both impossible and unnecessary.

To bring his differences with the Allies to the fore in the first few months of American belligerency, however, would have aroused serious dissension among the Associated Powers and gravely handicapped the propaganda campaign which Wilson hoped to wage against Germany. His decision not to make an immediate public issue of war aims was thus based on considerations somewhat similar to those which impelled the Allies to keep their treaties secret. He was, at it were, still pursuing the strategy of his war message: keeping his doubts to himself in an effort to concentrate on the war effort. His inability to share the easy optimism of some radicals that Germany might soon agree to a reasonable peace left no alternative but to work for decisive victory. True, this would make it impossible to rely for moderation at the peace conference upon a balance of power arising from the continued strength of each side. But it might well be argued that however much Wilson might desire peace without victory, Germany had shown she would not take a moderate peace without defeat. In this case any moderation would have to come from restraining influences on the Allied side, a part Wilson was prepared to play.

Meanwhile Wilson's policy cost the heavy price of disconcerting and alarming his liberal supporters, especially in Britain. Already, in July, he had to admit:

> The democratic feeling of the world is demanding more and more audibly an insistent statement from the nations associated against Germany which will show that the object of the war is not aggrandisement but the freedom of the peoples to secure independence . . . and free themselves from aggression whether by physical force or successful economic arrangement. . . . The sentiment of the world is now aggressively democratic, and will have to be met half-way.[27]

As the year lengthened, events conspired to convince the President that he must once more devote himself to the war-aims question.

On July 19, 1917, the German Centrist leader, Erzberger, succeeded in mustering enough support to carry a resolution in the Reichstag calling for a peace without "forced acquisitions of territories, forced requisitions and political, economic, or financial oppressions . . ." Though this made little impression on German policy, it temporarily raised liberal hopes that moderate elements in Germany might be gathering strength. Two weeks later, on August 1, 1917, the Pope addressed a peace appeal to all the belligerents. In the interests of Allied unity Wilson was at first inclined to return only a formal acknowledgment; but House, who was so closely in touch with radical opinion, urged him to make a reasoned reply. House believed that the President could seize the initiative from the Papacy and exercise it himself by making a statement of American aims. "The Allies," he reasoned, "must succumb to your judgment" and Germany would be put in an embarrassing position. Echoing his British correspondents, House told Wilson that the Allies had always frightened the German moderates with threats of dismemberment and economic discrimination. The President should take "a firm tone,

27. Unused draft, *Life and Letters*, 7, 204.

full of determination, but yet breathing a spirit of liberalism and justice that will make the people of the Central Powers feel safe in your hands." [28]

In the event Wilson did make a public reply to the Pope, combining firmness and conciliation. He excoriated the German government but held out the promise of a just peace, vigorously repudiating some of the pet schemes of Allied extremists: "Punitive damages [he wrote], the dismemberment of empires, the establishment of selfish and exclusive economic leagues, we deem inexpedient and in the end worse than futile, no proper basis for a peace of any kind, least of all for an enduring peace. That must be based upon justice and fairness and the common rights of mankind." [29]

The radicals recognized this as the Wilson they admired. The reply contrasted sharply with the Allied failure to render any answer at all and with the evasive answer given by Germany several weeks later. The *Times* and the Liberal-Imperialists of the *Round Table* tried to pass off the reference to economic discrimination as aimed at Mittel-Europa rather than "defensive measures planned at the Paris Economic Conference." But most of the radicals correctly accepted Wilson's remarks as a sharp rebuke to Allied chauvinists. Indeed, the President would have liked to be even more critical, especially of French and Italian territorial claims.[30]

What Wilson said in his reply to the Pope was less im-

28. House to Wilson, August 15, 17, 19, 1917, *Intimate Papers, 3*, 154–9; "House Diary," August 15, 18–23, 25, 1917; Seymour, pp. 273–8.

29. *War and Peace, 1*, 93–6; for the quotation, see pp. 95–6. In his first draft Wilson had written "childish" instead of "inexpedient." House persuaded Wilson this was too offensive to the Allies. Seymour, p. 277.

30. *Life and Letters, 7*, 231; Seymour, pp. 277–8; *Round Table* (December 1917), p. 77 (article written in October); Hammond, *Scott*, p. 234; *Nation*, September 1, 8, 29, 1917. For "correctly" see *Intimate Papers, 3*, 164, 168.

portant than the fact of his saying it. The incident signified his continued dissatisfaction with Allied intentions [31] and re-awakened his own interest in the formulation of terms. Wilson himself was still preoccupied with war preparations, but he immediately instructed House to get together an organization to collect materials for planning a peace settlement.[32] Several of the British radicals had recently drawn House's attention to the need for such preparations. As soon as America joined the war, Buckler had requested and received permission to study Balkan affairs, and had suggested that America should seriously prepare to make a "scientific peace." [33] House's study-group, which became known as the Inquiry, was therefore in harmony with the radicals' insistence that the peace must be planned for and based on the careful solution of questions in dispute. For the first Secretary, House selected Walter Lippmann.[34]

Wilson's chief reason for setting on foot the Inquiry was

31. The divergence between Wilson and House and official British opinion may be illustrated by their relative estimation of the reports of Page and Buckler as shown by a curious incident about this time. Page became annoyed at Buckler's sending reports to House and on August 28, 1917, ordered Buckler to desist and *not to tell House why*. House immediately inquired why he did not receive the information he valued and arranged to continue receiving Buckler's reports unknown to Page, through the medium of Henry White, Buckler's half-brother. See House to Buckler, September 28, Buckler to House, October 19, November 11, 1917, House Collection. At this time Wilson was again contemplating Page's recall. "House Diary," September 9, 1917. Cf. Buckler to White, August 28, 1917, Henry White Papers, Library of Congress.

32. September 2, 1917, *Life and Letters*, 7, 254.

33. Buckler to Page, April 30; Buckler to House, June 7; House to Buckler, June 10, August 21, 1917, House Collection. On October 1, 1917, Angell sent House detailed suggestions for the Inquiry's work, House Collection.

34. James T. Shotwell, *At the Paris Peace Conference* (New York, 1937), chap. 1; *Intimate Papers*, 3, 168–72; typewritten Progress Report of Inquiry, January 15, 1918, Wiseman Collection.

his expectation that the Allies would refuse his program and that he would have to force them to accept it. The letter in which he suggested the plan to House began with a comment on Allied disagreement with his answer to the Pope. Continuing, he described his scheme as intended to "ascertain . . . just what the several parties to this war on our side of it will be inclined to insist upon as part of the final peace arrangements, in order that we may formulate our own position either for or against them and begin to gather the influences we wish to employ." [35] In this way the President hoped to lay his plans without disrupting the war effort by bringing his differences with the Allies into the open. It was unfortunate for this purpose that the Inquiry immediately attracted public attention.[36] But in any case the demands for an open reformulation of aims soon became irresistible and forced Wilson to declare his purposes frankly.

Several circumstances now combined to lend weight to the radical cause. Throughout the fall anticipation of the Inter-Allied Political Conference, requested by the Russians but persistently postponed, kept interest in war aims alive. A very important series of events adding to the pressure began when the Bolsheviks, who seized power in November, launched a peace offensive. On November 8 they issued a decree on peace, followed two weeks later by a request for a ceasefire and a direct invitation to the Allied governments to join them in making peace on all fronts. This suggestion that peace could be had for the asking was all the more tempting in the light of Allied military failures. To cap the collapse of Russia and Rumania and defeats in France, the Italians suffered at Caporetto in October 1917 one of the most resounding de-

35. *Life and Letters*, 7, 254.
36. House to Wilson, September 29, October 3, 1917, House Collection. House had also warned Wilson of the danger that "in his desire to hit the [British] Government and the reactionary forces he might, if he were not careful, hurt the *amour propre* of the British people as a whole." "House Diary," August 20, 1917.

feats of the war, requiring diversion of large reinforcements from the Western Front. Lloyd George's efforts to secure unified military command to meet this crisis forced him to expose strategic failures in a way that caused further dismay. Underlying all these sources of disgruntlement was the onset of a fourth winter of war. This was by now the classic season for the war-aims campaign to reach a crest. The need for the radicals to turn to those who were merely disgruntled for support was one of the tragedies of the war-aims movement. For periods of Allied defeat were hardly likely to find Germany in a moderate mood.

The growing momentum of the demand for a restatement of aims manifested itself in the complaints of the radical press and in a marked addition of Parliamentary strength.[37] Asquith was too deeply committed to the secret treaties to take a lead, but such chiefs of the Liberal party as Walter Runciman and Lord Buckmaster adopted a palpably more moderate attitude toward the peace question, perceiving a possible stick with which to belabor the renegade Lloyd George.[38] They began to consult with the radicals and occasionally concerted debating strategy. Such cooperation took place in a major debate on November 6, 1917. The radicals moved that a peace ensuring restoration of Belgium, evacuation of occupied areas, an "equitable" solution of Alsace-Lorraine, and an international organization would be acceptable to Britain. They argued that the Government must decide between a stable peace or

37. Cf. *Manchester Guardian,* October 23, November 6, *Daily News,* October 26, November 24, *Nation,* September 29, October 13, 27, November 17, 1917; *Secret Diplomacy, No. 1* (U.D.C., 40b, 1918?), *Secret Diplomacy, No. 2* (U.D.C., 41b, 1918?), *Secret Diplomacy, No. 3* (U.D.C. 43b, 1918?). By this time the *Manchester Guardian* and the *Daily News* constituted part of the "radical press" inasmuch as they generally supported the radical position on war aims and negotiation. Cf. a secret report of the Ministry of Labour, dated August 9, 1917, referring to the growing influence of advocates of negotiated peace. Henderson Papers.

38. *Nation,* December 1, 1917; Masterman, p. 297.

imperialism and the Paris economic proposals. Though some of the Liberal party took a self-righteous position, one demanding "not only Belgium restored but the Ten Commandments," Runciman gave considerable support to the radicals. In reply Balfour skillfully combined home truths, pointing out that Germany showed no sign of being ready for the radicals' peace, and evasion, omitting any reference at all to the questions raised on British aims. The division went heavily against the motion—but Runciman went into the radical lobby.[39]

Much of this added support came from weariness rather than genuine conversion to the radical analysis of international relations. Similar influences produced even stranger bedfellows. There was a mounting fear among some Conservatives and Liberal-Imperialists that continued warfare would cause a collapse of social order or at least wreak a grievous injury on British power. Lord Milner, a member of the War Cabinet and perhaps the most eminent of Liberal-Imperialists, was widely reported to hold such views. In a conversation which Buckler relayed almost verbatim to House and which passed on to Wilson, Milner put his faith in the war-aims campaign and declared for House's benefit: "Our diplomacy has been in my opinion and still is deplorably weak in its attitude towards our enemies. . . . I hope that America will not imitate our timidity. How *are* we ever to know what our enemies will offer unless we keep our ears open. We ought to listen to every 'peace whisper.'" [40]

The supreme example of this kind of thought appeared on November 29, 1917, when the *Daily Telegraph* published a letter from Lord Lansdowne, the man who as Foreign Secretary had created the Entente. In his letter Lansdowne

39. *H. C. Deb., 98,* 2007–51.

40. *Life and Letters, 7,* 346; Buckler to House, November 3, House to Wilson, November 9, 1917, House Collection. Milner was of course using "weak" and "timidity" to refer to unwillingness to risk any exploration of the possibility of peace—as the last sentence quoted shows.

dragged into the light all the prudential arguments of the war-weary. He suggested—as in his earlier memorandum to the Cabinet—that it might be well to exchange the speculative advantages of victory for the reality of peace. Britain should be satisfied with certain minimum aims to be set by the standard of security. Borrowing radical arguments, he suggested that such a peace might be obtained by bargaining Allied economic power against German conquests and by renouncing schemes to dismember Austria-Hungary. As further evidence of his debt to the radicals, Lansdowne capped his proposals with an appeal for a joint Allied declaration of aims.[41]

What was new in Lansdowne's letter was the identity of the author. Nervous members of the right-wing had usually confined their agitation to the dinner table. Lansdowne's letter therefore gravely alarmed Government circles. A Reuter's message, generally believed to be officially inspired, hastened to declare that the Government agreed with Clemenceau's recent assertion that the war aims of the Allies were victory. It was a different story with the radicals and many other Liberals. C. P. Scott wrote two editorials supporting Lansdowne's appeal for moderate aims, and the *Daily News* and *Westminster Gazette* joined in. A Committee formed to pursue Lansdowne's proposals was active for several months and cooperated closely with the U.D.C. The secretary was F. W. Hirst, who lent the columns of his periodical *Common Sense* to the cause. The *Nation* stressed the support which Lansdowne's move would give to Wilson's aims. Britain must choose, it contended, between "Mr. Wilson's and Lord Lansdowne's 'covenanted peace'" or "Mr. George's peace of unconditional surrender." [42]

While pressure was mounting in Europe, Wilson had been

41. Newton, *Lansdowne*, pp. 464–8; Dugdale, 2, 182–3.

42. Newton, *Lansdowne*, pp. 473 ff.; Hammond, *Scott*, p. 218; *Nation*, December 1, 8, 1917; F. W. Hirst, *Consequences of the War to Great Britain* (London, 1934), pp. 17–19. Hirst had left the *Economist* in July, 1916.

hardening his resolve to take a new lead on war aims. Still impatient of pacifists who spoke as if Germany would make a Christian peace for the asking,[43] the President also retained his suspicions of the Allies' intentions and his belief that their failure to renounce publicly schemes against the ultimate welfare of the Central Powers was sustaining the German military party. As one remedy for this, Wilson planned to resume his public pronouncements. In October he accepted House's suggestion that his message to Congress in December should proclaim that economic freedom was as essential as territorial integrity.[44] As another remedy, Wilson decided to press for the joint Allied declaration of terms which the radicals had so consistently demanded. Thus when House came as Wilson's representative to an Inter-Allied Conference which met in Paris on November 29, 1917, he intended to persuade the Allies to agree upon a formal statement of terms in accordance with Wilson's principles, despite the fact that the conference was primarily designed not to discuss broad political objectives but urgent strategic and logistical problems.

On this visit House consulted the radicals from the first. Within less than two weeks he talked to Buckler, A. G. Gardiner, Massingham, C. P. Scott, Brailsford, F. W. Hirst, Lord Loreburn, Noel Buxton, and Josiah Wedgwood. House noted that Gardiner's views echoed his own parting remarks to Wilson. Massingham gave House "an insight into the situation here which I consider valuable." On November 14 House talked with Lansdowne, who was of course engaged in composing his letter. Lansdowne, whom House found in "a

43. *Life and Letters*, 7, 247–9, 383; speech at Buffalo, November 12, 1917, *War and Peace*, 1, 116–24.

44. All three of the chief British representatives in America felt Wilson's unrest sufficiently to send home warnings; Wiseman, August, 1917 (partly *Intimate Papers*, 3, 94); Northcliffe, August 30, Wiseman Collection; Reading to Balfour, October, 1917, *Intimate Papers*, 3, 180. Cf. *Life and Letters*, 7, 203, 286–7; "House Diary," October 24, 1917.

peculiarly pacific turn of mind," discussed the need for a declaration of aims and reassurances to Germany on economic scores. "Conservative that he is," House remarked, "we scarcely disagreed at all." Similar harmony prevailed when House and Loreburn talked: "Our minds run nearly parallel." [45] From all these men House heard one common argument: what was needed was a single statement of terms by all the Powers associated against Germany. Even those who were bringing direct pressure on their own Government looked to Wilson to promote such an announcement. On November 12 Noel Buxton wrote to House:

> I think it is true to say that the hopes of moving the British Government in the direction of reason, and of the American policy of encouraging the moderate factions in Germany depend on two main factors. The first is the influence which the President is disposed to exercise. This is far the most important. The second is Mr. Asquith's attitude on which again American views may be influential.[46]

These contacts left House more than ever convinced that some moderate declaration was necessary, but several conversations with Lloyd George suggested that it would be far from easy to obtain. The Prime Minister told the Colonel, on November 20, that Britain wanted Germany's African colonies, both East and West, and suzerainty over Arabia. An old handicap of American policy dogged these discussions, for though House argued for a declaration of aims he was unwilling to discuss particular territorial issues, partly because of reluctance to get involved in inter-Allied squabbles, partly because of belief that plans should not be crystallized far in advance and, probably, partly because of inadequate

45. "House Diary," November 9, 10, 12–15, 19, 21, 1917; November 14, 1917, *Intimate Papers, 3,* 232–3.
46. Buxton to House, November 12, 1917, House Collection. Cf. Buckler to White, November 30, 1917, White Papers.

knowledge of the matters in dispute.[47] To the British, who had a strong interest in many of the specific matters which would arise at the end of the war, this plan for an "announcement of general war aims" must have appeared impractical or highly disingenuous.

House concluded from his talks with British leaders that Britain's colonial ambitions and France's desire for Alsace-Lorraine made it impossible for them to satisfy the Russian ideal of "no annexations." The British leaders recognized the desirability of exacerbating Russo-German relations, but they were not prepared to accept House's methods. Consequently he decided it would be useless to try to obtain a declaration of war aims from the Inter-Allied Conference. Instead he would wait until his return to America and have Wilson bring pressure on the Allies—and particularly Lloyd George—from there. At Paris, House confined himself to proposing a declaration that America and the Allies were fighting to crush militarism and increase the freedom of nations. Wilson cabled to endorse this, adding: "You will realize how desirable it is for the Conference to discuss terms of peace in a spirit conforming with my January address to the Senate." Territorial questions, he went on, with special reference to plans to carve up Asia Minor, must be left to the decision of all belligerents at the Peace Conference. Even House's mild resolution was more than the conference would accept. Lloyd George agreed to vote for the resolution, but he would not actively support it. The Allied delegates agreed upon an Italian draft substitute, but House stood firm on Wilson's "progressive" principles. In the end the conference merely arranged for each belligerent to send the Russians a separate notification of willingness to discuss the revision of war aims with any stable Russian government.[48]

47. *Intimate Papers*, 3, 235, 281; House to Wilson, November 30, 1917, House Collection.
48. "House Diary," November 16, 1917; *Intimate Papers*, 3, 279–85; Kennan, chap. 6, passim.

House had now decided that Lloyd George "evidently thinks he had better tie his fortunes to the Conservatives rather than the liberal cause." But the Colonel's contacts with the radicals and his own predispositions gave him the opinion that in doing so Lloyd George was swimming against the tide. "If I am a judge of political conditions in England," he wrote, "he is only a mistake" (sic). House believed the time was very ripe for a restatement of policy and he was ready to use American influence freely to that end. Even in the conference he would have been in favor of—in his own words—"putting the steam-roller over" Sonnino, the Italian Foreign Minister. As he wrote his closing speech to the conference, House noted privately: "I wish I could say what I would really like to say, but with the reactionary crowd I find here I do not dare to do so." [49]

From the military point of view the conference was a great success and a major step on the road to Allied victory. But as to war aims House felt he had made little headway. On December 7, 1917, he sailed for America fully persuaded that Wilson must take a firm lead in the public reformulation of terms.

At Paris, House had concluded that Lloyd George was resolved in favor of the Conservatives: espousing the adamantine policy of his colleagues in the Government rather than the radical and American demand for a declaration of aims. But very soon after he returned to England the Prime Minister felt the pressure for a restatement of terms become irresistible. The Bolsheviks continued their pressure diplomacy, following to its logical conclusion the practice of public appeal to world opinion which had grown up during the war. This diplomacy, open indeed, proved a far cry from the liberal

49. For this and other quotations in the paragraph see "House Diary," December 1, 1917. Partly in *Intimate Papers*, 3, 291. Quotations omitted. The account of the war-aims aspect of this conference is much abridged in the *Intimate Papers*. The official report of the mission is in *Foreign Relations* (1917), Supp. 2, 1, 334–445. Cf. Wilson to House, November 16, 19, December 1, 2, 1917, Wilson Papers, File 2.

ideal of calm, rational discussion of the facts at issue. Lenin and Trotsky were out for revolution, not peace. On November 22 the Russian government began publication of the secret treaties, which appeared in British and American papers during the next two or three weeks. In England the U.D.C. did its best to disseminate the texts.

On December 15, 1917, the Bolsheviks signed an armistice and summoned all belligerents to join them at Brest Litovsk and make peace. For purposes of their own, the Central Powers accepted this invitation and thereby increased the onus on the Allies to show cause why they could not make peace. President Wilson gave another fillip to the war-aims movement when on December 4, 1917, he delivered his projected message to Congress in which he maintained his condemnation of the German government but held out to the peoples of the Central Powers a peace of reconciliation and a place in a "partnership of peoples." Explaining the purpose of his speech, Wilson recalled one of the earliest and simplest principles of the radical war-aims movement; it was, the President asserted, necessary to answer the question: "When shall we consider the war won?" [50]

This added fuel to the fire the radicals were building under Lloyd George. They and their new-found associates among the rest of the Liberal party exhorted Asquith to endorse Lansdowne's appeal. Asquith was too cautious to comply fully, but in a speech at Birmingham on December 14, 1917, he did defend Lansdowne's intention of clarifying British aims.[51] In Parliament on December 19, many who had not hitherto participated in the demand for reformulation of terms joined such stalwarts as Ponsonby and Noel Buxton in an extended debate. They contended that the publication of the secret treaties made it ridiculous to deny the need for re-

50. *War and Peace, 1,* 128–39. For an account of the relation between Bolshevik activity and Wilson's policy, see Kennan, chaps. 7 and 12; Mayer, pp. 396 ff.

51. Buckler to House, December 10, 1917; Buckler to Frazier, December 5, 1917, House Collection; Scott, pp. 206–10.

assuring the people. As Foreign Secretary, Balfour made an irritated and somewhat muddled defense of the treaties, but he could not squash the protest. Wedgwood branded Balfour's attitude as outdated. It was no longer sensible to remain imprecise in the hope of picking up advantages at the peace conference because now America would call the tune: "We are more or less bound by the terms that President Wilson will accept." And, he continued, "I am bound to say that I prefer the terms adumbrated by President Wilson to those that we have had from any speaker in this country, because I feel they are animated by the liberal ideas in which I have been brought up." Others made Wilson's pre-eminence a cause for complaint that no English leader had taken an equally clear and commendable stand.[52]

Feeling the pressure of these demands and himself not averse to exploring the possibility of peace, Lloyd George was yet subject to the unwavering determination of the Carsons and the Bonar Laws and to his Foreign Secretary's deep fear that Germany would negotiate merely to weaken the Allied effort.[53] Lloyd George also suspected that if he conceded to the radicals, Asquith would throw in his lot with the "patriots." To meet this situation, the Prime Minister tried to steer a middle course. On December 14, 1917, at Gray's Inn, he announced the Government's general agreement with "the Wilson policy" but vigorously attacked elements which "insidiously" suggested there was a "half-way house between victory and defeat." In Parliament on December 20, replying to the previous day's debate, Lloyd George veered toward the radicals again, going so far as to refer all colonial questions to the peace conference.[54]

The radicals were mollified but continued their pressure,

52. *H. C. Deb.*, *100*, 1997–2096; Buckler to House, December 21, 1917, House Collection; *Nation*, December 29, 1917.
53. *War Memoirs*, *4*, 2081–108; *5*, 2461–81, 2567; Dugdale, *2*, 181; Temperley, *Peace Conference*, *1*, 189.
54. Hammond, *Scott*, pp. 219–28; Scott, pp. 210–4; *H. C. Deb.*, *100*, 2219–28, 2234

seeing no reason why Lloyd George should begrudge a more precise, formal and orderly statement if his aims were truly so moderate. On January 5, 1918, the Premier responded by making the most comprehensive declaration of moderate terms yet made by any British statesman. He cast his pronouncement in the form of an address to a conference of the Trades Union Congress at Caxton Hall, London. The choice of occasion indicates the final compelling force which brought this success to the war-aims campaign. The same stresses of war which produced the peace hunger of Lansdowne compelled the Government to squeeze out still more military manpower. This could not be done without the cooperation of organized labor, especially as the Government had made pledges from which it now desired release. Labor's interest in war aims was at a peak. A special conference of the Labour party and T.U.C. had just adopted a memorandum on war aims which showed that although the bulk of the workers were by no means for peace at any price, they were deeply concerned that their sacrifices should be continued only for purposes they could approve. Lloyd George met with delegates to the conference and realized that he had to come to terms with this temper to get the support he needed. The speech of January 5 was intended to do this. "I went as near peace as I could," he confided to a friend. "The time had come to speak definitely." [55]

Lloyd George denied any desire to question Germany's right to a great position in the world or to dictate the form of her government—though he hoped to see a German democracy.

55. Riddell, pp. 304–5; *War Memoirs, 5*, 2483 ff., 2650 ff.; Maddox, p. 185; Jones, p. 124; Mayer, pp. 437–41; Winkler, pp. 179–82. For expressions of Labour's aims at this time see Henderson, "Labour and an After War Economic Policy," *War and Peace*, Supplement to the *Nation*, November 1917; idem, "Labour's Peace Terms," proof only (December(?) 1917), advocating "The Same Original Aims of 1914"; idem, *War Aims of Labour* (London, 1918); T.U.C. and Labour Party, *Memorandum on War Aims* (London, 1918), submitted to Labour Conference, December 25, 1917.

Proceeding to particular terms, he demanded the evacuation of Belgium, pointing out that Germany had not yet definitely promised even this. Belgium should also receive reparation, but the Prime Minister specifically withheld judgment as to whether the settlement should seek to shift the cost of war-like operations. Serbia, Montenegro, occupied France, Italy, and Rumania should be restored. For Alsace-Lorraine, Lloyd George required only "reconsideration." Russia would have to look out for itself, but Lloyd George did pronounce for an independent Poland. Austria-Hungary he was willing to leave essentially intact on condition there was self-government for its peoples. The Italians and Rumanians should be united under their respective sovereignties. Arabia, Armenia, Meso-potamia, Syria, and Palestine were "entitled to a recognition of their separate national identity." Colonial questions should be disposed of in the interests of the welfare of the inhabitants, precluding exploitation by "European capitalists." As to the secret treaties, Lloyd George conceded that the Russian debacle invalidated some of them and he was ready to discuss them with his Allies. In the matter of economic discrimination, the Premier thought it inevitable that in the period of recon-struction those controlling raw materials would help them-selves and their Allies first. Winding up his speech, Lloyd George summarized the principles of his peace as: sanctity of treaties, self-determination, and international cooperation.[56]

The Prime Minister's access of moderation surprised many people but perhaps none more than Woodrow Wilson, who was busily preparing a declaration of his own. On his return from the disappointments of Paris, House had at once urged Wilson to make a forthright statement to "knit together the best and most unselfish opinions in the world." [57] The Presi-

56. Scott, pp. 225–33; *War Memoirs*, 5, 2485. It seems certain that the speech was chiefly written by Robert Cecil. "House Diary," January 19, 1918; Memorandum by Cecil, January 2, 1918, Wise-man Collection.

57. *Intimate Papers*, 3, 317–9.

dent was already disposed toward this and immediately asked House to gather materials from the Inquiry.

Wilson and House had several purposes in mind as they prepared the speech containing the famous Fourteen Points: to meet the challenge of Bolshevik diplomacy and prevent its leading liberals into impractical courses; to try once more to arouse the German people against autocracy; and to fortify Wilson's leadership of Allied and particularly British liberalism. The address was also to be a reproof to the Allies for failing to declare moderate aims and a warning that Wilson would not countenance such extreme ambitions as those of the Treaty of London.[58]

It was not surprising that Wilson was especially heedful of the British radicals. House had just returned from contact with them. Henry White personally placed in Wilson's hands a report in which Buckler made plain the full extent of the support for Lansdowne, contradicting the belittling accounts of Ambassador Page.[59] As on other occasions, Wilson took the radical side against Page, telling ex-President Taft that he had to "discount whatever [Page] says about the situation in Great Britain." [60] Just as the previous December, Wilson was well aware of a body of liberal support in Britain, ready for leadership. With the Fourteen Points, the President reasserted that leadership with greater success than at any time

58. Ibid., pp. 322–3; *Life and Letters*, 7, 444, 513; Seymour, 283 ff. One of the Inquiry's reports advised Wilson to "show the way to Liberals in Great Britain and in France. . . . These Liberals will readily accept the leadership of the President if he undertakes a liberal diplomatic offensive . . ." Baker, *Woodrow Wilson and the World Settlement* (3 vols. New York, 1922), 3, 23–41.

59. Nevins, p. 341; Buckler to White, November 30, 1917, House Collection.

60. "House Diary," December 12, 1917, January 3, 1918. On December 22 Page sent Wilson a letter which must have arrived about the time the President was drafting his speech. "The cry continues here," he wrote, "for some summary that the man in the street and the man in the trenches can understand. All this will pass with the New Year mood." Hendrick, 3, 413.

since January 1917. It must be noted, however, that Wilson did not share the purposes of those on both the left and the right in Britain who were interested in reducing war aims solely to make peace quickly. Wilson intended to use his leadership of the liberals to force the Allies to accept reasonable terms and then to pursue the war vigorously until Germany, too, fell into line.

On the basis of reports from the Inquiry and detailed discussions with House, who was now giving a powerful lead, Wilson prepared his speech for delivery to Congress on January 8, 1918. News of Lloyd George's pronouncement, received on January 5, almost led him to abandon the project, but House convinced him circumstances were even more favorable than before.[61] As finally presented, Wilson's address began with a denunciation of the ambitions Germany had now revealed at Brest Litovsk and with high praise for Russian insistence upon open diplomacy. The President reiterated his belief that war aims should be publicly declared and freely discussed. No statesman should play a part in prolonging such a war unless "sure beyond a peradventure that the objects of the vital sacrifice are part and parcel of the life of Society and that the people for whom he speaks think them right and imperative as he does." The essential character of a worth-while peace was mutual accommodation of interests: "What we demand in this war is nothing peculiar to ourselves. It is that the world be made . . . safe for every peace-loving nation which, like our own, wishes to live its own life, determine its own institutions, be assured of justice and fair dealing by the other peoples of the world as against force and selfish aggression. All the peoples of the world are in effect partners in this interest, and for our own part we see very clearly that unless justice be done to others, it will not be done to us."

61. *Intimate Papers*, 3, 339–41; House suspected Lloyd George of deliberately getting in first, "House Diary," January 19, 1918.

Wilson then proceeded to outline an acceptable settlement in Fourteen Points. For the first time the President expressed official views on territorial questions. His proposals amounted to a modified application of self-determination. Thus he contented himself with asking merely "autonomous development" for the Hapsburg dominions, doubtless having in mind the Allies' high hopes of detaching Austria from Germany. Somewhat similarly Wilson chose to bolster sagging French morale by demanding correction of the wrong done to France in 1870, rather than accepting the Inquiry's recommendation of a plebiscite for Alsace-Lorraine.[62] On the other hand the President took a firm stand against Italy's claims to non-Italian territory, rejecting the Inquiry's suggestion of a strategic line.[63]

Wilson could neglect strategic frontiers because his whole territorial settlement assumed a new international order providing security for both great and small states.[64] The capstone of this order was to be a "general association of nations." To support it Wilson demanded an end to secret diplomacy—this first love of the radicals became Wilson's first point [65]—disarmament, freedom of the seas, and the "removal, so far as possible, of all economic barriers and the establishment of an equality of trade conditions" among members of the league.

The President devoted special attention to Russia. Unlike Lloyd George, he eloquently rejected the idea of abandoning Eastern Europe to the Central Powers. Wilson made this the subject of his first territorial point, demanding the evacuation

62. While redrafting the section on Alsace-Lorraine on January 7, 1918, Wilson went through the whole message inserting the words "should" and "must" to indicate the essential points. Alsace-Lorraine received merely a "should." *Intimate Papers, 3,* 329; cf. Progress Report of Inquiry, Wiseman Collection.

63. *Intimate Papers, 3,* 322–3; Baker, *World Settlement, 3,* 35 ff.; Wiseman memorandum, January 23, 1918, Wiseman Collection.

64. *Life and Letters, 7,* 506–7.

65. Subsequently Wilson explained that he did not mean to abandon secret discussions but to insist that all agreements should be open. *Life and Letters, 8,* 21–2, 208.

of Russian territory and an opportunity for Russia to determine her own institutions and freely enter the society of nations. The treatment of Russia he declared to be the "acid test" of the good will of nations.

For Germany, Wilson held out a full and free membership in the new international arrangements, grudging her no peaceful development or pre-eminence. He claimed no right to dictate Germany's constitution, but he drew attention to the differences between civil and military leaders in Germany and made it clear he would be more indulgent toward a German democracy than to representatives of the military party.[66]

There was little new in the Fourteen Points, but they constituted the most comprehensive and striking presentation yet of a liberal program, almost exactly endorsing the aims of the British radicals. In a few instances Wilson's program differed from that of the radicals. The latter had never shared the American emphasis on the freedom of the seas. On the other hand, Wilson's economic proposals fell short of the radical ideal, calling merely for the removal of restrictions and proposing no economic functions for the league and no positive arrangements for economic cooperation to minimize the disruptions caused by drawing new frontiers. But the President had at least pronounced against the radical nightmare of economic "war after the war," adding to his general "Point" a specific assurance to Germany against "hostile arrangements of trade." Perhaps most gratifying of all to the radicals was the breadth of Wilson's design, which was calculated to reach a reasonable solution of all problems in the hope of "removing the chief provocations to war . . ."[67]

British radicals gave both the Fourteen Points and Lloyd George's January 5 speech an enthusiastic reception. The Fourteen Points received somewhat the warmer welcome,

66. Text of speech, *War and Peace, 1,* 155–62; the Fourteen Points are in Appendix below.
67. Ibid., p. 161.

partly because of Wilson's already established reputation
for noble utterance. Lloyd George came under some criticism
for his coldness toward Russia and for his reference to trade
discrimination; but, on balance, radicals admitted that his
speech marked a signal victory for their cause.[68] Wilson's address encountered skepticism in some Conservative papers [69]
but from the radicals and most other Liberals and members
of the Labour party there was virtually nothing but praise.
"Mr. Wilson," the *Nation* exclaimed, "is fighting superbly
against all Imperialism and cynicism, and doing it with a
shrewdness and courage which stamp him as the leader of
civilization." [70]

Some were rash enough to speak as though the Fourteen
Points were a signed and sealed Allied policy: "Democracy,"
proclaimed the *Daily News*, "had secured its future." Others
were less sanguine and saw Wilson's terms as an aspiration
which must now be endorsed and realized. A Labour Conference at Nottingham on January 24, 1918, for example, called
again for a joint declaration of terms.[71] The effort to consolidate progress toward moderate war aims by securing formal and united Allied or at least British adhesion to the
Wilson program was to dominate radical activity in the remaining months of the war.

68. E.g. *Daily News*, January 7, 9, 1918; *Nation*, January 12,
19, 1918; Seymour, p. 291.
69. *Daily Mail*, January 7, 9; *Times*, January 9, 1918.
70. *Nation*, January 12, 1918. Some Liberal papers had reservations as to the freedom of the seas.
71. *Daily News*, January 25, 1918; Snowden, *Autobiography, 1*,
481.

6. The Dangers of Victory

THE PRONOUNCEMENTS made by Wilson and Lloyd George in January 1918 did not succeed in restoring Russian morale but signs of uneasiness appeared quite soon in Germany and Austria. This placed the Central Powers under the necessity of giving some response, especially after Lloyd George began to taunt them publicly for their silence.[1] On January 24, 1918, both the German and Austrian Chancellors made speeches in reply. The latter took much the more conciliatory tone; both directed their remarks primarily to Wilson rather than Lloyd George. These two speeches ushered in several weeks of public debate across the fighting lines and in Britain. Radical hopes soared for an imminent peace; the radical press and Parliamentarians united in urging that the Chancellors be granted a reasoned reply, pointing out that Czernin, at least, had shown readiness for conciliation.[2]

Lloyd George and his Government did not agree, fearing as usual that too much peace talk would uselessly sap British morale and apprehensive that Czernin was merely laying some plot in conspiracy with Germany. While they were willing to engage in secret *pourparlers* with Germany, they were reluctant to enter the public lists.[3] Britain's allies were even less

1. *War Memoirs*, 5, 2492–4.
2. *Nation*, February 2, 1918; Buckler to House, January 26, 1918, House Collection.
3. *War Memoirs*, 5, 2496–9; Reading to Balfour, February 15, 1918, Wiseman to Drummond, March 14, 1918, Balfour to House, February 7, 1918, Wiseman Collection. This reluctance may be connected with some indications that Lloyd George contemplated a deal with Germany in the East, a project that would hardly mature in public. Cole, pp. 111–15; Hammond, *Scott*, p. 232.

eager to consider a compromise peace at a time when American strength was about to make itself felt. As a result, a meeting of Allied prime ministers in the Supreme War Council at Versailles on February 2, 1918, issued a sharp rebuff to the Central Powers, declaring, "The only immediate task before them lay in the prosecution with the utmost vigor . . . of the military effort." [4]

The Council's action infuriated the radicals, who had seen in the incipient debate an opening for concession and reconciliation.[5] President Wilson was no less annoyed, regarding the incident as proof of his wisdom in remaining aloof from participation in the joint political decisions of the Allies. He shared Lloyd George's wariness of a "peace trap," but he thought it essential to explore fully any opening that promised an end to the war.[6] After much consideration, the President replied publicly to the Chancellors in an address to Congress on February 11, 1918, acknowledging Czernin's more moderate tone and assailing the extremes of Hertling's speech.[7]

Wilson rebuked the Allies severely for the Supreme War Council's action, not only by implication in his speech but by direct diplomatic communication. On February 5, 1918, he cabled to his Paris Embassy a protest against political statements which might implicate the United States. Exactly two weeks later he followed this up with a circular to Allied ambassadors in Washington threatening to reconsider the in-

4. The text is in *H. C. Deb., 103,* 148–9.

5. *Nation,* February 9, 16, 1918; Swanwick, *Builders,* p. 106; Buckler to House, February 4, 11, 1918, House Collection. On February 5 House drew Wilson's attention to the reaction of the *Daily News.* House to Wilson, Wilson Papers, File 2.

6. *Intimate Papers, 3,* 359, 378; *Life and Letters, 7,* 554.

7. "House Diary," January 27, 29, 30, February 5, 14, 1918; Wiseman to Balfour, February 4, 1918, Wiseman Collection; *Lansing Papers, 2,* 90–9. In the Wilson Papers there is a memorandum written by William Bullitt on February 3, comparing the positions of Wilson, Czernin, and Hertling in parallel columns. Text of speech in *War and Peace, 1,* 177–84.

structions of American representatives if the Supreme War Council continued to act politically. This note was, as Wilson confessed to Lansing, "a bit blunt, but I think it imperative that we should safeguard ourselves in this all-important matter." [8] Later Wilson made his dissatisfaction with Allied diplomacy even plainer to Lansing: "I am afraid of *any* expression of policy framed jointly at Paris. There has been none yet that seemed to me even touched with wisdom. . . . I am afraid that statesmen like our friend Lloyd George will not care to be guided and will rather rejoice in a somewhat crude and cynical rejoinder." [9]

For this stand, as revealed in Wilson's speech of February 11, and for four principles of settlement which the address contained, the President received wholehearted radical support.[10] During the following weeks the radicals managed to stage no less than five Parliamentary debates on peace terms and negotiation, driving the Government into positions of considerable embarrassment. On February 13, in particular, in a heated discussion of the Supreme War Council declaration, Balfour's rambling reply revealed that he was ignorant of the contents not only of Czernin's speech but of Wilson's.[11]

Through all the radical clamor rang a steady note of admiration for Wilson. He had partly designed his recent actions with

8. *Intimate Papers, 3,* 363; *Foreign Relations* (1918), Supp. 1, *1,* 70–1; *Lansing Papers, 2,* 95.

9. February 21, 1918, *Lansing Papers, 2,* 103. As it happened, both Lloyd George and Balfour declared they could see no difference between Czernin and Hertling, *after* Wilson spoke. *H. C. Deb., 103,* 22–4.

10. Buckler to House, February 11, 13, 1918, House Collection; *Nation,* February 16, 23, 1918. The principles were: (1) A peace of sufficient justice to ensure stability, (2) Peoples should not be regarded as chattels, (3) Territorial adjustments should be in the interests of the peoples concerned, (4) There should be the greatest possible degree of self-determination.

11. *H. C. Deb., 103,* 112–230; other debates in the Lords on March 19, 1918; in the Commons on February 12, 27 and March 4, 1918.

the British radicals in mind, and House kept in close contact with them during February and March.[12] Of course Wilson, for all his suspicions, kept in close touch with British government circles as well, being fully aware of the need to work hand in hand with the British leaders in prosecuting the war. But the radicals loomed sufficiently large in Wilson's. judgment to justify sending a special agent to supplement the liaison work of Buckler who was increasingly handicapped by Ambassador Page. Ray Stannard Baker was chosen for this new mission. Ostensibly Baker represented the *New Republic* and the New York *World,* but his real task, as he noted at the time, was "to report fully for the information of the President and the State Department on the state of radical opinion and organization, especially the attitude of labor in England . . ." His reports were sent first to Frank Polk, Counselor of the State Department, selections and sometimes complete documents being forwarded to the President and to House. Baker became as devoted as Buckler to the thesis that the radicals constituted the real source of Wilson's support in England.[13] The radicals amply repaid these attentions. In the big debate on February 13, Member after Member quoted, cited, and praised Wilson. Walter Runciman declared with reference to Czernin's speech, "President Wilson's opinion is good enough for me." [14]

Allied plans for military intervention in Siberia provided an added bond between Wilson and the radicals, who feared such schemes would further Japanese imperialism and needlessly provoke the Bolsheviks. The radicals looked to Wilson to oppose these plans, and after some hesitation he did so vigor-

12. Letters from Buckler to House on January 22, 26, February 1, 21, March 1, 10, House Collection. Cf. "House Diary," February 24, 1918.

13. "House Diary," February 2, 1918; "We find it impossible to get information on the liberals from Page," ibid., February 22, 1918; Baker's notes in Ray S. Baker, *American Chronicle* (New York, Scribner, 1945), pp. 306, 323, 342.

14. *H. C. Deb., 103,* 179; cf. ibid., cols. 1489–90; Conwell Evans, pp. 150–1.

ously. Although by the end of February he saw no way to avoid Japan's mounting guard over the Siberian railway, Wilson took the unusual step of withdrawing his first note of consent after it had been unofficially circulated, and substituted one which withheld positive acquiescence and sharply demanded safeguards. As added precaution Wilson took the occasion of the Soviet's meeting on March 12, 1918, to send a benevolent message purportedly condemning German encroachments on Russian sovereignty but really intended to caution Japan. The radicals well understood this inner purpose, and it won Wilson added favor in their eyes.[15]

As a positive program the radicals still concentrated on demanding the alignment of British and American aims and a declaration of joint Allied policy. This, thought Trevelyan, would provide a painless way out of the secret treaties.[16] It must be remarked, however, that there were some differences in the radical ranks, and some reservations toward American policy. Many moderate radicals feared that America was becoming naive and self-righteous in its idealism.[17] A few extreme peace-lovers, such as Snowden, were at one with the Lansdowne group in valuing peace itself so highly that they were probably willing to abandon Eastern Europe to German imperialism.[18] To these Wilson's conciliatory gestures were welcome; his determination to achieve his aims, decidedly

15. Kennan, pp. 479–83; *Intimate Papers, 3,* 396, 398–9, 419–20; Wedgwood to House, February 25, March 9, 1918; Buckler to House, February 28, March 1, 2, 11, 19, 1918, House Collection; *Nation,* April 13, 1918.

16. February 13, 1918, *H. C. Deb., 103,* 220–1; Buckler to House, March 10, 12, 1918, House Collection; *Nation,* February 23, March 23, 1918; *Peace Overtures and Their Rejection* (U.D.C., 27a, 1918).

17. Even the *Round Table* believed Americans were "firmly convinced of the unalloyed righteousness of their course," and that this brought "some danger of an indiscriminate condemnation and rejection of everything 'German.'" March, 1918, p. 261.

18. Cole, pp. 113–20; an extreme pacifist exclaimed to Scott that "only Wilson's copy book morality stood between the world and peace." Hammond, *Scott,* pp. 214–15.

less so. A much larger group of radicals were inconsistent, constantly demanding moves toward peace yet denouncing on principle any suggestion of the kind of compromise—such as a deal in the East—which there was any chance of Germany's accepting.[19]

For to the radicals' misfortune, Lloyd George was quite right in saying that Germany was not in a conciliatory mood, although he might perhaps have done more to improve the situation. Throughout the winter German demands at Brest Litovsk slowly revealed the ugly shape of a German peace to the most stubbornly myopic eye. The treaties of Brest Litovsk, published on March 12, 1918, were as harsh a peace as could well be imagined. Six days later Ludendorff launched his greatest offensive in the West, which not only signified Germany's determination to win a peace of victory but rolled Allied armies back so far that the Allies faced the danger not of too much success but of disastrous defeat and a second Brest Litovsk.

As the German offensive swelled into a mighty battle of several months' duration, the war-aims campaign subsided. The radicals perforce admitted that the Germans were in no mood to reason. But although they now reluctantly conceded that it might be necessary to defeat Germany thoroughly, they remained anxious that Allied terms should be moderate. These were trying days for such men, for the need to keep up national morale gave free rein to the proponents of a punitive peace.[20] At the same time, the disintegration of the Liberal party progressed even further. While some Liberal-Imperialists tacitly

19. E.g. the *Nation*, February 9, March 2, 9, 23, 1918. Arthur Henderson identified 3 groups in England for Baker: (1) Pacifists, Lansdowne followers, and radicals; (2) "Bitter-enders," Lloyd George and the government; (3) Labor and the "sanely liberal group." Baker, *American Chronicle*, p. 314.

20. On May 13, 1918, e.g., Bonar Law assured Carson that immediate steps would be taken to implement the Paris Economic recommendations. *H. C. Deb., 106,* 30–1.

formed a weird combination with Lansdowne and Morel to favor a peace bought at Russian expense,[21] the official party leadership devoted itself to attacks on Lloyd George's military policy, making the split in the party irremediable.[22]

Nor could the radicals draw their usual comfort from Wilson. As in the previous spring, he was immersed in military preparations. In the only two major speeches which he did make, he was concerned to encourage the Allies by emphasizing the strength of American reinforcements. The eloquence with which he did this suggested that he, too, was not untouched with the anger of the time. From him came words that could never be pleasant to a liberal ear: "Force, Force to the utmost, Force without stint or limit, the righteous and triumphant Force which shall make Right the law of the world."[23]

Without doubt Wilson intended to fight unrelentingly until Germany agreed to an acceptable peace. But he did not relish this task as much as his public utterances might suggest. Privately he explained the near impossibility of combining pleas for moderation with exhortations to battle. He was, he said,[24] no convert to the "Knock-Out Blow" and, in fact, in both his speeches he took care to hold out the promise of a peace of reconciliation. But the bulk of the press emphasized the warlike passages and Wilson once more faced the danger

21. Buckler reported on May 9, 1918, that Philip Kerr, Liberal-Imperialist right-hand man to Lloyd George, had described the war as one between Wilson and the *Round Table,* adding "and in the end we shall beat him." House Collection. Baker, *American Chronicle,* p. 330, attributes the same remark to Wedgwood.

22. Cf. Jones, *Lloyd George,* p. 149; Wilson Harris, *Life So Far,* p. 112.

23. At Baltimore, April 6, 1918, *War and Peace, 1,* 202; the whole speech, pp. 198–202; the other speech at New York, May 18, 1918, ibid., pp. 205–10; for Wilson's intention to bolster Allied morale cf. Reading to Balfour, March 27, 1918, Wiseman to House, May 11, House to Wiseman, May 12, 1918, Wiseman Collection.

24. In a private address on April 8, 1918, *Life and Letters, 8,* 79–80.

of arousing a spirit which would thwart his cooler intentions. Most of the radicals still trusted Wilson [25] but they perceived this danger. "Given victory," the *Nation* inquired on May 11,

> how would Mr. Wilson cope with Allied statesmen who would claim their respective portions . . . ? He can have no security he could cope with them at all . . . it is not the idealist tendency which anywhere rules today and war is not the school from which idealism springs. . . . The idealist stakes much on victory, and then again stakes the fruits of victory on the character and intellect of statesmen.

Radical misgivings increased as a result of a series of declarations in May, June, and the following months, by which the Associated Powers promised full independence to Poland, Czechoslovakia and Yugoslavia. The exposure of the secret treaties had made it essential to reassure the submerged nationalities which might serve as a barrier to the Bolsheviks as well as a threat to the enemy, and the complete collapse of efforts to secure a separate peace with Austria removed the main strategic reason for dealing gently with the Hapsburg Empire. Wilson accepted this new policy somewhat doubtfully and strove to keep his part distinct from that of the Allies.[26] But, partially for this reason, he took an energetic lead as soon as his mind was made up and by August was fully committed to the break-up of Austria-Hungary.

25. *Life and Letters*, 8, pp. 38–9, 71–2; Buckler to House, May 4, 1918, May 9, 1918, House Collection; *Manchester Guardian*, April 7, 1918; *Daily News*, May 11, 18, June 15, 1918; *Nation*, May 11, 1918.

26. For Wilson's doubts see in particular Wiseman's report of interview with the President, May 20, 1918, Wiseman to Drummond, May 30, 1918, Wiseman Collection; for his efforts to keep apart see esp. *Lansing Papers*, 2, 130–9. In general, however, Wilson did not take the divisive and conflicting aspects of self-determination nearly so seriously as the radicals. This was partly, perhaps, another result of his less careful attention to the economic problems of the settlement.

The radicals had always been cautious in their approval of movements for national independence. Their fear that self-determination would require the total defeat of the Central Powers was no longer so compelling now that such a defeat was generally accepted as necessary and, as the German offensive crumbled, possible. A more fundamental objection to "Balkanization" sprang from the conviction that it emphasized national separateness at the expense of international cooperation and that it would produce a multitude of states that could not survive economically. Furthermore, the radicals—who had given more thought to the subject than most—had concluded that complete national self-determination was geographically impossible and must result in new irredenta or "Ulsters." [27] The radical solution was to combine moderate self-determination with political and economic international cooperation. This, they thought, not only would make new states more stable but would often make them unnecessary. Consequently, many radicals, giving perhaps too little attention to the political necessities facing Wilson and to the fact that in any case the rebellious nationalities were probably beyond restraint, viewed the President's patronage of the new sovereignties as a regrettable error of judgment.[28]

In the late summer of 1918, as the military tide turned on all fronts and the Allies rolled convincingly toward victory, several other portents intensified radical misgivings. Conservatives and Liberal-Imperialists showed unmistakable intentions of annexing the German colonies, whatever plans others might have for the postwar world. In August, Balfour openly declared that Germany's colonies could never be returned.[29] Advocates of permanent economic discrimination

27. A particularly careful study of this was G. P. Gooch, *The Races of Austria-Hungary* (U.D.C., 23, July 1917).

28. *H. C. Deb.,* 106, 599–602; *Nation,* September 7, 1918; Angell, *The Conditions of Allied Success* (New York, 1918), p. 30.

29. *H. C. Deb.,* 109, 1633. With regard to proposals for international trusteeship the *Round Table* declared: "We should be sorry

against Germany were also active and receiving aid and encouragement from the Government. On July 29 Bonar Law announced that the Cabinet had definitely decided in favor of imperial preference, and he curtly dismissed questions intended to bring out the discrepancies between this policy and Wilson's pronouncements.[30]

Discussion of a league of nations also began to develop in ways unfavorable to the radicals. Plans to establish a league of Allies before the peace gained increasing support, lending weight to fears that the league might become a disguise for a permanent anti-German combination. The Government was known to have accepted the idea of some kind of international organization and to have worked out a plan in the so-called Phillimore Report. This, although ready in March 1918, was not published until after the war, but it was fairly widely known to suggest little more than the formalization of the European Concert, a scheme which seemed very inadequate to the radicals. Of all the members of the Government, only Robert Cecil displayed much real interest in a league, and even his views were only slightly more enterprising than the Phillimore Report.[31] A debate in the Commons on August 1, 1918, revealed the full measure of radical disappointment and of the Government's coolness toward the league idea.[32]

For all these reasons radicals saw little cause to abandon their doubts about the Government's approach to the coming

---

indeed to see the Empire exchanging the substance of possession for such a shadowy security as this." September 1918, pp. 656–8.

30. *H. C. Deb.*, *109*, 39–40, 612–15; for further protectionist statements cf. Lloyd George to National Union of Manufacturers, August 1, 1918, New York *Times*, August 2, 1918; Robert Cecil, interview in *Times*, July 19, 1918.

31. Winkler, pp. 70–1, 236–8, 248–50; Forster, pp. 169–70; Lippmann to House, August 9, 1918, House Collection.

32. *H. C. Deb.*, *109*, 678–737; cf. ibid., 1412–36. It is surely permissible to read much significance into the selection of "Christian Science" as the British code words for the league project. Wiseman Collection.

settlement. Lloyd George veered and tacked with the breeze: on July 5, 1918, he declared that Germany could have peace on Wilsonian terms; on September 19 he pugnaciously demanded that the "image of victory" be stamped on the peace. On June 23 Balfour resolutely affirmed that British honor was bound up with the secret treaties. Politicians encumbered with less responsibility, chiefly Conservatives, did not try to hide their eager anticipation of condign punishment for Germany.[33] This vengeful talk coincided with predictions of reaction in domestic as well as foreign policy.[34] To combat this a group of radicals formed a Liberal Democratic Union while the official Liberal party, anticipating an early general election, made feverish efforts to put together a program.

The radicals thus saw the war rapidly nearing a decision at a time when their hopes of moderating national policy seemed to be at their lowest ebb for many months. They did not renew their demand for negotiations, being forced to admit that the military were firmly in control of German policy. They did, however, take up once more the agitation for yet another reformulation of terms and in particular for a unified Allied program. Pointing out that there had been no Allied endorsement of the Fourteen Points and subsequent Wilsonian principles, they were anxious to secure this before the complete collapse of German power removed all external restraint upon Germany's enemies.[35]

33. Scott, pp. 381–3; *Round Table,* September, 1918, p. 678; *H. C. Deb., 109,* 1592; W. S. Lilly, "Vengeance," *Nineteenth Century, 84* (1918), 401 ff.

34. In July the *Nation* complained: "Mr. George and his Government . . . are in full reaction against the Liberalism of Mill, Gladstone, Cobden, Bright, C. B., Morley and Asquith, and their later American affinity, Mr. Wilson."

35. See Debate August 8, 1918, *H. C. Deb., 109,* 1583 ff., *Daily News,* June 15, October 2, 1918. The radicals did resent their Government's going out of its way to discourage overtures. Thus on May 4 the *Daily News* sarcastically declared that "it may be impossible permanently to avert [peace]." The British government

Endorsement of the Fourteen Points seemed particularly desirable because the radicals believed that prospects of a liberal peace depended on American leadership. Here again the radicals were uneasy, because Wilson's comparative silence on war aims continued. True, the President made a brief speech on July 4, 1918, outlining four "ends" for a settlement which won general liberal acclamation.[36] But the speech also contained an uncompromising demand for victory which encouraged the opposition to the radicals almost as much as the four ends reinforced them.[37] Wilson sharpened radical fears by giving his consent in June to further intervention in Siberia, this time including American troops. Radicals correctly viewed this as a surrender to Allied pressure and were apprehensive that the United States might become the tool of Japanese ambitions.[38]

The radicals dreaded to think that Wilson's failure to speak out might mark a profound retreat from his liberal views. Fears of a failure in American liberalism increased at the news of the intolerant war spirit developing in the United States.[39] Most British radicals still trusted Wilson's intentions but others wondered whether he might not underestimate

feared that all peace offers were ruses intended to encourage the "partisans of peace by agreement" in Britain. Cf. a series of four secret memoranda, May to September 1918, in the Wiseman Collection. For some evidence of official qualms about a "Wilsonian" peace, see Wiseman to Arthur Murray, cable, July 4, 1918, commenting on Wilson's July 4 speech: "We should realize that we are up against a new conception of foreign policy which no amount of argument will reconcile with, for instance, traditional British policy." Wiseman Collection.

36. (1) The destruction of arbitrary power, (2) Consent of peoples to arrangements affecting them, (3) Acceptance between nations of standards of private honor, (4) An organization of peace.

37. Text of speech, *War and Peace, 1,* 231–5.

38. *Intimate Papers, 3,* 386–422; *Life and Letters, 8,* 283–5; for radical fears see the *Nation,* August 10, September 7, 1918.

39. *Nation,* July 8, 20, August 17, 1918; *Round Table* (September, 1918), pp. 692–3.

the weight of opposition to his ideals. Some of the President's utterances certainly contained an easy optimism which gave an appearance of overconfidence. The lack of a clear lead from Washington was particularly disturbing as the war obviously neared a conclusion. The *Nation* prophetically expressed this feeling:

> The hour to look to is that in which an utterly disillusioned German democracy in fact if not in form, turns from her rulers (and enemies) to the Alliance and awaits its word. On the response depends not her fate only but that of the world . . . the decision, and therefore the moral responsibility rests with America.[40]

Once more Wilson had not strayed as far from the radicals as they feared. Alert to the danger of falling into a trap by conceding Germany victory in Eastern Europe, the President nevertheless intended to make a moderate peace. He still placed high priority on forming a league of nations. His reluctance to develop detailed plans for a league stemmed from his conviction that no elaborate paper scheme could endure. Instead, Wilson favored a simple but universal agreement to guarantee political independence, territorial integrity, and the observance of treaties, adding elaborations only in the light of experience. By July 1918 he acquiesced in the need for preparation at least to the extent of cooperating with House in drafting a "covenant," but he still refused to publish his plan.[41]

For all its simplicity, Wilson intended his league to be a real force in the postwar world and expected it to aid in the

40. *Nation*, August 31, 1918. Cf. "Wayfarer," *Nation*, September 14, "C.K.C." to *Nation*, September 28, 1918. British labor groups were similarly impressed by what Beatrice Webb called "the sanctimonious self-righteousness" of American labor delegates. Cole, p. 130.

41. *Life and Letters*, 8, 17, 43, 74–5; *Intimate Papers*, 4, 15–54; Wiseman to Arthur Murray, July 9, 1918; Wiseman to Cecil, July 24, 1918, ibid., Wiseman Collection.

solution of difficult questions in the settlement. It was, for
instance, to be more powerful than the Phillimore proposal,
which Wilson declared had "no teeth." [42] He inserted provision
for military cooperation in House's draft, which had only
provided for economic sanctions. Similarly in harmony with
the radicals, Wilson explicitly opposed making the league
an anti-German combination and warned that forming a league
before the peace would damn it in German eyes.[43] As a practical safeguard against such discrimination, the President asserted that the league could only set out to safeguard territorial
integrity if the territorial peace terms were "fair and satisfactory and *ought* to be perpetuated." [44] Further indication that
Wilson did not view the league as a device to freeze an Allied
victory was given by provision in his scheme for changes
of frontier to meet shifts in racial aspiration, the peace of the
world being "superior in importance and interest to all questions of boundary." This provision stayed in Wilson's scheme
until after the end of the war.[45]

Again in conformity with the radicals, Wilson continued to
suspect the British government of plotting permanent economic war against Germany and, indeed, of a bid to gain
economic supremacy everywhere. In July 1918, hearing that

42. Interview with Wiseman, Wiseman to Reading, August 16,
1918, Wiseman Collection. *Life and Letters*, 8, 328, "House Diary,"
September 24, 1918.
43. *Intimate Papers*, *4*, 38; Wiseman to Murray, August 10,
1918, reporting that Wilson wanted Germany in the league, Wiseman Collection; Wiseman to Reading, August 16, 1918. The relevant portions are omitted from the *Intimate Papers*, *4*, 52–4. Wilson's scheme still fell short of radical hopes by making no provision for positive economic functions.
44. Wilson to House, March 22, 1918, *Life and Letters*, 8, 43–4.
45. *Intimate Papers*, *4*, 35 and n. 1; Baker, *World Settlement*, *1*,
223–4. This insistence upon the need for change was of course directly in line with British radical thought, particularly with Brailsford's *League of Nations*, which Wilson had read. For a full account of House's part in the drafting see *Intimate Papers*, *4*, chaps.
1, 2.

Walter Hines Page had designated an American observer to an Inter-Allied Parliamentary Conference on Commerce, Wilson pulled his ambassador up sharply, declaring: "These are dangerous conferences, because the nations which are engaging in them have some purposes which are in no respect our own." [46] A month later the President told E. N. Hurley that America was not "like the English . . . planning to dominate everything and to oust everybody we can oust." The British government was well aware of Wilson's opinion and knew that it was shared by a large group in England. This knowledge exercised an appreciable restraining influence on British policy. [47]

Even on the Siberian question Wilson shared radical suspicions. Only with great reluctance did he agree to the joint intervention and he was acutely conscious of the dangers. The President confessed to Masaryk that he felt no confidence in the policy and had merely taken what seemed the least dangerous course. At the outset he demanded assurances that the operation would be limited, casting his demand in terms strong enough to evoke a highly indignant protest from Balfour. [48]

Thus Wilson retained his belief that the Allies sought a peace markedly different from the one he desired. Many reports reached him suggesting that the British government

46. July 30, August 29, 1918; *Life and Letters*, 8, 306, 365. In August Wilson warned that he might disassociate himself from Allied economic pronouncements as sharply as he had from the Supreme War Council's answer to the two Chancellors. Wiseman to Reading, August 16, 1918, *Intimate Papers*, 4, 62–3.

47. Zimmern-Percy Memorandum, July 12, 1918, Wiseman Collection.

48. Wilson to Masaryk, August 7, 1918; *Life and Letters*, 8, 322–3; *Intimate Papers*, 3, 403; "House Diary," September 19, 1918; *Foreign Relations* (1918): *Russia*, 2, 287–90, 315–17, 392-4. Wiseman to Murray, July 12, 1918, pointing out that Americans noticed that conservative Britons favored the Siberian venture while liberals did not. Wiseman Collection.

was in reactionary hands. House was alert to the differences between Wilson and the Allies and remarked on "Lloyd George's inability to act in any other but a thoroughly selfish way . . . a way indeed which approaches dishonesty . . . Both he and Clemenceau dislike the President and the President dislikes them and all of them are partly justified in their feeling." [49] Wilson also knew that not all of his opponents were in Europe. He saw that the belligerent mood of his own country would not conduce to a peace of "right, reason, and justice" and might combine with kindred spirits in Europe to defeat his policy.[50] Sometimes the President attempted to cool the national temper, urging moderation on his correspondents and taking occasional stands in defense of civil liberties. But these efforts were perfunctory and hardly commensurate with the danger. Ironically when, early in 1918, Lincoln Steffens sought to promote the idea of a peace without victory by means of a speaking tour approved if not instigated by Colonel House, he encountered such fierce hostility that he was eventually refused a hearing at all.[51]

Sensing the opposition ahead, but not perhaps the sheer technical complexity of the coming settlement, Wilson admitted that he probably could not completely fulfill the expectations of his European admirers.[52] He was, however, thoroughly determined to try to persuade or compel the Allies to accept his kind of peace. To do this he relied in part upon the

49. "House Diary," August 22, 1918.

50. "House Diary," June 11, 1918; *Life and Letters*, 8, 518.

51. House to Steffens, May 14, 1918, in Lincoln Steffens, *The Autobiography of Lincoln Steffens* (New York, 1931), pp. 773–7.

52. *Life and Letters*, 8, 154, 251. Illustrating the idea that the chief obstacles would be willful opposition, House wrote that the difficulties need not be "almost insuperable . . . if those having the settlement in hand were entirely unselfish and without jealousy." "House Diary," September 19, 1918. Earlier he had written, "The Great Powers at the Peace Conference should put out a plan so just that all the smaller nations will be glad to concur in it." July 5, 1918. *Intimate Papers*, 4, 25, cf. Ponsonby's remark above, p. 67, and Hobson, above, p. 66.

European liberals. He declared: "I know that Europe is still governed by the same reactionary forces which controlled this country until a few years ago. *But I am satisfied that if necessary I can reach the peoples of Europe over the heads of their Rulers.*" [53] This strategy required that Wilson keep his hold on the liberal forces. Reports of his loss of prestige among British radicals during the summer of 1918 were therefore extremely alarming.

These reports flowed in freely. Buckler continued to send comments until mid-August, particularly relaying talk of economic warfare. But the embarrassment of continuing this channel of communication unknown to Ambassador Page was considerable, and in July, House arranged for the reports to cease. Two new sources of information on radical sentiment made it possible to dispense with Buckler. Ray Stannard Baker was now well established on his intelligence mission, and Polk was conveying selections from his reports to House and to Wilson.[54] Baker also wrote directly to House. Also sending reports to House was Walter Lippmann, in Europe on behalf of military propaganda. In August and September the two sent several voluminous dispatches. They confirmed Wilson's suspicion that the reactionaries were in full cry in England, and relayed the radicals' anxiety on that account. Even more significant, they laid great stress on Wilson's loss of prestige.

On August 21 Lippmann forwarded a memorandum in which Eustace Percy expressed the prevalent belief that American war fever now surpassed that of the Allies. Percy

53. Italics inserted. Wilson to Oscar F. Cushing, July 5, 1918, as related to R. S. Baker, *Life and Letters*, 8, 253; cf. Wilson to Axson, June 30, 1918, ibid., 241.

54. House to Henry White, July 27, 1918, House to Baker, July 18, 1918, House Collection. Polk to Baker, September 13, 1918, Polk Collection; Baker, *American Chronicle*, p. 346. Baker began reporting in the spring. As early as May 28, 1918, he had urged that "Mr. Wilson must often blow upon the embers of liberalism and democracy here." Baker to Polk, Polk Collection.

urged Wilson to take an active lead as the "only way of pre-
venting a similar bankruptcy in constructive Allied policy
as . . . took place in the summer of last year." This sentiment, Lippmann himself reported, "exists practically universally among the Liberals and Radicals from C. P. Scott down
. . . there is a growing feeling that the leadership of the
President has not been exercised sufficiently in the last few
months." Lippmann strongly recommended that Wilson make
one of his great speeches before the middle of October if the
reaction was to be checked. This speech, Lippmann suggested,
should cover three main points: a reaffirmation of the league of
nations, the preservation of a free Eastern Europe, and a
renewed refusal to enter a selfish economic league against a
reformed Germany.[55]

Two days earlier, on August 19, 1918, Baker had sent House
a letter of advice, enclosing a copy of a long report sent to Polk
on August 10. In the report Baker had emphasized the anxiety
of British radicals concerning American policy. "I am putting
these questions," he explained, "as they come to me as I
circulate among the liberal and labor groups here. Some of the
people believe it is not enough for America to assert her ideals,
but that she must get them down in black and white and
have them adopted as allied policy." In the letter to House,
Baker warned that unrest was growing in Britain and that
a "message of interminable war" without a clear declaration
of constructive purposes would do little to improve matters.
He had tried to convince radicals that American motives
were idealistic but was forced to report "a decided tendency
to question our purposes and wonder whither the American
war-spirit." The "only group," he continued, "which believes

55. Lippmann sent an earlier assessment of Percy's views on August 15. Percy Memorandum enclosed in Lippmann to House, August 21, 1918, House Collection. Wilson distrusted Percy personally.
Wilson to House, August 31, 1918, Wilson Papers, File 2; cf. C. P.
Scott's account of interview with Lippmann, Hammond, *Scott*, p.
243.

sincerely in the Wilson program is this labor and liberal group. . . . We ought never to let these liberal groups get away from us. Never was there such a need of constructive and idealistic leadership. . . . the leadership must positively come from us—from Mr. Wilson." [56]

Buckler sent a similar appeal from Henderson, and Lippmann sent one from Angell. These reports had a threefold significance for American policy. They confirmed suspicion of the British government and they reassured Wilson of the radicals' existence, at the same time warning him that he might forfeit their trust. Spurred on in this way, the President did reassert his liberal leadership in these final days of the war. Baker's report and letter of August 10 and 19 contributed very directly to this. On September 3, 1918, House forwarded them to Wilson, commenting: "Do you not think the time has come for you to try to commit the Allies to some of the things for which we are fighting?" When House visited Wilson on September 22, he found that the President had been thinking the matter over and had written a speech to fill the bill. This was the address delivered on September 27, 1918, at a Liberty Loan drive in New York City.[57]

Wilson designed the speech to allay radical fears and to press on the Allies his own design of a peace. The speech represented, he wrote, "the very great anxiety I have that the whole temper of the nations engaged against Germany should be a temper of highminded justice." He thought it necessary to be "brutally frank" with friends and foes alike. There were, therefore, in the speech "many things . . . which will doubt-

56. Baker to Polk, August 10, 1918, Baker to House, August 19, 1918, House Collection. Baker to Polk partly printed in Baker, *American Chronicle*, pp. 353–5, and in *Life and Letters*, 8, 345–6. A sign of growing labor dissatisfaction with the Lloyd George regime was the decision of the Labour party Conference in June 1918 to dissolve the party truce, preparatory to fighting the coming election on party lines. Curiously the party did not call on Labour members to resign from the Cabinet. *Times*, June 27, 1918.

57. *Intimate Papers, 4,* 64–8.

less displease the Imperialists of Great Britain, France and Italy." [58]

The address conveyed a direct response to the radical appeal. Wilson said that as hopes of victory sprang high, it was natural to want definite assurance as to the results: "plain workaday people" were rightfully demanding such assurance. The President insisted that the Associated Powers must do justice to all and establish a virile league. The establishment of this league Wilson made one of five "particulars," of which the others were impartial justice, the subordination of special interests which conflicted with the general interest, no alliances within the league, and no "special, selfish economic combination within the league and no employment of any form of economic boycott or exclusion" except as an international sanction. Wilson drove home this sweeping endorsement of the radical program by denouncing alliances and economic rivalries as "the prolific source in the modern world of the plans and passions that produce war." In a thinly veiled attempt to compel Allied acceptance of his principles, the President invited Allied statesmen to speak out if they disagreed.[59]

With this speech Wilson successfully stayed the doubts of the British radicals and reassured them as to his intentions. The *Nation* acknowledged that the President had dealt with all the points on which it was concerned. Massingham noted that the Allies were still uncommitted and urged Wilson to continue his effort to tie them down. Even the mistrustful General Council of the U.D.C. sent Wilson a resolution of approval. This single speech refurbished the President's honor and rehabilitated his leadership of the radicals.[60]

58. *Life and Letters*, 8, 442; Tumulty, pp. 301–2.
59. *War and Peace*, 1, 253–61.
60. *Nation*, October 5, 1918; Baker to House, November 1, 1918, House Collection; Lippmann to House, October 2, 1918, ibid.; U.D.C. resolution, October 22, received November 5, 1918, *Foreign Relations* (1918), Supp. 1, 1, 469–70; Swanwick, *Builders*, p. 49.

He was just in time. Two days later Bulgaria surrendered. On October 5, 1918, Germany's new Chancellor, Prince Maximilian of Baden, announced to the Reichstag that he had that day requested President Wilson to bring about an armistice preliminary to a peace based upon the President's pronouncements. In desperation, German leaders turned to Wilson in the hope that his devotion to a moderate peace might save them from complete disaster. This appeal placed Wilson in some embarrassment, for his "Associates" had still not formally subscribed to the program Germany invoked; nor did it seem wise to take the genuineness of the appeal for granted.[61] To complicate the situation, the bulk of the Allied and American press revealed itself vehemently opposed to parleying with the enemy at all.[62] Despite this, Wilson agreed with House that the opportunity to end the war—and on his terms—should not be lightly cast aside. He was encouraged in this decision by the fact that the British radicals were also strongly in favor of making the most of this chance to negotiate and were willing to entrust their fate to the President's keeping.[63]

Wilson therefore determined to pursue the negotiation cautiously and to pin the Germans tightly to their pledges before taking any steps toward the conclusion of hostilities. Following this plan, he engaged in a series of exchanges in which he demanded assurances that Germany really accepted the Fourteen Points and subsequent principles as a basis for peace, that reforms in Germany ensured that the agents of foreign policy truly represented the German people, and that the Germans realized an armistice must guarantee continued Allied military supremacy. By a Note dated October 20, 1918,

61. See account of Cabinet meeting, October 22, 1918, Houston, *1*, 311; *Intimate Papers, 4*, 74–9.

62. *Life and Letters, 8*, 476; *Intimate Papers, 4*, 76–7; Harry R. Rudin, *Armistice, 1918* (New Haven, 1944), pp. 89, 101–2, 124–5.

63. Wilson read comments of the *Manchester Guardian* and *Daily News* before answering Germany. "House Diary," October 9, 1918, partly *Intimate Papers, 4*, 77–8.

Germany satisfied Wilson to the extent that on October 23 he formally communicated his correspondence to the Allies, recommending that the German request for armistice be granted, subject to military approval.[64]

The President now turned to persuading his Associates to accept his program; in effect to endorse the radical peace aims, finally, formally, and unitedly. He had already sent House to Europe with full powers to perform this delicate task.[65]

It was high time that Wilson did turn to the Allies. While he had been playing his lone hand with Germany, Allied statesmen had become alarmed and exasperated. They feared that either the Germans would trick Wilson into allowing German troops to disengage and regroup or that his principles might lead him deliberately to aid Germany to escape the full consequences of her military plight. On October 9, 1918, these fears inspired the Allied prime ministers, then meeting in Paris, to cable Wilson emphasizing their interest in the negotiations and insisting that armistice terms must depend on military opinion.[66]

Neither Wilson nor House wished to dispute this last point. The President contented himself with urging that military terms should be adequate but not unnecessarily humiliating.[67] House, upon whom chief responsibility for executing policy now devolved, remained quiescent in the meetings which discussed military conditions, and the terms that emerged were an Anglo-French product.

Wilson and House believed the formal Allied endorsement

64. *Intimate Papers, 4,* 75 ff.; Rudin, pp. 89–132, 170–6; *Foreign Relations* (1918), Supp. 1, *1,* 383.

65. House was commissioned a special representative of the President on October 14 and sailed on October 17, arriving in Paris October 26, *Intimate Papers, 4,* 86–7.

66. *War Memoirs, 5,* 3281–3.

67. *Intimate Papers, 4,* 83, 110; Geddes to Lloyd George, October 13, 1918, Wiseman Collection; Newton D. Baker to Pershing, October 27, 1918, *Life and Letters, 8,* 520–1.

of the Fourteen Points [68] was much more important than military terms. Both men, it has been seen, were prepared to meet strong opposition to their demand that the armistice be an all-round commitment to a "Wilsonian" peace.[69] British radicals shared, echoed, and reinforced these hopes and fears. The radical press unanimously demanded a formal Allied agreement on the Fourteen Points, the U.D.C. passed a resolution of encouragement, and Wedgwood exhorted Wilson to remember that "more than ever, he is the leader of all liberals and labor throughout the world." At the same time the radicals warned once more that reaction was strong and harbored many schemes incompatible with a liberal peace of moderation. "The jingoes everywhere will soon be out for spoils," wrote Wedgwood in a later letter. "It is then that Wilson's last act must come." [70]

In Paris, House found the British less fundamentally opposed to the Fourteen Points than their continental colleagues. The latter were apparently willing to let the question slip by on the assumption it would not greatly influence the future.[71] Perhaps because he was aware that a large part of the British electorate took the Fourteen Points too seriously to forgive a broken pledge to them, Lloyd George shared House's determination to discuss the matter. In particular the Prime Minister wanted to object to the point calling for "freedom of the

68. From now on, the term "Fourteen Points" refers to all the President's principles of settlement enunciated in his speeches of January 8, February 11, July 4, and September 27, 1918.

69. And cf. "House Diary," October 15, 28, 29, 1918, partly *Intimate Papers, 4,* 150–1; *Lansing Papers, 2,* 157; *Life and Letters, 8,* 500, 512, 523; Houston, *1,* 316–18.

70. Wedgwood to House, October 25, 28, 1918, House Collection; *Daily News,* October 8, 19, 21, 22, 1918; *Nation,* October 12, 19, 26; *Manchester Guardian,* October 16, 24; C. P. Scott to L. T. Hobhouse, October(?) 31, Hammond, *Scott,* p. 243; Swanwick, *Builders,* 113; *Foreign Relations* (1918), Supp. 1, *1,* 413; R. S. Baker's "Notebook," October 15, 1918; *Life and Letters, 8,* 481.

71. Rudin, pp. 106–7, 137; Seymour, p. 368.

seas." At a meeting of the prime ministers with House on October 29, Lloyd George declared that Britain could never abandon the methods that brought her victory. Seeing the Fourteen Points under serious debate, the other Allies hastened to add their own objections.[72]

Over the next five days House fought for an explicit acceptance of the Fourteen Points. He received the full support of Wilson, who cabled that he could never compromise on the freedom of the seas, that Points 1, 2, 3, and 14 were the "essentially American terms in the programme," [73] and that, if the Allies remained intractable, he would air the dispute before world opinion.[74] Wilson and House, counting on liberal support, believed that such publicity was a powerful weapon in their hands.[75]

House decided to try to win over Britain first, believing that if he could reach agreement on the freedom of the seas, she would prove accommodating on the rest of the program. With Britain satisfied, House felt the other opposition would crumble. Events seemed to vindicate his judgment. At the October 29 meeting House met Allied objections by threatening that America might make a separate peace. Quickly changing his tone, Lloyd George agreed to formulate his grievances with a view to further discussion.[76]

Lloyd George had two special reasons to be accommodating,

72. *Intimate Papers, 4,* 159–64; Wiseman to House, "Diary," October 28, ibid., p. 160; Rudin, pp. 266–84. The British and American *Procés Verbaux* of the pre-Armistice negotiations are to be found in the House Collection.

73. I.e. open diplomacy, freedom of the seas, economic freedom, and a league of nations. In truly radical language Wilson added, "We are pledged to fight not only Prussian militarism but militarism everywhere." Wilson to House, October 30, 31, 1918, *Intimate Papers, 4,* 168, 182–5.

74. October 29, November 1, 1918, *Life and Letters, 8,* 529, 542.

75. Cf. "House Diary," October 30, 1918.

76. Ibid.

in addition to his awareness of radical opinion at home and the need for continued American cooperation.[77] First, British statesmen were alarmed at the crescent ambitions of France and Italy and were not averse to a plausible way of avoiding the implications of the secret treaties.[78] Second, the British government had reason to believe that the "freedom of the seas" might be an empty phrase. On October 15, 1918, Lloyd George read to the Cabinet an account of an interview between Sir Eric Geddes, First Lord of the Admiralty, and President Wilson. Geddes had sounded Wilson on the freedom of the seas and reported: "His views are obviously unformed but his intention appears to be to deal with it if possible in generalities." [79] In addition, on October 16, Wilson had given Wiseman an extended exposition of the Fourteen Points. He spoke highly of British seapower and gave the impression that he had no desire to impair it. Lloyd George and House were both aware of this before they met in Paris.[80]

On October 30, then, Lloyd George gave way to House's pressure and reappeared with a memorandum couched in moderate terms, declaring merely that "what is usually described as the Freedom of the Seas is open to various interpretations, some of which [the Allies] could not accept. They must therefore reserve to themselves complete freedom on this subject when they enter the Peace Conference." The

77. A typewritten memorandum of the British Economic Defence and Development Committee, under the initials of Robert Cecil, dated September 1918, emphasizes British concern to secure American aid in reconstruction, Wiseman Collection.

78. Seymour, p. 378 ff.

79. *War Memoirs, 6,* 3290; cable from Geddes to Lloyd George, October 13, 1918. Wiseman Collection.

80. Wiseman's account of the interview has been published with notes by John L. Snell, "Woodrow Wilson on Germany and the Fourteen Points," *Journal of Modern History, 26* (1954), 364 ff. For Lloyd George's knowledge see ibid., p. 366, n. 1; for House's knowledge, "House Diary," October 17, 1918.

memorandum, of which Wiseman was probably the chief author, added one further qualification to the Fourteen Points, namely, that by "restitution" the Allies understood "that compensation will be made by Germany for all damage done to the civilian population of the Allies, and their property." House had no objection to this important addition, and he urged Wilson to accept the British formula. With some verbal changes this formula did become part of the Allied answer to Germany. Meanwhile, however, House pressed Lloyd George for a more definite assurance and on November 3 received a confidential acknowledgment that the freedom of the seas was fully open to discussion at the conference. This did not constitute part of the reply to Germany.[81]

Given the hard-fought British compromise, things fell out much as House hoped. Further questions were raised but were brushed aside or left unanswered. The Belgians began a discussion of Point 3, which declared against economic discrimination. This discussion was settled by transposing the words "so far as possible" to the head of the article to stress its flexibility. Italy opened up the whole territorial settlement in the East and South by objecting to Point 9. But Britain and France cut off the Italian protest by asserting that the German armistice did not concern Austria-Hungary.[82] Again House acquiesced. Thus it was that no more formal reservations emerged and on November 4, 1918, the Supreme War Council approved two important documents: one to be transmitted to Germany by Wilson, accepting the invitation to make an armistice under the Fourteen Points, subject to the Lloyd

81. *Intimate Papers*, 4, 170–4; Snell, p. 365. During these debates House used an interpretation of the Fourteen Points written by Cobb and Lippmann and tentatively approved by Wilson. *Intimate Papers*, 4, 153–8, 192 ff.

82. *Intimate Papers*, 4, 172–8, Rudin, pp. 275–7, 280–1. Wilson had already informed Austria that events had outdated Point 10, Lansing to Ekengred, October 19, 1918, *Foreign Relations* (1918), Supp. 1, *1*, 368.

George reservations; the other a detailed set of armistice terms ready for transmission when a German emissary crossed the lines.

Wilson and House congratulated each other on a signal triumph of liberal diplomacy.[83] The radical peace program had indeed taken a mighty stride. From now on, all parties to the war were pledged to base the peace on standards of equity. These standards now had a legal as well as a moral status. No one could avoid measuring the peace against the Wilsonian program.[84]

The British radicals were full of admiration for Wilson's achievement. They had viewed the pre-armistice debate as a battle of liberalism against reaction and were well pleased at the outcome. But, although perpetual optimists such as those of the *Daily News* behaved as if the day were won,[85] those who had long carried on the struggle for liberal war aims had been too often disappointed to believe that their opponents would easily yield. The Democrats had lost the midterm elections after Wilson had appealed for a Democratic Congress to support him at the peace conference. Wilson's defeat and Lloyd George's preparations for the Khaki Election alarmed and dismayed the radicals. The *Nation* pointed out there was much room for maneuver in the interpretation of the President's principles. At the very beginning of armistice negotiations the *Nation* had warned its readers that the Fourteen Points were "merely the titles of Bills, which

83. "You have a right to assume," wrote House, "that the two great features of the Armistice are the defeat of German military imperialism and the acceptance by the Allied Powers of the kind of peace the world has longed for." November 10, 1918, *Intimate Papers*, 4, 142.

84. It is worth noting that the Allies did not attempt to escape this implication when, in June 1919, they answered German objections to the Peace of Versailles. Rudin, p. 396.

85. Cf. *Daily News*, November 7, 11, 12, 16, 1918.

have yet to be drafted and enacted."[86] Now, on November 16, while rejoicing at the end of the fighting, the *Nation* cautioned that the Fourteen Points "may be thought through, and worked out, with courage or with timidity, with conviction or with scepticism."

Wilson and House also revealed apprehension that powerful opposition still lay ahead. The President suspected the British government of intriguing against him and of attempting, for instance, to undermine his prestige in Italy.[87] House was also aware of contrary forces, and he sent Frank Cobb to Britain in an apparent attempt to organize a campaign to secure endorsement of the Fourteen Points by candidates in the General Election.[88] The Colonel also urged Wilson to put the armistice agreement in a message to Congress in an effort to solemnize it. This Wilson was glad to do, for he was increasingly afraid that his own people were "too much in love with force and retribution."[89] The President confessed he foresaw great difficulty in "holding together the best sentiment of the world while the process of reestablishment could go forward."[90]

The British government had not overlooked the possibilities for maneuver within the pre-armistice agreement. Perhaps this may partly explain Lloyd George's comparative meekness at Paris. Well before the negotiations the Government had carefully considered the relation of the Fourteen Points to peace-making and had concluded that their extreme generality left ample scope for interpretation, particularly in the points most closely touching British interests. The Geddes and Wise-

86. *Nation*, October 12, 1918.
87. *Life and Letters*, 8, 579–80.
88. Cobb to House, November 9, House to Cobb, November 11, Baker to House, November 1, 1918, House Collection.
89. *Intimate Papers*, 4, 142; *Life and Letters*, 8, 587. For the address see *War and Peace*, 1, 294–302.
90. *Life and Letters*, 8, 581.

man reports on the freedom of the seas must have considerably strengthened this conclusion. Just before the pre-armistice negotiations Lloyd George went through the Fourteen Points with Philip Kerr and expressed the view that "The Fourteen, five and other points are not very definite. They leave a large margin for interpretation." [91] This belief that the Points did not bind Britain with much precision to any particular settlement may partly explain Lloyd George's comparative meekness at Paris. He may have been chiefly concerned with securing a quick agreement which would leave questions open for future exploitation after the fighting ceased. His initial firmness on the freedom of the seas was consonant with this strategy because, as Lloyd George pointed out during the discussion, that Point had aroused much popular alarm in Britain, where freedom of the seas had acquired the very precise meaning of abolishing the right of blockade.

Wisely or not, Wilson had persistently refused to translate his principles into precise terms, or even agreements, before Germany collapsed. Upon completion of the pre-armistice agreement House had commented to Wilson, "I doubt whether any other heads of the governments with whom we have been dealing realize how far they are now committed to the American peace programme." [92] Apparently House thought this gratifying but, even if it were true, the situation was clearly full of possibilities for future discord.

91. Seymour, p. 369. Two reports of similar import are: Lord Hardinge to Balfour, October 10, 1918, and Political Intelligence Department, October 12, 1918, Wiseman Collection. Another report drawn up by the Policy Committee of the British War Mission (i.e. now Northcliffe's organization in Britain), October 9, 1918, suggested the Fourteen Points were outdated. *War Memoirs*, 5, 3285.

92. House to Wilson, November 5, 1918, *Life and Letters*, 8, 554. It should be remembered that the Germans were aware of the generality of the Fourteen Points and could have held out for more precise explanations had they wished to do so. Seymour, p. 325.

As the history of British war aims suggests, there were many powerful elements in Britain which would welcome the chance to make a peace within the letter but not the spirit of the Fourteen Points. Their views received several notable expressions during the period of the armistice negotiations. The vengeful attitude of most of the press has already been mentioned. In the Foreign Office plans were afoot for keeping the German colonies. On October 23, 1918, Balfour reiterated that the colonies should not be returned. Privately he declared on the same day that Britain would not even discuss the matter.[93] Even more ominous to radical eyes were plans for economic discrimination. As early as September, Lloyd George had again spoken in favor of imperial preference. This struck at a pillar of both radical and traditional liberalism. In his interview with Wiseman, Wilson had specially emphasized the importance of avoiding commercial partiality. Yet on November 2, in a bid for Conservative support at the polls, Lloyd George wrote to Bonar Law formally renewing his pledge to imperial preference.[94]

This offer, made public within a few days, was a concession to the dominant section of the Conservative party, which was frankly hostile to Wilson's program. Lloyd George showed jealousy of Wilson on his own account.[95] After a meeting between Lloyd George, Milner, Balfour, Churchill, and General Sir Henry Wilson on October 14, 1918, the latter reported that all were "angry and contemptuous of Wilson." Next day Curzon submitted a memorandum to the Cabinet urging that

93. Dugdale, *Arthur James Balfour*, 2, 193; Bennett, *Journal*, 2, 270; cf. memoranda, Percy to Wiseman, June 18, Wiseman to Percy, June 19, 1918, Wiseman Collection. In the Commons on October 21, 1918, Balfour, when asked whether he approved or disapproved of the Fourteen Points, replied merely, "It is not desirable at the present moment to discuss the matter . . ." *H. C. Deb., 110*, 417–18.

94. Jones, *Lloyd George*, p. 159.

95. Murray to Wiseman, October 23, 1918, Wiseman Collection.

a Wilsonian peace would be inadequate and that negotiations should not be left in Wilson's hands.[96] An Imperial War Cabinet meeting on December 30, 1918, well portrays the vigor of the opposition to Wilson. Reporting a conversation with the President, Lloyd George agreed with Curzon that Wilson would be "only one voice" at the Peace Conference. Discussing economic discrimination and Point 3, Lloyd George suggested, "President Wilson meant nothing particular by that Article anyhow, and since he had brought it forward he had lost the election." Fiery Prime Minister Hughes of Australia declared that by demanding a fair share of spoils in return for sacrifices made, Lloyd George could carry all of Britain and half of America. Then, he said, "The League of Nations should be the gilded ball on the dome of the cathedral, and not the foundation stone." [97]

Clearly the armistice was not a universal conversion to radical and Wilsonian war aims but the opening of a new phase in the struggle. This was true for Britain and all the more so for the other Allies. Some British radicals forecast in remarkable detail the lines on which the struggle would be waged. At the time the armistice was made, the *Nation* warned against the danger of invoking the principle of self-determination without permitting Austrian and Bohemian Germans to unite with Germany. Reparations, the *Nation* continued, provided another field for error: Europe's economy was too shattered to support large indemnities, and the new Europe could be "wrecked on its Budget." To annex the German colonies and try to cover it with some internationalist fiction would likewise be fatal; the Germans would say, "When they took a German colony they called themselves 'trustees.' Nonetheless the net economic result was that all the concessions and other

96. Seymour, p. 367; *War Memoirs, 6,* 3291.
97. This account is based on the confidential minutes of the meeting in the Wiseman Collection. They are printed in large part in Lloyd George, *Peace Conference, 1,* 114–24.

valuable considerations fell to them and theirs." Unilateral disarmament would arouse similar resentment. Most important of
all, the *Nation* believed, was to permit Germany a genuine voice
in the Peace Conference. Anything less would create a special
alignment at the very outset of the new order. The defeated
Powers must be convinced that the treaty was based on a consistent effort to reach a reasonable settlement. As the *Nation*
saw it, the chief question before statesmen was, "What
measure of moral force can we attach to the peace?" [98]

In his speech of September 27, 1918, President Wilson had
proclaimed there must be "no discrimination between those
to whom we wish to be just and those to whom we do not
wish to be just." British radicals acclaimed this sentiment as
both right and expedient: an endorsement of their desire that
the peace should be a manifestly reasonable effort to remove
sources of international friction and to end the war by eradicat-
ing its causes. The radicals would readily support Wilson in
efforts to obtain such a peace. He, in turn, counted on liberal
support, believing that an appeal to it was one of his most
potent weapons. But Wilson had recently suffered electoral
defeat. In Britain, Lloyd George and the Conservatives were
sweeping all before them in a campaign against liberal forces.
On the Continent the cry for revenge went almost unchal-
lenged. Would Wilson have the power, the courage, and the
wisdom to carry out his plans?

At the time of the armistice his record of achievement surpassed all reasonable expectation. He had sketched a new
pattern of international politics which combined the designs
of leading liberal thinkers and seized the imagination of millions. Failing in his efforts to remain neutral, he had mobilized
his nation energetically for war and skilfully used his designs
for a new world order to penetrate the ranks of the enemy and
weaken their will to resist. So effective was this campaign that
in their time of defeat the Germans turned to Wilson for hope

98. *Nation,* October 26, November 2, 9, 16, 1918.

and protection. With the President triumphant in this respect, his agent House had adroitly brought the Allies to an undertaking that the peace would indeed be based on Wilson's principles.

Unfortunately for Wilson, his principles, like most rallying cries, were vague in many respects; and much hard thinking would be required before they could be fitted to the myriad, tangled, specific problems presented by the coming settlement. There was need of such a rebuilding of foundations, such adjustment of details as the world had never seen. There were issues centuries-old which defied all reason, and might at best yield to makeshifts, patience, and time. Thus, even if everyone agreed with Wilson and shared all his aspirations, the sheer complexity of peacemaking would tax the shrewdest heads. As it was, of course, there were many who disputed the President's principles and abhorred his purposes. Not the least articulate of these opponents were numbered among Wilson's countrymen. As the days passed after the armistice, Germany's power crumbled, the memory of Wilson's utterances faded, and his adversaries mustered their strength.

But Wilson had vowed it could be done; had promised a peace to fulfill his designs. So, at least, millions believed. Should he fail, the radicals would be his earliest and most damaging denunciators. During the war years they had developed meticulous standards by which to judge a peace. Over the last eighteen months they had made it plain that their allegiance to the President was not unquestioning. They had equipped themselves with all the habits and organs of opposition. Should the settlement fall short of liberal aspirations, the whole war-aims campaign might prove to have been a training for revisionism.

7. Epilogue

WE NOW KNOW that by and large the Treaty of Versailles did fail to satisfy liberal aspirations and that a storm of criticism immediately arose. In retrospect this is not surprising, for the task which Wilson undertook in Paris was one of over-powering difficulty. To what extent criticism was justified and how far the treaty measured up to Wilson's principles are important questions which, by their nature, cannot be given a final answer.

Wilson and his liberal supporters wanted a peace founded on the general spirit of reconciliation expressed in his Four-teen Points and subsequent principles, now part of the armistice agreement. Such a peace, they thought, must be one of mutual benefit derived from reasonable compromise. But the Four-teen Points were at once dangerously vague and embar-rassingly precise. Broad declarations of this kind could not serve as terms of peace, though Wilson had on occasion un-wisely referred to them as such. Even the expert staff of the Inquiry, to whom Wilson had necessarily delegated the work of detailed application, had perforce to work without full knowledge of the policy of other nations and without knowing the circumstances under which the conference would meet. Yet the Points were sufficiently explicit to afford ample room for accusations that they had been violated in this or that particular.

The most superficial and hasty effort to apply the Points to the map of Europe revealed inevitable contradictions be-tween them. Thoroughgoing pursuit of "free and secure access to the sea" for one nation conflicted with self-determination for others. Complete national self-determination was in any case impossible, given the distribution of population in Europe. Frontier-drawing, on the scale required in 1919, also raised obstacles in the way of establishing the harmonious and efficient patterns of economic life envisaged in Wilson's Point 3. The ramifications of modern industrial life presented problems unknown to the boundary-makers of Vienna.

A reasonable and unusually clever man might, with much difficulty, have devised a set of compromises calculated to achieve the best possible application of Wilson's principles. But the unavoidable element of compromise made it certain that other men, no less reasonable, could raise objections amounting to a charge of failure. In reality, reasonableness was at a premium in 1919. Even with the best of intentions it was only to be expected that when controversial points had to be settled, the benefit of doubt should go against the defeated enemy. The very experts employed by the victors were chiefly versed in the affairs of the rising nationalities of Europe, with a consequent tendency to perceive the needs of the new "succession" states rather than those of the Central Powers.

Allied aspirations compounded the already complex problem of merely applying Wilson's principles. The hitherto suppressed nations of central and eastern Europe were set on independence and on obtaining generous frontiers. Their fears of some future *revanche* on the part of their old masters also led them to favor any measures to weaken the Central Powers. The new nations were heartily seconded in these designs by the French, who saw in a large Poland and Czechoslovakia a possible substitute for the Russian watch on Germany's eastern flank. Clemenceau had personally experienced the events of 1870 as well as 1914 and was intent on precluding a repetition. In addition to the repossession of Alsace-Lorraine, French plans for their own aggrandizement therefore envisaged the detachment of large slices of German territory, by annexation if possible; if not, then by· erecting a buffer state in the Rhineland. France also demanded the wealthy Saar valley for her own. To complete the work, Clemenceau wanted Germany disarmed and compelled to shoulder a crippling burden of reparation for the grievous sufferings of the French land and people during the previous four years.

To the south, Italy had entered the war as a business venture and now awaited her dividend. For her share she claimed the Brenner line, sweeping acquisitions on the shores of the Adriatic, and colonial gains as available. Italian claims in the Adriatic ran counter to the interests of the new nation of southern Slavs arisen from the ruins of the Dual Monarchy. In the Far East, Japan's resolve to retain Germany's concessions in China, as well as her islands in the Pacific, also impinged embarrassingly on the interests of a friendly power, for China was now one of the Allies. The disposition of one of the concessions, that in Shantung, was destined to be one of the most bitterly assailed portions of the treaty.

Lloyd George's demands on behalf of Great Britain were relatively modest. He was concerned to reach a formula whereby Britain would receive a sizeable share of reparations; and, of course, the German fleet, then at Scapa Flow, could not be permitted to leave again under its own flag. But Britain also had to reckon with the ambitions of her dominions, several of which had conquered German colonies and did not mean to relinquish them. These aspirations combined with Britain's own interests in Africa and the Near East to produce a strong pressure for favorable adjustments in colonial areas.

It would be a mistake to condemn these various demands out of hand as motivated simply by greed, though no doubt some of them bore such a character. As the case of France clearly showed, fears for future safety were a powerful and perhaps the primary driving force. One would have had to be singularly blinded by the happy immunity long—but no longer—enjoyed by Britain and America to believe that the victorious statesmen would readily abandon their plans in favor of the projected but untried methods of collective security. The greatest distinction between Wilson and the Allied prime ministers was one of circumstance and faith in the new order. Yet every concession to strategic necessity and to a balance of power unregulated by collective control played into the hands of those prepared to condemn the peace as merely another exercise in outmoded diplomacy.

The problem of applying liberal precepts to the real world of fear, ambition, and unaccommodating geography was aggravated, of course, by the conditions under which the attempt was made. The temper of the Allied governments was not conciliatory. Their nations had suffered long and hard in a war which the overwhelming majority sincerely believed the Central Powers had needlessly provoked and conducted with revolting barbarity. Oppressed nations looked back on centuries of ungenerous rule. France, overrun and bleeding, sought vengeance. Italy had military humiliation to avenge and leaders needing nationalistic triumphs to combat danger of revolution at home. In England the Coalition had just won a resounding electoral victory on a platform of retribution and, whether or not Lloyd George had fully participated, he found himself at the head of a majority of "hard-faced men," who were not accustomed to self-denial. Wilson, who had developed to a high degree the liberal's faith that, given time, the people would reach reasonable conclusions, had the misfortune to meet his greatest challenge at a juncture when time was short and the public everywhere was enraged or desperate.

Circumstances favored this vengeful mood. The Allies were well placed to dictate their will. Germany had greatly impaired its claim to sympathy by imposing the harsh Treaty of Brest Litovsk on Russia. The Allied armies remained formidable while Germany was in turmoil and her army melting away. Moreover the arrangements worked out in the secret treaties provided a basis on which the Allies might cooperate in establishing their own version of a desirable peace.

Defects in the organization of the conference offered favorable conditions for such log-rolling. Only when the conference was far advanced did the powers decide to proceed immediately to a final settlement instead of making a preliminary treaty. Wise or not, this decision greatly curtailed the time available to the specialized commissions, deprived them of any insights they might have drawn from a prolonged consideration of the German case, and dispensed with the rechecking which a second congress would have entailed. Inadequate planning apparently complicated the inevitable congestion arising from the scope of the conference's task and the number of delegations engaged. It was impossible for even those at the top to maintain an over-all view, while the experts had to make their contribution from the narrow confines of specialized commissions. Such a fragmented process provides the most favorable circumstances under which the advocates of special interests can work.

This may have been unavoidable; perhaps no organization could have coped satisfactorily with so great a task and ensured the logical, coherent settlement demanded by liberal opinion. It was certainly unavoidable that many aspects of the world situation were beyond the control of the negotiators. The new states of Europe, for instance, had called themselves into existence and had to be accepted. Russia had no stable government, went unrepresented at the conference, and remained an unknown but menacing quantity. Some of the Allies were actually engaged in hostilities against the Bolshevik regime. In many other areas anarchy, war, or famine raged, providing constant distraction for the Allied negotiators who now disposed of most of the world's food and transport.

This, in barest outline, was the situation Wilson faced. To add to his handicap he confronted it with defective armor. The memory of his speeches and the prestige of his achieve-

ment at the armistice faded in the weeks before the conference convened. Wartime solidarity and the spirit of common sacrifice had time to wear thin. Most important of all,
Wilson's opponents had time to develop the charge that he
could neither speak for nor commit America. The allegation
was correct. Wilson had lost the midterm election and by his
own late appeal for a mandate for the peace conference had
made it easier to represent the result as a vote of no confidence. Taft had called for a Republican victory to avert a
"negotiated" peace. Senator Lodge wrote directly to Clemenceau warning him of Wilson's repudiation. Opposition to the
President came into full view during his visit to America, half-
way through the conference. The Democratic party was rapidly
crumbling, and its opponents, scenting a win in 1920, were in
full cry. To make matters worse, Wilson had selected a delegation containing no Republican of first rank. Nothing could
do Wilson more harm than doubt as to his ability to carry his
country at a time when he was trying to establish a new world
system which depended for much of its appeal upon the
promise of continued American participation and concern.

Under all these adverse conditions, some but by no means
all of his own making, did Wilson secure a fair approximation
to his principles? Every answer must depend largely on the
outlook of the observer. "Under the conditions" is a proviso
which many enthusiastic converts to Wilson's eloquence were
not prepared to admit. By persistently expounding his aspirations for the future without an equally vigorous indication of
the difficulties he foresaw, Wilson had encouraged a great
many liberals to expect that Germany's defeat would immediately usher in a perfect settlement. Disillusionment was the
inevitable fate of such blind optimism. Yet if it be once conceded that perfection was not to be expected, it is possible to
advance a strong argument that Wilson achieved remarkable
success in an extremely difficult task.

To begin with, the Treaty contained the League Covenant.

This established the first comprehensive international organization to keep the peace and to symbolize that tension and war anywhere were the concern of all nations in the indivisible world of the 20th century. Writing the Covenant and securing its adoption by the conference was essentially Wilson's personal achievement. In the age of the United Nations his contribution to the League alone exerts a powerful, continuing, and, it may be hoped, beneficent influence on world affairs.

The more particular provisions of the Treaty also bore witness to the liberal moderation championed by Wilson. In the West, France yielded its extreme territorial demands in exchange for the guarantees of the Covenant and a special commitment by Britain and America. The Rhineland remained German and France secured only temporary possession of the Saar, subject to a subsequent plebiscite. In the East, Czechoslovakia and Poland were compelled to curb their wilder ambitions; a plebiscite was arranged in Upper Silesia, and Danzig, though wrested from Germany, was given autonomy. Lloyd George played a notable part in these dispositions. But those who make out the case for Wilson may argue that without the President's pervasive influence the mercurial Welsh tactician might well have taken a different role. The Polish Corridor itself, probably the most disputed single provision of the Treaty, was confined to areas of predominantly Polish race. Indeed the new map of Europe was fairly close to the ethnographic possibilities, the most notable exceptions being the denial of *Anschluss* between Germany and Austria and the award of the Brenner to Italy on strategic grounds. Italy's other hopes were thwarted to an extent sufficient to embitter her attitude to the whole settlement.

Outside Europe the conference distributed colonies in a manner which aroused charges of disguised imperialism. But the institution of mandates at least introduced promising new guarantees for the natives and prospects for their future. The outcome of this experiment depended on the fortunes of the League. Somewhat the same could be said in regard to reparations, the least defensible part of the Treaty, for the final determination of the burdens placed on Germany was left to a commission which America could dominate as the world's chief creditor. But the financial clauses invited excesses, and American rejection of a proposal that war loans and indebtedness be approached as a unified world problem did not augur well for financial statesmanship. On balance, the Treaty justified liberal fears that economic problems would be neglected or mishandled.

In addition, the reparations provisions were associated with the so-called "Guilt Clause" by which Germany was compelled to acknowledge that she and her allies had "imposed" the war on their enemies by aggression. This ran directly counter to the tenets of those who, like the radicals, believed the problem of war could not be explained away simply by the iniquity of one nation and who therefore hoped that the peace would provide a patently reasonable, "scientific" adjustment of conflicting interests and establish a mechanism for meeting future contingencies. The demand that the Kaiser be brought to trial and the exclusion of Germany from the League strengthened these misgivings. Even more, the denial of any significant German participation in the deliberations of the conference increased the uneasiness of those who feared that there had not been a full discussion of the issues from all sides.

It cannot be denied that the Treaty, besides being open to criticism in detail, lacked that obvious spirit of generous conciliation and patent fairness which liberals deemed essential for a lasting peace. Very likely no settlement could have maintained such a character after so great an upheaval. On any interpretation the Fourteen Points would have involved a startling number of simultaneous adjustments. When all the detailed demands on Germany were added together at the very end of the conference, they made a formidable collection, no matter how defensible each may have been in itself.

But the Treaty bore the imprint of Wilson's moderating influence on all its parts. Much of its disastrous aftermath resulted from the way in which its provisions were implemented. Probably Wilson's greatest failure lay not in the Treaty but in his failure to secure ratification by his own nation as a step toward continued American participation in the new order. It appears that the completeness of this mishap was largely due to the stubborn streak in Wilson which had made it so difficult for him to bargain during the conference, which made him reluctant to retrace his steps even to improve the Treaty, and which encouraged him to disguise compromises in language that smacked of hypocrisy and deceit.

Nevertheless, Wilson and the liberalism he represented ensured that the negotiators at least professed an obligation to base their terms on standards of justice and the requirements of world order, rather than the preponderance of military power. Plebiscites, historical research, all the apparatus of the settlement paid formal respect to the welfare of peoples affected by diplomatic decisions. That this exposed the Treaty to criticism for falling short of its pretensions should not obscure the restraint induced by them. It seems reasonable to conclude that the settlement would have conformed much less to liberal ideals had it not been for Wilson's moderating influence.

Be that as it may, liberals who had been the most fervent of Wilson's supporters were bitterly disappointed and outraged by the Treaty. Some were surprised and shocked; others considered their gloomy warnings vindicated. The grounds for their complaint were numerous and varied. General Smuts, who had become exceedingly anxious for what he called a "Wilson Peace," and who greatly admired Wilson's efforts, expressed the general theme of liberal discontent when he warned the President of the disillusionment the Treaty would arouse by its deviation from the general spirit of his program. In Smuts' estimation the treaty did not square with Wilson's 1918 speeches and therefore represented a breach of the armistice agreement. "This war began with a breach of solemn international undertaking," he wrote to Wilson bluntly, "and it has been one of our most important war aims to vindicate international law and the sanctity of international engagements. If the Allies end the war by following the example set by Germany at the beginning, and also confront the world with a 'scrap of paper,' the discredit on us will be so great that I shudder to think of its ultimate effect on public opinion." [1]

Arthur Henderson expanded the same idea in a pamphlet entitled *The Peace Terms:* [2] "The Treaty is defective, not so much because of this or that detail of wrong done, but fundamentally in that it accepts, and indeed is based on, the very political principles or premises which were the ultimate cause of the war."

The critics also objected to specific provisions of the Treaty. J. M. Keynes fired the most telling shot of the whole revisionist campaign when he assailed the economic clauses on both moral and practical grounds in his *Economic Consequences of the Peace*. Henderson's pamphlet offers a convenient summary of other objections. Wilson's declarations on the right of self-determination were clearly violated, declared Henderson, by the refusal to allow *Anschluss* between Germany and Austria, by the inclusion of German minorities in Czechoslovakia, Italy, and Poland, by the disposition of Danzig, and by the separation of East Prussia from Germany. Commercial restrictions on Germany and the confiscation of German shipping and property, as well as the impractical and unjust reparations

1. Smuts to Wilson, May 30, 1919, Baker, *World Settlement, 3,* 466 ff.
2. London, 1919.

clauses, were incompatible with promises of equality of economic treatment. Above all, Henderson denounced the general intent of the Treaty. "The Treaty is obviously based," he concluded, "on a principle which President Wilson has repeatedly repudiated, namely, that peace will best be secured by the mere destruction of German military power and the punishment of the German people. It responds in this to the theory . . . that the main obstacle to permanent peace and a better organization of the world was German military power and the special wickedness of the German race."

No one familiar with the radical war-aims campaign can read these complaints without a sense of complete familiarity. The wave of resentment which rapidly arose in Britain moved the French publicist Fabre-Luce to comment that the British were revisionist from the moment the Treaty of Versailles was signed. But, as we have seen, even this striking commentary understates the case. The radicals had begun to criticize the Treaty before it was drafted; in anticipation during negotiation of the Armistice, by implication throughout the war.

It was ironical that those of Wilson's supporters who had shown the keenest awareness of the problems involved in making the peace should be among the most outspoken critics of his achievement. There had, of course, been some differences of emphasis between Wilson and the radicals before the conference opened. The radicals showed greater concern for economic affairs and greater awareness of the possible dangers of self-determination. They had also deplored the parts of Wilson's utterances which seemed likely to encourage the view that the mere defeat of Germany would be sufficient guarantee of stable world order. But these differences were entirely outweighed by general agreement with Wilson on the main lines of advance. The really important distinction between the radicals and the President was one of responsibility. For although the radicals did their best to promote liberal principles, they did not share Wilson's onerous duty of putting them into practice. They therefore felt free to criticize, and their disappointment made it difficult for them to appreciate Wilson's accomplishment. Drawing upon their wartime experience, the radicals were well qualified to become the leaders of revisionism.

In this role the radicals achieved remarkable success. Their analysis of international affairs quickly won widespread acceptance among the majority of the Liberal party, who suffered a reaction after Versailles similar and consequent to the one they had experienced in August 1914. Radical ideas enjoyed an even more vigorous popularity in the Labour party, now second only to the Conservatives. By 1920 such promising young Labour leaders as the new Mayor of Stepney, Clement Attlee, were in the chair at revisionist meetings of the U.D.C. Two years later, E. D. Morel, as a Labour candidate, symbolized the startling reversal of fortunes by defeating no less a man than Winston Churchill in a Parliamentary election.

The upsurge of enthusiasm for radical views on foreign policy and the speed with which a revisionist program was formulated would be scarcely comprehensible were we not aware that this outlook was directly related to the war-aims campaign and to a long-established tradition of British and American liberalism. Given this understanding, it becomes clear that left-wing revisionism in the postwar years was not, as it is often depicted, a spontaneous and inexplicable phenomenon but rather the outgrowth of enduring Anglo-American attitudes to foreign affairs.

For the future it was of even greater import that the Labour party so warmly embraced the radical theory of international relations. Most of Labour's prewar ideas about foreign policy had been borrowed from the radicals. During the war, several prominent Labour leaders worked with the U.D.C., and the rank and file of the party made the most vigorous response to the war-aims campaign. After the war MacDonald and Snowden, the two Labour leaders most closely identified with the radical cause, reassumed their dominant position in the party, and at the same time many of the radicals who had broken with the majority of Liberals on the war-aims issue found a new political home with Labour. They were the vanguard of a numerous migration accompanying the decay of the Liberal party.

Once in the Labour party, the education and the articulateness of the radical leaders ensured them great influence on party doctrine. Nowhere was this influence greater than in their chief field of interest, foreign affairs, an aspect of policy on which the average trade unionist party leader had comparatively little to contribute. In this way the radical analysis of international relations became firmly engrafted on the Labour party.

In the immediate postwar years revisionism did not succeed in bringing about concessions to Germany which, made from strength, might have stabilized the new order. But the radical approach to foreign affairs, once merely that of an influential minority, now dominated a party which would eventually govern the nation. Moreover, the great influence of the British left upon the rising nationalist élite of Asia transmitted much of this heritage to the leaders in states which have been formed from former British possessions. Even in midcentury these leaders and those of the Labour party are still much affected by the radical analysis of foreign affairs. Many an otherwise enigmatic declaration by Bevan or Nehru takes on new meaning when viewed in the context of the radical tradition as it flowered in the first World War. Without knowledge of the war-aims campaign it is, therefore, impossible to understand adequately one of the most important ideological forces affecting the foreign policy of the free nations.

On the American side, Woodrow Wilson's policies and his theory of international affairs become more comprehensible when his relationship to the British radicals is unearthed. It develops that there was not just a sympathy and similarity of general purposes between Wilson and the radicals; they agreed even on most points of detail and of method. Direct and frequent exchanges nourished this affinity, and these associations cast a revealing new light on several aspects of Wilson's wartime diplomacy—his persistence in mediation, his efforts to rally public opinion in the belligerents, his emphasis on obtaining statements of terms—and on his tactics at the peace conference, particularly his appeals to the peoples of Europe.

Study of Anglo-American war aims from a liberal perspective can illuminate other issues, for example the problem of the proper relation between military effort and national objectives. For the American or Englishman of today, however, the war-aims campaign is perhaps most interesting as evidence of the nature and vigor of our hopeful and would-be rational tradition in foreign affairs. Even the radicals, who derided the naive attempt of most liberals to blame the war on the exceptional villainy of one nation, remained convinced that reasonable solutions could be found for the problem of war. They appreciated the conflict of interests but did not despair of designing methods for peaceful adjustment.

Some decades later we are more inclined to doubt our rational capacity to achieve the satisfactory compromise of conflicts without violence. Yet if we feel inclined to abandon the confidence of our liberal predecessors, we should be aware that we turn our backs on a heritage of some antiquity. Whatever its shortcomings, the liberal view of international relations was at least a spur to action. It may well be that we cannot dispense with such a leaven of hopefulness. A sound politics requires an ultimate optimism which has entertained all the grounds for pessimism. For those seeking a diplomacy of this quality, the liberal war-aims campaign of the first World War has great practical importance.

Appendix

The Fourteen Points
(*from President Wilson's address to Congress on January 8, 1918*)

1. Open covenants of peace, openly arrived at, after which there shall be no private international understandings of any kind, but diplomacy shall proceed always frankly and in the public view.

2. Absolute freedom of navigation upon the seas, outside territorial waters, alike in peace and in war, except as the seas may be closed in whole or in part by international action for the enforcement of international covenants.

3. The removal, so far as possible, of all economic barriers and the establishment of an equality of trade conditions among all the nations consenting to the peace and associating themselves for its maintenance.

4. Adequate guarantees given and taken that national armaments will be reduced to the lowest point consistent with domestic safety.

5. A free, open-minded, and absolutely impartial adjustment of all colonial claims, based upon a strict observance of the principle that in determining all such questions of sovereignty the interests of the populations concerned must have equal weight with the equitable claims of the government whose title is to be determined.

6. The evacuation of all Russian territory and such settlement of all questions affecting Russia as will secure the best and

freest cooperation of the other nations of the world in obtaining for her an unhampered and unembarrassed opportunity for the independent determination of her own political development and national policy and assure her of a sincere welcome into the society of free nations under institutions of her own choosing; and, more than a welcome, assistance also of every kind that she may need and may herself desire. The treatment accorded Russia by her sister nations in the months to come will be the acid test of their good will, of their comprehension of her needs as distinguished from their own interests, and of their intelligent and unselfish sympathy.

7. Belgium, the whole world will agree, must be evacuated and restored without any attempt to limit the sovereignty which she enjoys in common with all other free nations. No other single act will serve as this will serve to restore confidence among the nations in the laws which they have themselves set and determined for the government of their relations with one another. Without this healing act the whole structure and validity of international law is forever impaired.

8. All French territory should be freed and the invaded portions restored, and the wrong done to France by Prussia in 1871 in the matter of Alsace-Lorraine, which has unsettled the peace of the world for nearly fifty years, should be righted, in order that peace may once more be made in the interest of all.

9. A readjustment of the frontiers of Italy should be effected along clearly recognizable lines of nationality.

10. The peoples of Austria-Hungary, whose place among the nations we wish to see safeguarded and assured, should be accorded the freest opportunity of autonomous development.

11. Rumania, Serbia, and Montenegro should be evacuated; occupied territories restored; Serbia accorded free and secure access to the sea; and the relations of the several Balkan states to one another determined by friendly counsel along histori-

cally established lines of allegiance and nationality; and international guarantees of the political and economic independence and territorial integrity of the several Balkan states should be entered into.

12. The Turkish portions of the present Ottoman Empire should be assured a secure sovereignty, but other nationalities which are now under Turkish rule should be assured an undoubted security of life and absolutely unmolested opportunity of autonomous development, and the Dardanelles should be permanently opened as a free passage to the ships and commerce of all nations under international guarantee.

13. An independent Polish state should be erected which should include the territories inhabited by indisputably Polish populations, which should be assured a free and secure access to the sea, and whose political and economic independence and territorial integrity should be guaranteed by international covenant.

14. A general association of nations must be formed under specific covenants for the purpose of affording mutual guarantees of political independence and territorial integrity to great and small states alike.

Bibliographical Essay

THERE ARE numerous bibliographies to assist the student of Wilson's diplomacy during the first World War. The first resort is to Samuel F. Bemis and Grace Gardner Griffin, *Guide to the Diplomatic History of the United States, 1775–1921* (Washington, D.C., 1935), and to Miss Griffin's *Writings on American History, 1906–* (New York, New Haven, or Washington, D.C.—imprint varies—1908–). Centering around these are many special works, of which the most useful for the present purpose are Laura S. Turnbull, *Woodrow Wilson, A Selected Bibliography of His Published Writings, Addresses and Public Papers* (Princeton, 1948), and three historiographical articles: Robert C. Binkley, "Ten Years of Peace Conference History," *Journal of Modern History, 1* (1929), 603–29; Paul Birdsall, "Second Decade of Peace Conference History," *ibid., 11* (1939), 362–78; and Richard W. Leopold, "The Problem of American Intervention, 1917: an Historical Retrospect," *World Politics, 2* (1950), 404–25.

Nothing comparable exists on British diplomacy, though there are excellent indexes of official publications. The Royal Historical Society's *Writings on British History, 1934–* (London, 1937–) are too limited in number as yet to be of more than slight help. For the study of the British radicals there is little better than the review columns of the London *Nation* and the lists of U.D.C. publications contained in Helen M. Swanwick's *Builders of Peace* (London, 1924) and in Charles P. Trevelyan's *Union of Democratic Control* (London, 1919). The latter is a more generous but less accurate listing than the former. Two general checklists which assist in identifying wartime writings are the British Museum's *Subject Index of the Books Relating to the European War 1914–1918, Acquired by the British Museum, 1914–1920* (London, 1922) and G. M. Dutcher, *Selected Critical Bibliography of Publications in English Relating to the World War* (Philadelphia, 1918).

Relatively few works treat the question of war aims in general. Recently A. J. P. Taylor has contributed a brief essay, "The War Aims of the Allies in the First World War," to *Essays Presented to Sir Lewis Namier,* edited by Taylor and Richard Pares (London, 1956). This essay is sometimes illuminating, but its value is limited by a complete absence of references. Charles Seymour's *American Diplomacy during the World War* (Baltimore, 1934) is still one of the few major studies which consistently relates American policy to the question of war aims. Hans W. Gatzke's *Germany's Drive to the West (Drang nach Westen), a Study of Germany's Western War Aims during the First World War* (Baltimore, 1950) and Henry R. Winkler's *The League of Nations Movement in Great Britain, 1914–1919* (New Brunswick, N.J., 1952) are two useful works bearing obliquely on the present topic. Lord Beaverbrook's *Politicians and the War, 1914–1916* (2 vols. London, 1928, 1932) vividly describes the politics of high command in Britain and is the chief, though by no means unquestionable, source of information on the cabinet crisis of 1916. The same author's *Men and Power, 1917–1918* (London, 1956) does not continue the story in the same detail but presents personalities with even greater zest and some acidity.

On the British radicals the main account is Swanwick's *Builders of Peace,* which profits from its closeness to events. Trevelyan's pamphlet called *Union of Democratic Control* makes frequent errors of fact. Irene C. Willis, *England's Holy War* (New York, 1928), a reprint of three short works originally published in 1919, 1920, and 1921, is a polemical attack on the conduct of the Liberal party by a member of the U.D.C.'s Executive Committee. Part of Henry Pelling's recent

America and the British Left (London, 1956), deals with the period of the first World War as it concerned labor groups. William P. Maddox, *Foreign Relations in British Labour Politics* (Cambridge, Mass., 1934) is an older work which is informative on the early development of the Labour party's ideas on foreign affairs. Since the present book went to press an assessment of liberal dissent from national policy over the last two centuries has appeared in a series of broadcast lectures published as A. J. P. Taylor, *The Troublemakers*, London, 1957.

Two books deserving special mention are Harry R. Rudin's *Armistice, 1918* (New Haven, 1944), a valuable guide to a complicated event, and George F. Kennan's *Russia Leaves the War* (Princeton, 1956), a splendidly convincing account of the Russian crisis and its effect on American policy.

Fortunately there is a wealth of biographies and memoirs to compensate for the comparative lack of historical studies. Of memoirs one may single out David Lloyd George's huge *War Memoirs of David Lloyd George* (6 vols. London, 1933–36), which, though frequently discounted, prove singularly useful and contain numerous indispensable documents. His *Memoirs of the Peace Conference* (2 vols. New Haven, 1939) merit less respect. Sir Edward Grey's *Twenty-Five Years, 1892–1916* (2 vols. New York, 1925) must also be mentioned. Several of the British radicals have written autobiographies which bear upon the war-aims movement. Three of these are Norman Angell, *After All* (London, 1951), Philip Snowden, *An Autobiography, 1864–1934* (2 vols. London, 1934), and Charles P. Trevelyan, *From Liberalism to Labour* (London, 1921).

On the American side, Robert Lansing's *War Memoirs of Robert Lansing, Secretary of State* (Indianapolis, 1935) must be checked carefully against the *Lansing Papers* (see below). David F. Houston's *Eight Years with Wilson's Cabinet, 1913–1920* (2 vols. Garden City, N.Y., 1926) gives valuable accounts of several cabinet meetings, while William J. Bryan's *Memoirs of William Jennings Bryan* (Philadelphia, 1925) are of interest with regard to the genesis of early American thoughts on mediation.

There are many excellent biographies. Blanche E. C. Dugdale's *Arthur James Balfour, First Earl of Balfour* (2 vols. New York, 1937) prints many documents and offers a sober view of its subject. Of the radicals, Wedgwood and both the Buxton brothers are the subjects of modest but competent biographies: T. P. Conwell Evans (on Noel Buxton), *Foreign Policy from a Back Bench, 1904–1918* (London, 1932), Victoria de Bunsen, *Charles Roden Buxton: a Memoir* (London, 1948), and C. V. Wedgwood, *The Last of the Radicals, Josiah Wedgwood, M.P.* (London, 1951). Two other valuable British biographies are E. M. Forster, *Goldsworthy Lowes Dickinson* (London, 1934), and J. L. Hammond's *C. P. Scott of the "Manchester Guardian"* (London, 1934). F. Seymour Cocks' *E. D. Morel, the Man and His Work* (London, 1920) is untrustworthy on many facts.

There are a great many biographies of Wilson. At the moment, Arthur Link's *Woodrow Wilson and the Progressive Era* (New York, 1954) is more useful than the volumes of his major biography of Wilson, which are now appearing. H. C. F. Bell, *Woodrow Wilson and the People* (Garden City, N.Y., 1945) is an enlightening short interpretation of the President's career. Ray Stannard Baker's *Woodrow Wilson, Life and Letters* (8 vols. Garden City, N.Y., 1927–39) is still the most complete single source of published information on Wilson. The last two volumes fortunately print a great many documents verbatim. Harley Notter's *Origins of the Foreign Policy of Woodrow Wilson* (Baltimore, 1937) is the standard account of Wilson's early thought on foreign affairs. Alexander L. and Juliette L. George, *Woodrow Wilson and Colonel House* (New York, 1956) is an extended examination of Wilson's temperament, particularly as manifested in relation to House.

Charles Seymour's *Intimate Papers of Colonel House* (4 vols. Boston, 1926–28) achieves a very skillful balance between biography and printed source. *Woodrow Wilson, The New Democracy, Presidential Messages, Addresses, and Other Papers, 1913–1917*, edited by Ray Stannard Baker and William E. Dodd (2 vols. in one, New York, 1926) and the later volumes, *War and Peace, Presidential Messages, Addresses and Public Papers, 1917–24*, edited by Baker and Dodd (2 vols. in one, New York, 1927), are standard works of reference. Other printed unofficial sources include Stephen Gwynn's *Letters and Friendships of Sir Cecil Spring-Rice, a Record* (2 vols. Cambridge, Mass., 1930), Burton J. Hendrick's *Life and Letters of Walter H. Page* (3 vols. Garden City, N.Y., 1922–26), and George A. Riddell, *Lord Riddell's War Diary, 1914–1918* (London, 1933). G. Lowes Dickinson, *Documents and Statements Relating to Peace Proposals and War Aims* (London, 1919), and James B. Scott, *Official Statements of War Aims and Peace Proposals, December 1916–November 1918* (Washington, 1919), are two other fruitful collections.

Of the official American sources which have been printed, the Department of State, *Papers Relating to the Foreign Relations of the United States; The Lansing Papers* (2 vols. Washington, D.C., 1939–40), are probably the most helpful. In Britain the *Parliamentary Debates, Official Report* (fifth series) is, of course, indispensable.

We have inherited an almost embarrassingly generous legacy of writings from the British radicals. From the prewar period, Norman Angell's *Great Illusion* (London, 1910), J. A. Hobson's *Imperialism* (London, 1902), and E. D. Morel's *Morocco in Diplomacy* (London, 1912) are essential. Of the wartime books the most important are H. N. Brailsford, *League of Nations* (London, 1918), C. R. Buxton and others,

Towards a Lasting Settlement (New York, 1915), G. Lowes Dickinson, *The Choice before Us* (London, 1917) and *Economic War after the War* (London, 1916), and E. D. Morel, *Truth and the War* (London, 1916). Dickinson and Brailsford provide a necessary balance to the more enthusiastic and less critical writings of Morel, Ponsonby, and others. Very important are the approximately sixty pamphlets and leaflets issued by the U.D.C. during the war.

Almost as indispensable is the London *Nation*, which served as a central radical forum and which provides a guide by which to measure the swings of Liberal opinion. *War and Peace*, a supplement to the *Nation* in the later months of the war, and *U.D.C.*, early journal of the U.D.C., are unfortunately hard to find. For the Liberal–Imperialists the best source is the *Round Table*. The *New Europe* was the chief organ of those who strongly supported the aspirations of rising national movements. The *Daily News* and the *Manchester Guardian* provide the best approach to moderate Liberal opinion. Other information on Liberal views can be secured from the *Westminster Gazette* and *Daily Chronicle*.

Several manuscript collections which supplement the printed sources are essential for uncovering the relations between Wilson and the radicals. Most important of all is the House Collection in the Yale Library. The vital source here is the files of correspondence between House and W. H. Buckler. This material is absolutely necessary to the study of liberal war aims. Colonel House's voluminous typewritten Diary also provides a great deal of information on his contacts with the radicals. Because the large majority of Wilson's communications with the radicals was channeled through House, and because Buckler has now placed his own files in the House Collection, the Papers of Woodrow Wilson in the Library of Congress are less helpful than might be imagined. However, the Wilson Papers do contain documents which House forwarded without taking a copy for himself. The Wilson Papers are, of course, invaluable for a well-rounded understanding of the President's general policy. Also in the Library of Congress are the Papers of Henry White, which contain numerous communications from Buckler. There is, however, comparatively little of significance that cannot be found in the other collections. The Papers of Frank Polk, lodged with the House Collection in the Yale Library, contain Ray Stannard Baker's reports from England in 1918. Yet another neighbor to the House Collection and a source of great importance is the Sir William Wiseman Collection. Wiseman's papers have a double value: they contain considerable material on liberal forces, and, even more important, they make it possible for the student to read many official British documents which would not otherwise be available, the British archives for the first World War being still firmly closed. These papers are particularly enlightening on the Armistice. The few boxes of Arthur Henderson's papers in the Library of the Labour party at Transport House also contain official documents which are not to be found elsewhere.

Index